Content Marketing Strategies

FOR DUMMIES®

A Wiley Brand

by Stephanie Diamond

Content Marketing Strategies For Dummies®

Published by: **John Wiley & Sons, Inc.,** 111 River Street, Hoboken, NJ 07030-5774, `www.wiley.com`

Copyright © 2016 by John Wiley & Sons, Inc., Hoboken, New Jersey

Media and software compilation copyright © 2016 by John Wiley & Sons, Inc. All rights reserved.

Published simultaneously in Canada

For general information on our other products and services, please contact our Customer Care Department within the U.S. at 877-762-2974, outside the U.S. at 317-572-3993, or fax 317-572-4002. For technical support, please visit `www.wiley.com/techsupport`.

Wiley publishes in a variety of print and electronic formats and by print-on-demand. Some material included with standard print versions of this book may not be included in e-books or in print-on-demand. If this book refers to media such as a CD or DVD that is not included in the version you purchased, you may download this material at `http://booksupport.wiley.com`. For more information about Wiley products, visit `www.wiley.com`.

Library of Congress Control Number: 2015957831

ISBN: 978-1-119-15454-9

ISBN 978-1-119-15456-3 (ebk); ISBN ePDF 978-1-119-15463-1

Manufactured in the United States of America

10 9 8 7 6 5 4 3 2 1

Contents at a Glance

Table of Contents

Foreword

. . . .

*T*raditional advertising is in turmoil. Online advertising is increasingly expensive, and consumers are becoming cautious of what they click next.

The reality is that today's customers will make a buying decision only after arming themselves with research that gives them enough confidence that they're making an intelligent decision.

Educational-based marketing (a.k.a. content marketing) is the new driver for online sales. It's also proving to be the most effective technique in engaging an audience with your brand early in the purchase cycle — so much so that thought leaders in online marketing have said, "Content Marketing is the only marketing left."

The growth of content marketing continues to revolutionize the way that we communicate and engage with existing and perspective clients. It is the only form of marketing today that capitalizes on educating customers and actually addressing customer problems by publishing relevant content.

Content marketing is about publishing interesting media that is of high value to your readers. Through quality content, this marketing positions you as an authority in your market, building trust and loyalty that translates into lifelong customers.

Content marketing is complex, which makes deciding where to start challenging. There are many moving parts, which makes learning it quite difficult. This book simplifies all the key elements and lays out strategies and formulas that take you through the process no matter what level or size of organization.

Combining this strategy with the right tools enables you to build and scale a marketing plan that works well with your business.

When Stephanie approached me about her writing this book, I could not think of anyone more suited. She not only is experienced in the field but has also already cowritten the successful *Social Media Marketing For Dummies* book in several editions. With her deep knowledge of the topic, she has managed to distill a complex subject perfectly for readers of all kinds, small businesses, brands, and newcomers.

Paul Clifford
CEO & Founder, Kudani.com

Introduction

Much has been written about content marketing in the last few years. It's a hot topic that continues to attract attention. If done correctly, it can help grow your business and add revenue to your bottom line. But very little has been written about how to develop the underlying content marketing strategy that is crucial to your success.

The quality of the questions you ask yourself about your business will determine how well you serve your customers and your community. So the first question you need to ask yourself is, "How do I create a content marketing strategy so that I can serve my customers?" *Content Marketing Strategies For Dummies* is written to help you answer this and many other crucial questions about content marketing.

About This Book

Content marketing is how you provide your customers with the information they need to make decisions and solve problems. So why are so many content marketers falling short in this critical area? More specifically, what problems hold you back from creating the content you need you?

According to several reports, including the 2014 B2B Spotlight Report (https://www.brighttalk.com/webcast/1166/137365), the three greatest problems you have as a content marketer are:

- **You don't have enough time:** As a business person, your schedule is already full. Adding content marketing to the mix makes it almost impossible to get that marketing done right.

- **You can't create enough content:** No matter how much content you create, it's never going to be enough.

- **You don't know what to write about that will engage your audience**: You run out of ideas and don't have the time to spend researching new ones that will resonate with your specific audience.

Here's the good news: You can tackle — and solve — all these problems with the strategic content marketing plan that this book helps you develop and execute. The book is full of resources and solid, research-backed advice.

Sprinkled throughout are the book are pointers to downloadable worksheets that help you customize and implement your own content marketing strategy. Each chapter also ends with a mind map (a great learning tool), of the chapter's contents. You can refer to these mind maps to help you assimilate all the key points of your ongoing content marketing efforts. As you read this book, use them to develop a solid framework and assimilate the key points for your ongoing content marketing efforts.

You can find all the downloadable worksheets and mind maps at www.dummies.com/extras/contentmarketingstrategies.

Foolish Assumptions

I wrote this book to serve as an invaluable guide, and I wondered what you would need to know to find this book interesting. Here are some of the assumptions I've made about you:

- ✔ You work for or run a business with an online component
- ✔ You've considered using content marketing as a strategy but aren't sure where to start
- ✔ Your competition is using content marketing, and you need a solid strategy to beat it
- ✔ You have accounts on social media platforms but aren't sure what content to send to your followers
- ✔ You sell online products or services and you need to figure out what content will attract new buyers at every stage of the buyer's journey
- ✔ You're curious about how developing content marketing strategies can add revenue to your bottom line

Icons Used in This Book

In the margins of the book, you'll find these icons helping you out:

Whenever I provide a particular idea that will make content marketing easier for you, I mark it with a Tip icon.

The Remember icon marks paragraphs that contain a friendly reminder.

This icon points you to downloadable materials associated with this book.

Note the paragraphs marked with the Warning icon to avoid potential disaster.

Beyond the Book

In addition to the information you find in the book, I have included these online bonuses:

- **Cheat Sheet:** The cheat sheet for this book contains a checklist for content for a typical blog post; details about the roles that content marketing team members should play; the metrics to consider tracking; and the different types of influencers you should approach. Find it here:

  www.dummies.com/cheatsheet/contentmarketingstrategies

- **Dummies.com web extras:**

  Find out how to avoid content marketing strategy mistakes, reevaluate your business model, and create consistent content. You'll also learn how to document your buyer's journey, encourage your followers to share your content, and see reminders about what things you need to do when creating your content. Find the web extras here:

  www.dummies.com/extras/contentmarketingstrategies

- **Worksheets and mind maps:** I include a mind map at the end of each chapter that outlines what's in the chapter. Use these to help you assimilate what the chapter covers, and annotate them with your own ideas. You can also find downloadable worksheets to serve as hands-on aids in developing your own content marketing strategies. Find these items here:
  www.dummies.com/extras/contentmarketingstrategies.

- **Updates:** If I have any updates for this book, they will be posted at
  www.dummies.com/extras/contentmarketingstrategies.

Where to Go from Here

This book is designed so that you can quickly jump to a specific chapter or section that most interests you. You don't have to start with the first chapter — although if you're new to content marketing strategy, I recommend that you do so. Understanding the Five *C*s framework of Content Marketing, explained in Chapter 1, helps you better apply the techniques that you learn in subsequent chapters of the book.

Part I

Getting Started with Content Marketing Strategies

getting started
with

Content Marketing Strategies

In this part . . .

- ✔ Find out about the Five *C*s process that will help you develop a successful content marketing strategy.

- ✔ Learn how your business model and brand is perceived by your ideal customers.

- ✔ See why getting attention is critical to building a large fan base on social platforms.

- ✔ You need buy-in from all parts of the organization for your content marketing project. I show you how to get it.

- ✔ Putting your content marketing plan together requires that you collect the information that will persuade your stakeholders. See how to present the data that will get buy-in from your audience.

Chapter 1

Establishing Your Content Marketing Strategy

Companies have finally recognized what their customers have always known. If they can't find the content that makes your product easy to use and enjoy, they are off to seek out your competitor. You've missed the opportunity to impress them or, in some cases, even get on their radar screen. As marketing expert Seth Godin has said, "Content marketing is the only marketing left."

This chapter covers what goes into creating a content marketing strategy. Without it, you can't get the traction you need to beat the competition. You also discover each of the "Five *C*s" that must be included to make your strategy complete.

Understanding the Components of a Content Marketing Strategy

To understand how the pieces of a content marketing strategy fit together, I have organized the components into a framework called the Five *C*s. They are (1) company focus; (2) customer experience; (3); channel promotion (4) content creation, and (5) check-back analysis.

Working with the Five *C*s framework helps you cover all the bases as you create your content marketing strategy and implement your content plan. You can choose to go sequentially through the chapters, or pick the ones that relate to your company's present status.

I also present a mind map created with iMindMap software (`http://imindmap.com`) at the end of every chapter to help you take notes and organize your thoughts. You can download these maps (and see them in color) at `www.dummies.com/extrascontentmarketingstrategies`.

The following sections walk you through each of the Five *C*s in more detail.

Determining the company focus

The first *C* is company focus. To create a content marketing strategy, you need to begin by looking at your company's business goals. The question to ask yourself and your team is, "What do we want the company to achieve and how do we make it happen?"

You should direct your attention to your goals and business case for undertaking this effort. To that end, Part I of the book covers the following topics:

- **Components that go into creating a content marketing strategy:** You're in that topic's chapter now, and aspects of that strategy are covered in more detail in subsequent chapters.

- **Getting your customers' attention:** Content marketers are fiercely competing for your customers' attention. Find out why attention is important and how to capture it.

- **Understanding your business model and your brand:** Learn about a variety of business models and how to determine what "job" your product does. You look at brand components and access a downloadable brand worksheet to use.

- **Getting buy-in from your teams:** Getting buy-in from everyone on your team, not just the executives, is important. I tell you how to present your proposal to encourage participation and provide a downloadable worksheet that uses what I call the Five-Prong Approach (FPA).

- **Putting your content marketing plan together:** Find out how the organization of your company can affect the success of your content marketing efforts. You also see how the work you do on the Five-Prong Approach in Chapter 4 helps you put your plan together.

Uncovering the customer experience

The second of the Five *C*s is customer experience. You need to learn what your prospects will think, feel, and do when interacting with your brand. The question for your marketing team to ask is, "Who are our prospects and how will we serve them as customers?"

You must define your audience and analyze the customer experience. You do this by

- **Collecting and analyzing customer data:** Before you define your audience, you need to evaluate the kind of data you will use. In Chapter 6, you look at the benefits and challenges you may face when dealing with big data to analyze your audience.

- **Creating personas:** Chapter 7 helps you define the characteristics of your perfect audience by investigating several different types of information. You find out what actions you need to take, and I point you to a worksheet for creating a persona template to use as a model to document your findings.

- **Developing the customer journey:** You want to understand the journey your prospect takes from being interested in your product to sold on it. Chapter 8 looks at the buyer's mindset and gives you a model to help you document your customer's touchpoints.

- **Assisting with sales enablement:** Your sales team is facing an empowered customer. Find out in Chapter 9 how your content can assist in making the job easier and more powerful. I also show you how to determine where your company falls on the content maturity scale.

Creating quality content

The third *C* is content creation. You need to focus on creating quality content (based on your story) that you know your customers want and need. The question to ask is, "How will we create quality content, who will do it, and what will that content be?"

You need to develop a strategy for content, define your messaging, and establish your systems and governance rules. The chapters in this part take you through:

- **Creating a content strategy:** You should have both a content plan and a content marketing strategy. In Chapter 10, you see how to take an audit of your content to determine what you have and how you can leverage it to develop a true corporate asset. This chapter is chock-full of maps and worksheets: a downloadable content audit worksheet; a downloadable content plan worksheet; and examples of maps that you can use to visualize your own content ecosystem and websites.

✔ **Content types:** You want to ensure that you take full advantage of all the types of content available to you. Chapter 11 covers various types including long- and short-form original content, curated content, and visual content.

✔ **Writing and storytelling:** You have a story to tell that will connect with your audience. How do you incorporate it into your content? See Chapter 12 to get a feel for the science behind why stories work and how to develop your own powerful corporate stories.

✔ **Processes and systems:** You know that without a documented workflow and procedures, your content marketing efforts fail. Chapter 13 spells out the roles and responsibilities of your content team and shows you the benefits of using an editorial calendar.

Developing channel promotions

The fourth *C* is channel promotion. To have your content make the greatest impact, you want to decide where and by whom your content will be distributed. The question to ask is, "How will our prospects and customers find our content so that they can choose us?"

You want to make your content easy to find and share. You need to know how to promote your content so that prospects can find it.

✔ **Channel plans:** Developing a content plan is not enough. After you have created your content, you need to get wide distribution. Chapter 14 explores how to understand your channel needs and shows you a model you can use to put together individual channel plans.

✔ **Sharing content:** Sharing is key to any content plan. Chapter 15 looks at why you should embrace share-ability as a strategy and borrow from journalism's Five *W*s and one *H* (who, what, why, where, when, how) as applied to sharing.

✔ **Paid, earned, shared, and owned media:** Making the most of all types of media is the only way to ensure that your brand voice will be heard. Look to Chapter 16 to learn about the value of these types of media and why earned media is gaining in importance.

✔ **Syndication and guest posting:** Do you think syndication is "old school"? Maybe it's not. Chapter 17 shows you how to get the most from syndication and why you need to be guest posting.

✔ **Influencers:** Influencers wield a great deal of power with online audiences. Find out in Chapter 18 how to pick the right influencers for you. I also supply a downloadable worksheet to help you put together your plan for working with individual influencers.

Deploying check-back analysis

The fifth *C* is check-back analysis. The focus here is on the metrics you choose to determine successes or failure. The question to ask is, "Have we met our goals?"

You want to reevaluate your plans and make revisions as necessary. Chapters 19 and 20 work with you to

✔ **Reassess your business model and brand value** You know that it's important to frequently assess how things are working. Find out how you can determine whether business model changes are warranted and whether you need to revise brand plans.

✔ **Reexamine your content marketing strategy:** Obviously, a determination of how well your content marketing strategy is working is essential. See why even failing is a springboard to success and why you need to get buy-in for making changes.

So that's an overview of the Five *C*s. Each chapter also includes far more information and working plans than listed here. If you do the hard work required to create and implement your plans, you can expect to be on the road to content marketing success.

Don't be left out

When creating your strategy, knowing what other companies with high growth do is helpful. According to a 2014 study done by Accenture called "CMOs: Time for digital transformation or risk being left on the sidelines" (`https://www.accenture.com/us-en/insight-cmos-time-digital-transformation-risk-left-sidelines.aspx`), a large percentage of high-growth companies:

✔ Use data and analytics to improve the impact of their marketing (86 percent)

✔ Know that digital channels are of strategic importance (84 percent)

✔ Make sure that customers get a similar experience across all channels (80 percent)

Communicating Your Mission

When you hear the term *mission statement,* you probably want to skip to the next section in this chapter. I understand. At some point while you were in school, you were taught about mission statements and you found it boring. But the good news is that now, when you look at communicating the reason your company exists, a mission statement becomes important and personal.

Crafting your statement

In his book *Epic Content: How to How to Tell a Different Story, Break through the Clutter, and Win More Customers by Marketing Less* (McGraw-Hill Education, 2013), Joe Pulizzi, "the godfather of content marketing" and head of the Content Marketing Institute (see Figure 1-1), offers an easy way to craft a content marketing mission statement.

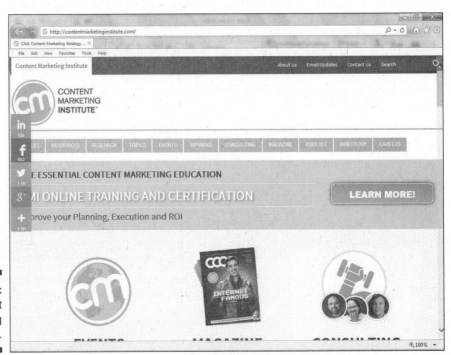

Figure 1-1:
Content
Marketing
Institute.

Pulizzi says to break down the statement into three parts:

- ✔ **Whom you will serve:** The core audience you are targeting
- ✔ **What solution you will offer:** What you will deliver to that audience
- ✔ **The outcome:** How it will make them better

Here's a breakdown of what goes into each of these sections:

- ✔ **The target audience:** Before you determine the characteristics of your personas (Chapter 7 covers personas in detail), you have to identify the niche(s) that work best for you. Aside from doing market research, you need to pick a very narrow group to target. When defining their niche, some companies are afraid to rule anyone out. They think that they may eliminate an important customer segment. But narrowing down the target is exactly what makes this tactic so powerful. By defining your niche carefully, you know that you're speaking to the people who are interested in hearing your message.

  You can always add segments later, but remember this: When you target everyone, you don't connect with anyone.

- ✔ **Your solution:** This may seem like the simple part of the formula, but it's only deceptively simple. You know what your product does. But in your mission statement, you want to communicate the solution as a promise to meet your customer's needs.

- ✔ **Your desired effect:** In this section, you want to spell out what need your product satisfies. Clearly identifying this need is key to determining whether customers believe you fulfilled your promise to them.

As you look at your company's goals, you want them to align with your content marketing strategy. If those goals don't align with your strategy, you need to determine what revisions to make.

Reviewing real mission statements

Now that you've looked at what goes into creating a mission statement, let's see how it plays out in real life. In her article "12 Truly Inspiring Company Vision and Mission Statement Examples," as shown in Figure 1-2, Lindsay Kolowich gives some examples to work with (`http://blog.hubspot.com/marketing/inspiring-company-mission-statements`).

Figure 1-2:
HubSpot
blog.

You can deconstruct a few that hit the mark by looking at their mission statements and seeing how the formula fits.

- **Patagonia mission statement:** "Build the best product, cause no unnecessary harm, use business to inspire and implement solutions to the environmental crisis" (http://Patagonia.com; see Figure 1-3.

  - *Who the company serves:* People who love outdoor activities

  - *What the solution is:* High quality clothing to fight the elements

  - *What the outcome is:* Deliver excellent clothing under superior working conditions that do not damage the environment

  This is an effective one-sentence mission statement that is clear and defines Patagonia's commitment to its customers and the environment.

- **Warby Parker mission statement:** "Warby Parker was founded with a rebellious spirit and a lofty objective: to offer designer eyewear at a revolutionary price, while leading the way for socially-conscious businesses" (http://warbyparker.com; see Figure 1-4).

  Who the company serves: Fashion-forward eyeglass wearers

  What the solution is: Designer eyewear at a revolutionary price

Figure 1-3:
Patagonia.

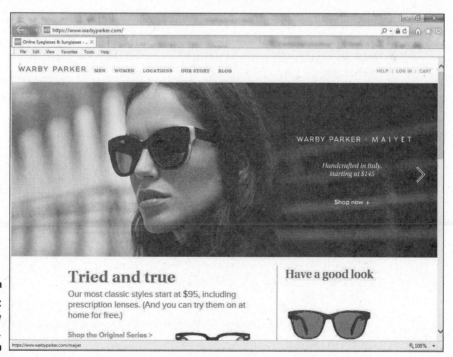

Figure 1-4:
Warby
Parker.

> *What the outcome is:* Fairly priced eyewear to customers and a program that teaches people in underdeveloped countries to prescribe free eyewear to those in need.

This is another one-sentence mission statement that succinctly communicates Warby Parker's desire to provide well-priced designer eyewear and a commitment to help fund socially-conscious businesses.

✔ **Ikea mission statement:** "At Ikea our vision is to create a better everyday life for the many people. Our business idea supports this vision by offering a wide range of well-designed, functional home furnishing products at prices so low that as many people as possible will be able to afford them."

- *Who the company serves:* People who want well designed products but can't afford expensive items.

- *What the solution is:* Functional home products at low prices

- *What the outcome is:* Create a better everyday life for as many people as possible.

With this statement Ikea clearly communicates its desire to help people afford well-designed products.

These companies make crafting mission statements look easy. But I'm sure they spent a lot of time and effort to get them just right. A mission statement can help employees serve their customers and feel pride in their organization.

In her article, Kolowich quotes Simon Sinek, author of the book, *Start With Why,* as saying, "Customers will never love a company until the employees love it first."

Establishing Your Goals

After you've established your mission statement, you can focus on your company goals. In Chapter 3, you take a close look at your business model and create a business model canvas. Doing the exercises in that chapter should prepare you to articulate your goals. Here, I give you a brief look at how to formulate goals.

Uncovering your goals

When looking at formulating your own goals, it can be useful to see what other marketers set as their top goals for B2B content marketing. According to the

"2015 Benchmarks, Budgets and Trends — North America" report by the Content Marketing Institute/Marketing Profs, (`http://www.slideshare.net/CMI/2015-b2b-content-marketing-benchmarks-budgets-and-trends-north-america-by-content-marketing-institute-and-marketingprofs`; see Figure 1-5), the top organizational goals for B2B content marketing are the following:

✔ **Brand awareness:** 84 percent

✔ **Lead generation:** 83 percent

✔ **Engagement:** 81 percent

✔ **Sales:** 75 percent

✔ **Lead nurturing:** 74 percent

✔ **Customer Retention/Loyalty:** 69 percent

✔ **Customer Evangelism:** 57 percent

✔ **Upsell/Cross-sell:** 52 percent

The report indicates that 2015 was the fifth year that brand awareness came in at the top spot and that customer evangelism shows up on the list.

Next you find out how to set measures to track your goals.

Figure 1-5:
2015 Benchmarks, Budgets, and Trends — North America Survey.

Picking KPIs

After you establish your goals, you need to develop Key Performance Indicators (KPIs). KPIs are the measures you choose to help you determine whether you're reaching your business goals. You need them to keep your strategy on track. If you don't measure yourself against your business goals, you won't know whether your content marketing strategy is working and supporting your larger business goals.

To help you think about how to craft your KPIs in relation to your marketing goals, check out Table 1-1. You can apply the table to your marketing plan as well. List your goals and then choose some metrics. Then refer back to this list when you check your progress.

Table 1-1	Choosing KPIs
CMI/Marketing Profs B2B Top Goals	*Suggested Metrics*
Increase brand awareness	Social media shares, social media likes, email forwards, referral links
Lead generation Lead nurturing	Blog signups, blog comments, conversion rate, form completions
Increase engagement	Comments, page depth (how many pages consumed), downloads, page views, back links, time on site, click through rate
Grow sales revenue by *X* percent	Revenue influenced by content (which content was consumed before sale), offline sales
Improve customer retention/loyalty	Bounce rate, followers, retention rate
Encourage customer evangelism	Social media shares, comments, follower count, word of mouth
Increase upsells/cross-sells	Measure conversions in shopping cart and on landing pages, number of conversions

Expanding Your Corporate Mindset

Every company has its own culture. The culture dictates how and why tasks get done. If your culture is a positive one, you're probably focused obsessively on serving your customers, and you're proud of your reputation. Have you thought about how your culture, reputation, and customer service impact your content marketing strategy? You can examine that next.

Creating a culture of content

Does your company have a culture of content (CoC)? Content creation and marketing is front and center in today's businesses, so it's no surprise that it could become part of an organization's DNA.

The term *CoC* was popularized by the Altimeter Group's authors Rebecca Lieb and Jessica Groopman in their 2014 study cited here: `http://rebeccalieb.com/blog/2014/12/04/the-three-components-of-a-culture-of-content`. (See Figure 1-6.)

Figure 1-6: Rebecca Lieb.

So what is a culture of content? It's one in which:

- ✔ Content is championed.
- ✔ Content is shared throughout the organization.
- ✔ People are encouraged to be creative with content.
- ✔ Staff from every department can contribute content.
- ✔ The company has a tolerance for risk and failure with content.

Does this sound like your organization? Or a better question might be, "Wouldn't you like your organization to function like this?" Trying to move your organization in this direction would be worthwhile. Your organization can benefit from a CoC in several ways. It can get:

- ✔ **Better quality content (and quantity):** People who are encouraged to be creative and become part of a content team create better content and contribute more often.

- ✔ **More content sharing:** People who are proud of the content the organization (and they) are creating are more likely to share it.

- ✔ **A competitive edge:** A company that champions content and places a high value on its creation stands out from the crowd.

- ✔ **More valuable data to analyze:** More and better content provides valuable data.

How can you foster a CoC? Dawn Papandrea details in her article, "How to Create a Culture of Content Marketing from the Top Down" (`http://www.columnfivemedia.com/how-to-create-a-culture-of-content-marketing-from-the-top-down`; see Figure 1-7), some of successful entrepreneur Marcus Sheridan's (`http://www.thesaleslion.com`) steps for creating a content culture.

Figure 1-7:
Column Five
Media.

Here are a few of those eight tips:

- ✔ **Get buy-in from the top.** Make sure to have support from your executives if you are going to undertake a content marketing strategy. No project can survive the disinterest of management.

- ✔ **Share the same vision.** All good company cultures thrive because they have a shared vision of what they want to achieve. This is especially crucial for a culture that needs to rely on content contributions from staff.

- ✔ **Appoint a Chief Content Officer.** You need a champion to encourage content marketing efforts. Have a person dedicated to the program's success. It's important to show employees that you are investing in the program.

- ✔ **Support and maintain the content culture.** Make sure that everyone on the team is convinced of the importance of content and keeps the culture at the forefront.

Most companies that have a content culture agree on one important ingredient: training. They believe that without training their staff to recognize, create, and share content of value, they will not succeed.

Thinking about reputation

The importance of reputation is obvious to almost everyone. But you probably don't think about how your company's reputation contributes to the acceptance of your content and vice versa. When readers see your branded content, they need to make an immediate decision. They have to decide whether you're trustworthy enough to continue reading. If they decide that you're not, they click away. If they see a review of your business, they can be swayed by negative comments. But how much does this really matter to your bottom line?

According to a press release by IC Media Direct, shown in Figure 1-8, "It has been calculated by the Harvard Business School that each star in a Yelp rating increases a business' sales by 5 to 9%. And a bump up from 3.5 to 4 stars on Yelp typically results in a 19% increase of restaurant bookings during peak business hours" (http://www.reuters.com/article/2015/06/29/idUSnMKWnWknGa+1d2+MKW20150629).

That's quite an impact. Yet companies are typically very lax about reputation management as part of their content marketing strategy.

In her article for *Connote Magazine* shown in Figure 1-9, Rebecca Bilbao reports that only 13 percent of businesses have a fully integrated reputation management program. She also reminds us that a company's reputation among its employees is crucial to recruiting and retention, which impacts the bottom line (http://connotemagazine.com/features/the-reputation-report-set-kpis-or-perish/).

Figure 1-8:
IC Media
Direct.

You need to monitor online content to ensure that your reputation stays intact. Here are a few habits to consider building into your content marketing strategy:

- ✔ **Continually listen:** The conversation about your business is going on 24 hours a day. You need to be ready to respond to anything that could affect your customer's perception of you. Make sure to read review sites and other user-generated content about your business regularly, right along with your customers.

- ✔ **Monitor your brand names and products:** Set up alerts for your product and brand names. You don't want to miss a brewing problem.

- ✔ **Link to all your sites to create a wide perspective:** Don't make your customers dig for information about you. Be sure to link to all your owned media and social media sites.

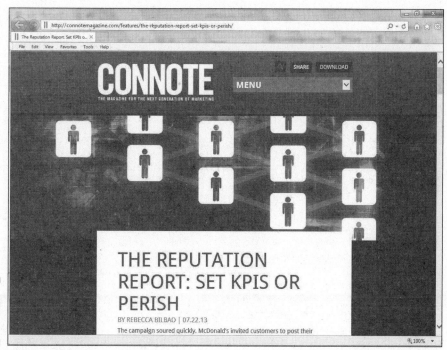

Figure 1-9:
Connote
Magazine.

✔ **Maintain strict content governance:** You should have a content governance system set up (see Chapter 14 to learn about governance systems.) Make sure that your system is in force so that erroneous or poor quality content doesn't have a lasting effect on your reputation.

✔ **Create and distribute case studies and testimonials:** Blow your own horn so that others can form a positive opinion about your company. Case studies and testimonials should be a staple on your website.

Using content to serve customers

Get ready to hear something you won't like: You need to make customer service a part of your content marketing strategy. See, I knew you wouldn't like it. Why? Because it's not as sexy as creating great blog posts that get you buzz, plus it requires extra effort.

If your organization takes this section's advice to heart, though, you will see several important benefits including:

✔ An increase in customer loyalty and retention

✔ Happier, more educated customers

✔ A better understanding of your customer's problems

✔ An opportunity to provide real solutions

All these benefits go straight to the bottom line.

Tony Hsieh applied this customer service strategy to his company Zappos (`http://zappos.com`), and it was acquired by Amazon for $1.2 billion. Perhaps you should consider trying it.

So how should you apply your customer service strategy to your content marketing strategy? Think for a moment about how you provide customer service now. You probably provide data sheets, product documentation, email support, and, if you're ambitious, social media platform support. But here's the truth: This approach is wholly inadequate for the content-intensive world you live in today. You need to look at your website, your other owned sites, and your social sites to see how you can focus on adding customer service content to each one.

You likely believe that customers are at the center of your strategy. However, you might have that wrong. You might be customer *centric* rather than customer *focused,* according to J-P De Clerck in his article, "Content marketing: a customer-centric manifesto" (`http://www.i-scoop.eu/content-marketing-customer-centric`; see Figure 1-10).

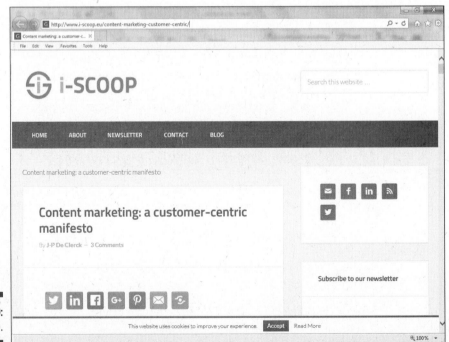

Figure 1-10:
I-Scoop.

De Clerck cites Peter Fader's book *Customer Centricity: Focus on the Right Customers for Strategic Advantage* (Wharton Digital Press), which says that customer centricity means focusing on the high-value customer and marketing to that segment. This is not to say that you completely ignore your other customers. It means that you focus a great deal of effort on the customers with the highest potential customer lifetime value. Customer Lifetime Value (CLV) refers to the profit you expect to make over the lifetime of a specific customer.)

Monetate's infographic cited in the article is found here `http://content.monetate.com/h/i/12311808-what-does-it-mean-to-be-customer-centric`. (See Figure 1-11.) Monetate is a customer analytics firm.

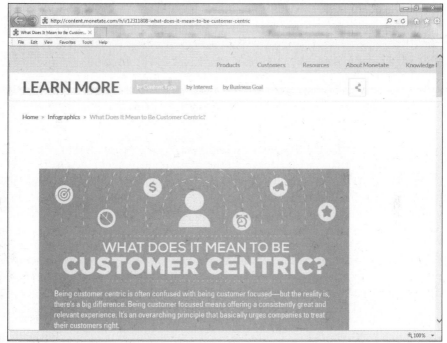

Figure 1-11: Monetate's Infographic showing what it means to be customer centric.

So what should you do regarding customer service content after you identify these high-CLV customers? You should create content that addresses their specific needs and distribute it on the following:

✔ **Support sites:** Look at the content you provide for support sites. Is it dull and boring? Your customers want to be entertained as well as educated. Think about how you can make this content more appealing.

✔ **Social media platforms:** You may already answer support questions on these sites, but do you provide links to interesting help content? Probably not. Try to think about putting links to all the content you create for your customers.

✔ **Guest postings:** You're probably not thinking about customer service when you send guest posts. But aiming your post toward customer service isn't hard to do. Just make it something that is "in service" to the reader.

✔ **Webinars:** You likely have webinar content that serves customers. Repurpose it as podcasts or video to spread your message.

Your strategy should include content targeted at helping your most valuable customers find the information they need.

Dipping into User Design and Habits

Two additional issues to be aware of when you are constructing your content marketing plan are the user experience (UX) and your customer's habits. Both are related to content in a very specific way:

✔ **The UX:** The UX I am referring to here is not about the buyer's journey that the user takes on the road to making a purchase. (I cover the buyer's journey in Chapter 8.) The UX is the experience the user has while navigating your sites and reading your content. It's about the design elements you employ to communicate your content marketing strategy.

✔ **Habits:** Your customer's habits impact the adoption of your product. When you know how to attach the use of your product to customers' habits, you're more likely to persuade them to buy. The content you create to get your customers on board with your products will have a big effect and must be part of your strategy.

Read on to find out how both of these issues impact your content.

Recognizing the importance of UX design in your strategy

When you think of developing a strategy, issues about design probably don't immediately come to mind. Yet when you look at conducting business online, you can find evidence of design choices in everything you do. Not only is the product itself impacted by design, but the way you have customers interact with the brand is completely driven by design.

This point in driven home by John Moore Williams in his article, "The New Design Process: Why Designers Should Be Shaping Business Strategy," in the InVision blog (`http://blog.invisionapp.com/why-designers-should-be-shaping-business-strategy/`).

Williams makes a very important point that's worth quoting in full: "Designers understand the business landscape differently than the business guys. Where an exec sees lifts in conversion rates, a designer sees a more delightful user experience. Where an exec sees increased time on site, a designer might wonder if some interactions could produce less friction. Where the business guy sees users, designers see people."

Are you guilty of the narrow vision that Williams describes? I'm not suggesting that you shouldn't think about metrics. In fact, I cover the importance of tracking metrics in "Picking KPIs," earlier in this chapter. The key is to keep an eye on metrics and the UX at the same time. Your user experiences content visually, and design either impedes or enhances that experience — and enhancing it makes all the difference.

Observing product habits

Most habits develop without our realizing it. We find that we perform some of the same routines every day without much thought. In fact, stopping a habit is more difficult than starting one, as I'm sure you've discovered.

Having the topic of habits may seem strange in a chapter on strategy, but it really isn't when you look at how habits impact your customers' use of your product. Do you know whether using your product requires a habit change? If it does, you're going to have an uphill battle luring customers. Conversely, if you can attach the use of your product to an existing habit, you will find fostering product adoption much easier.

An interesting perspective on the benefits of habits as they relate to products was discussed by Dina Chaiffetz in her article series on the InVision blog (`http://blog.invisionapp.com/how-to-build-habit-forming-products-building-on-the-loop/`).

Chaiffetz points out two significant benefits of focusing on habits: (1) when your product establishes a habit, you establish a permanent relationship with a customer; and (2) if you know about a habit your customer already has, you can piggy-back on that to become part of the customer's routine.

Doesn't that sound good? Habits can help you develop an ongoing relationship with your customer that will be hard to break, plus you can become a part of your customers' everyday life.

So how can you add habits to your strategy? Nir Eyal tackles this question in his book *Hooked: How to Form Habit-Building Products,* in which he presents the four steps to product habit formation.

You can find an example of this process in Nir Eyal's SlideShare presentation that diagrams how a Pinterest habit is formed at `http://www.slideshare.net/nireyal/hooked-model` (see slide #110).

Here's how the Pinterest habit is formed:

- **Trigger:** First, you need to have both an external and internal trigger that cause you to use the product. An external trigger might be that you are reading your emails online, so going to another site is easy. The internal trigger could be your boredom or desire to socialize.

- **Action:** You log in to a social platform and look around for something entertaining.

- **Variable Reward:** While on the platform, you are rewarded by discovering something of interest, or sometimes you find nothing and you log off. The key to this reward is that it doesn't happen every time; it's on a variable interval schedule.

  A variable interval schedule is a concept borrowed from behavioral psychology. It refers to the fact that you are more likely to keep going back for a reward when your reward is given intermittently, rather than each time you do something. If you're used to getting a reward every time and then you miss one or two, you will stop going back. If you are unsure when you will be rewarded because it's variable, you keep trying again. Slot machines work on the same principle.

- **Investment:** You make an investment in the product by personalizing it. In the case of Pinterest, you might pin things and share other pins. You are not only investing your time but also building a body of content, so you're likely to return.

So now you see how easily a product habit can be formed if it has the right ingredients. It helps you understand why your friends play certain games until they drop. You can find more about habit formation by looking at Stanford Professor BJ Fogg's work on changing behavior: `http://www.foggmethod.com/`.

Mind maps are a great learning tool. Check out the next page for a mind map of this chapter's content, and download a color version at `www.dummies.com/contentmarketingstrategies`.

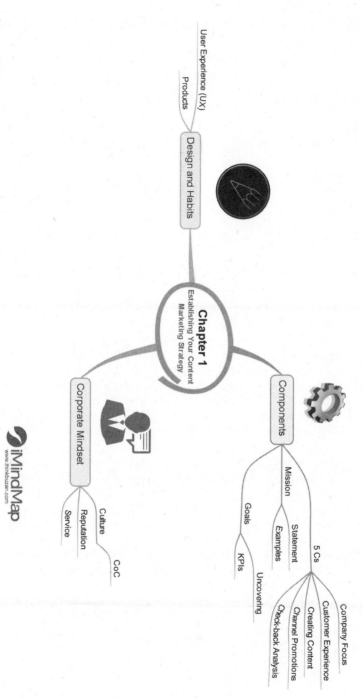

Chapter 2

Capturing Your Customer's Attention

Do you know the thing that all marketers desperately want in 2016? It's your attention — to what they have to say and sell. Since the advent of our "always on" culture, the competition for your attention has been fierce. In fact, most of the content created by companies is never seen by its prospects.

It wasn't always hard to get people's attention. In the previous century, when you wanted to get a customer's attention, you would send him your marketing material and give him a call. The prospect was usually receptive because you were the keeper of all product information. Those days, however, are over.

But conversations do help develop relationships, and relationships help you get and keep your customer's attention. So what can you do to compete with other producers for consumers' attention? There is no shortage of content from your competitors that identifies each one of them as the one to choose. Your content probably does the same. How do consumers decide?

In this chapter, you look at how getting prospects' attention involves developing the kinds of conversations that help your prospects say yes to you. You may or may not have the opportunity to meet your customers face to face, but you must engage them with quality content that addresses their needs and provides valuable information.

Focusing on Attention

Unsurprisingly, technology has negatively impacted our attention span. The Statistic Brain Institute defines attention span as "the amount of concentrated time on a task without becoming distracted" and reports that our attention span in 2000 was 12 seconds but by 2015 had gone down to 8.25 seconds (`http://www.statisticbrain.com/attention-span-statistics`; see Figure 2-1).

The Statistic Brain Institute also reports that an office worker checks her email Inbox approximately thirty times per hour. That's a shocking statistic if you multiply that by an 8-hour day. Two hundred and forty times a day!

Figure 2-1: Statistic Brain Institute.

Seeking the "attention web"

So why should the attention span and distractibility of the average customer matter to you as a content marketer? Obviously, it matters because you want to get your prospect's attention, and doing so becomes more difficult with each passing day. In addition, what marketers have come to believe about engagement metrics (that they consist of measures like page views or clicks) may not be true. That's why marketers started to consider whether the time people spend engaging with content or the scrolling they do might be better ways to measure their interest. This led to what is called the "attention web" movement that involves selling ads based on attention measures rather than sheer numbers (of clicks, for example).

An article on Time.com looks at the myths we hold about how we consume online content. Authored by Tony Haile, CEO of Cheatbeat (`http://Chartbeat.com`), it's called "What You Think You Know About the Web Is Wrong" (`http://time.com/12933/what-you-think-you-know-about-the-web-is-wrong`; see Figure 2-2).

Figure 2-2:
Time.com.

Haile derived his findings based on an investigation his data analytics company conducted by reviewing 580,000 online articles. Central to Haile's argument is that fact that using the click as the most important measure of attention is flawed. Following are two of the four myths he presented:

> ✔ **Myth: We read what we've clicked.** This seems like a common sense assumption, but it may not be true. You assume that the reader clicks the article with the intention of reading it. This may be true, but it doesn't necessarily mean that the reader actually spends time reading that article. She may glance at it and move on. The content marketer

rejoices in the number of clicks he gets, but the reader may actually make no connection with the brand. The content marketer then creates more content just like it in the mistaken belief that his reader was engaged. You can see how this would negatively impact your entire content program.

✔ **Myth: The more we share, the more we read.** You would expect that a person would share only an article that he found compelling. This is another fallacy. As discussed in Chapter 10 about sharing content, people share for all kinds of reasons. Haile found no correlation between the amount of time spent with an article and its number of shares, once again shattering the assumption that such articles have hit their target. It may be more likely that people share articles based on their headlines and source. From these factors, they make a guess about how pertinent the content is to their audience.

You probably find this information disheartening, as most serious content marketers do. So what can you do to deal with audience members with short attention spans? Tonya Wells provides some suggestions in her article "Micro Content: Capturing Readers with Short Attention Spans" on the Infographic World blog (`http://infographicworld.com/blogs/micro-content-capturing-readers-with-short-attention-spans/`; see Figure 2-3), a graphic design firm.

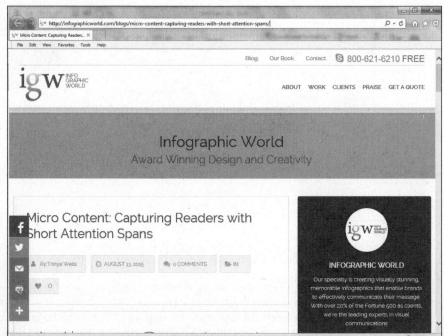

Figure 2-3:
An Infographic World article about short attention spans.

Wells suggests using the following:

- ✔ **Mini-graphics:** These would be graphics that focus on only a piece of data rather than present a long infographic. This approach has value because it does use a visual to capture attention but doesn't make the reader spend a long time figuring it out.

- ✔ **Short lists:** A short list appeals to someone who is on the go. You impart information in small chunks, like a bite-sized snack.

- ✔ **How-to articles:** Again, you can see how to make this format work for a reader with a short attention span. You can do what you did with the mini-graphic and focus on learning how to do one thing.

- ✔ **Tips and tricks:** This is a popular format for all audiences. By limiting the content to a few items, you have captured attention but not slowed down your reader.

- ✔ **Frequently asked questions (FAQs):** Keep them short and answer one specific question in each one. That way, you help readers make progress and don't slow them down with fluff.

- ✔ **Social media posts:** By definition, some of these posts should be short and to the point, like Twitter's 140 characters. Don't miss an opportunity to write short content that links out to a longer form post if the reader is interested.

Aside from specifically developing content for short attention spans, marketers and researchers have been looking for ways to improve their metrics so that they can gauge true reader interest. One example of this effort is the work of Christoph C. Cemper, the CEO of Impactana `http://impactana.com`, shown in Figure 2-4. Impactana is a software tool that measures buzz versus impact.

Cemper explains his approach to buzz versus impact in his article on the Marketing Land blog, as shown in Figure 2-5 (`http://marketingland.com/measuring-real-impact-content-marketing-131823`).

Cemper says that each marketer should ask herself, "Did our content resonate with the audience?" This is exactly the question content marketers must ask to ensure that their content strategy is hitting the mark. Here's the difference between *buzz* and *impact:*

- ✔ **Buzz:** Buzz is something that all content marketers like to have. It highlights their brand and gets the attention of their peers. It clearly has value. But if you're looking for true engagement, you need to go further than likes and retweets.

- ✔ **Impact:** Impact is measured by the amount of attention your reader gives your content. For example, comments on a blog post or downloads of content signal real interest. That's because the reader stopped to write something in relation to the content or downloaded content that he wanted to look at later.

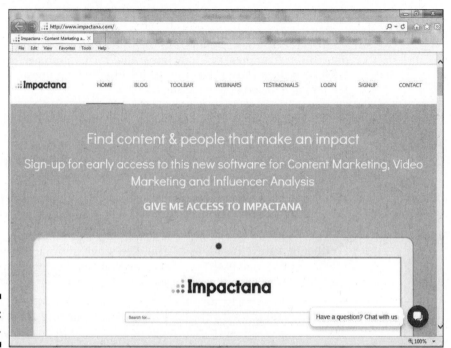

Figure 2-4:
Impactana.

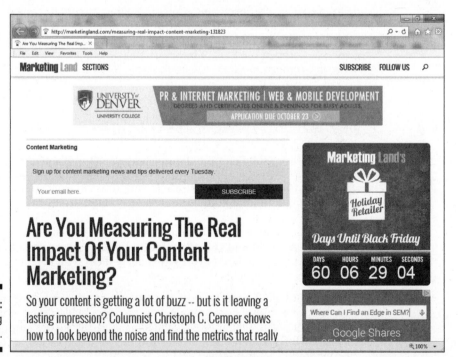

Figure 2-5:
Marketing
Land.

Cemper's prescription is to evaluate these concepts on a matrix, as shown in Figure 2-6. The original matrix can be seen on the article on Marketing Land (see Figure 2-5). The matrix shows that you obviously want to aim for both high buzz and high impact, but that average buzz can still be valuable if you have high impact.

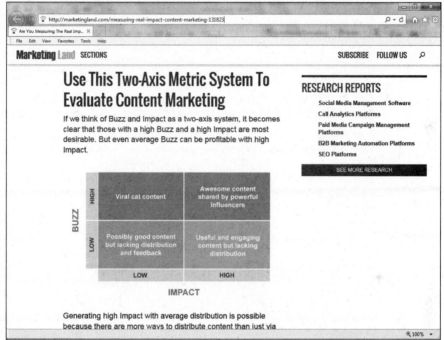

Figure 2-6:
Matrix of Christoph C. Cemper explaining buzz vs. impact.

Looking at attention triggers

Although some may treat attention as an unknowable commodity, there are actually codified ways to capture it. In his book *Captivology: The Science of Capturing People's Attention* (HarperOne, 2015), Ben Parr, former Mashable editor, details seven triggers that you can employ to get attention.

These triggers have been drawn from the fields of psychology and neuroscience and help you understand how and why people pay attention (sometimes without a conscious thought.)

The triggers are

- ✔ **"Automaticity":** This trigger relies on the automatic response people have to sensory cues, such as color.

- **Framing:** This trigger gets people to pay attention by challenging their world view. This means that when you present something in a way that is unexpected or doesn't match people's understanding, you get their attention. You have framed the problem in a way that doesn't match their understanding.

- **Disruption:** When you use the disruption trigger, you upset a person's expectations, which causes them to pay attention.

- **Reward:** By using the reward trigger, you tap into the inherent desire people have for rewards.

- **Reputation:** This trigger relies on the fact that people believe the words of experts and will give them their attention.

- **Mystery:** When people are unsure about what will happen or they don't understand something, they pay attention until they get an answer.

- **Acknowledgement:** People freely give their attention to those who nurture and support them.

In looking at this list, you probably think that getting attention is less mysterious than you thought. The problem you have when creating content is the fact that you have to know your audience well enough to know what constitutes a trigger. Table 2-1 lists questions you can ask yourself to determine the triggers for your audience.

If you have completed the development of your personas (see Chapter 7), you will be able to ask yourself specific questions directed at each one.

Table 2-1	Parr's Captivology Triggers
Trigger	*Some Questions to Ask*
"Automacity"	Are there specific senses related to your persona that you want to tap into, such as school colors or songs?
Framing	How can you change your personas' view to convince them that you are the only right choice to solve their problem?
Disruption	Can you challenge expectations? Shatter some myths?
Reward	What constitutes a real reward for your personas? For example, perhaps you can offer access to your new product in advance instead of a discount.
Reputation	Have you done your homework on influencers? (See Chapter 18 for more about influencers). If so, you will know who your personas take advice from.
Mystery	Can you develop a series of stories about your topic that will keep personas coming back for more?
Acknowledgement	Can you provide valuable customer service that goes beyond the expected?

Using these triggers as the basis for your content should help you get more attention for your brand. Give this list of questions to your teams to help guide them.

Making Your Content Easy to Consume

Do you want to help readers consume your content? Then make it easy! If you're like me, you've given up in frustration when an article wasn't readable. I'm not referring to the logical sequence or writing style, but rather to the design elements. If your article font is too small or lacks skimmable headings, you're sending your reader away.

Reading in patterns

A good starting point for making your content alluring to readers is to understand how people read. Eye-tracking studies have determined that people use two eye patterns when viewing content, as follows:

- **The Z pattern:** Picture a Z. Using this pattern, readers' eyes move from left to right and then down, and then left to right again.

- **The F pattern:** Using an F pattern, readers' eyes move left to right, and then back moving from right to left, and then right, and then down. Both patterns are shown in Figure 2-7.

  You can find the original images at Smashing magazine (`http://media.mediatemple.netdna-cdn.com/wp-content/uploads/2015/03/f-pattern-z-pattern-opt.png`).

  To further clarify, three versions of the F pattern as heat maps are shown in Figure 2-8. The originals can be seen at `http://www.nngroup.com/articles/f-shaped-pattern-reading-web-content/`.

When you're composing your blog posts and web pages, it's helpful to know how readers will be scanning your content. Using either an F or Z pattern, you know they will start at the top and read the headline. Then their eyes will scan down and across in some fashion. Put the most important content in the area of the page where you know they will look first.

Instead of trying to force your readers to read every word, facilitate their need for speed. As noted in the "Focusing on Attention" section, earlier in this chapter, your readers aren't likely to spend a long time poring over your articles. According to the Nielsen Norman Group, they'll read about 27 percent of the words on a page (`http://www.nngroup.com/articles/how-little-do-users-read`). Therefore, one of your jobs as a content marketer is to make your articles easy to skim.

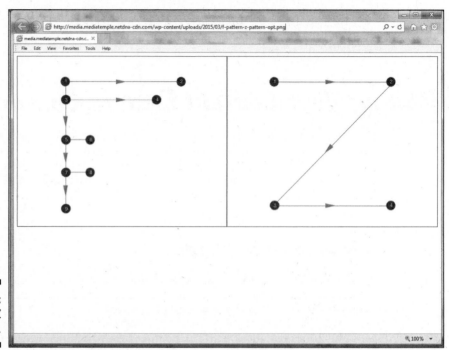

Figure 2-7:
The F and Z
patterns.

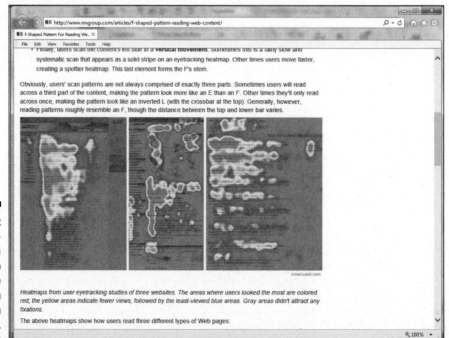

Figure 2-8:
The F Pat-
tern on a
heat map
from the
Nielsen
Norman
Group.

Considering design elements and typography

Whereas Chapter 13 discusses writing style, this chapter focuses on holding your reader's attention by using good design. So what are some things you can do to help your readers focus their attention? Consider using the following:

- **Headings and subheadings:** You want to make it easy to read your headline. (For more on the importance of headlines and tools you can use to improve them, see Chapter 12). But after your readers' eyes move from the headline, they are going to be skimming your headings and subheadings. If you leave these out, your reader will have to try to pick out words or phrases that have meaning to them. You shouldn't make them have to guess what and where those words are. If you do, you're banking on the fact that your reader has all the time in the world to assess your content. Considering what we know about attention spans, that's not likely.

- **Short paragraphs:** Keeping your paragraphs short really helps readers make progress through your article. When they see a dense article with no breaks, they are inclined to click away. It's not a conscious choice. They make a quick assessment about how long it will take to read an article, and they either commit to give it a try or move on.

- **Bullet lists:** As an author of many *For Dummies* books, I believe in the power of bullets. Some people are afraid to use bullets because they have seen too many bad examples. If you thoughtfully organize your material (as in this list!), bullets are a great way to help the reader quickly understand complex topics.

- **Numbered lists:** Everyone loves lists. It's one of the most popular formats on the web. Readers can instantly understand how the material is organized and gauge the amount of time they need to spend with it. In Figure 2-9, you can see the effective use of a list right in the blog post by Larry Kim (`http://blog.hubspot.com/marketing/design-content-remarketing-campaigns`). It sets up the content and provides structure to the post.

- **Type size and font color:** Designers often forget about differences in readers' vision. Some readers can't see tiny type. If the type is in a light color, it compounds the problem. It may look great in the design as a whole, but it can be a turn-off to many readers. Figure 2-10 shows a great example of an article by Maya Luke in the Influence & Co. blog that doesn't require you to squint or make your text larger (`http://blog.influenceandco.com/3-bulletproof-techniques-to-avoiding-writer-s-burnout`). You can't see the font color in this book, so go to the link here if you want to check it out.

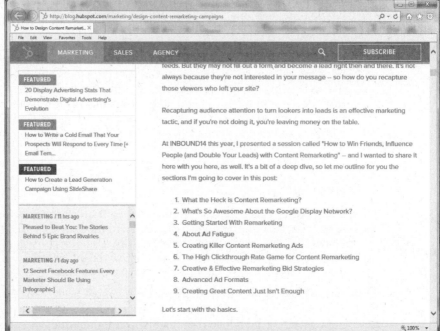

Figure 2-9: Numbered list example on the HubSpot blog.

- **Visuals:** Using visuals is a well-known way to advance understanding. If you can provide a photo, a map, a graph, or some kind of diagram, your reader will more easily connect to it. In the BarkBox blog (`https://barkbox.com/`), shown in Figure 2-11, you can see a wonderful example of a picture that works perfectly with the headline. It demonstrates a love for animals while displaying the "BarkGood For a Good Cause" banner.

- **White space:** The Contently blog is designed to make great use of white space, as shown in Figure 2-12 (`http://contently.com/strategist/2015/09/04/13-stats-that-should-terrify-cmos/`).

Figure 2-10:
Type size
and font
color on the
Influence &
Co. blog.

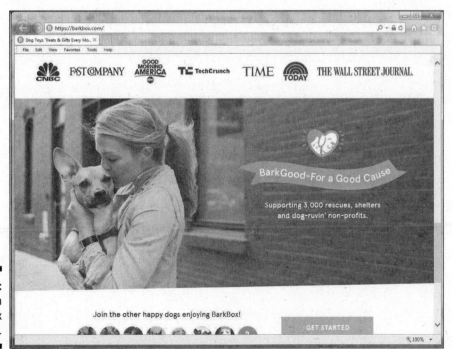

Figure 2-11:
Visuals on
the BarkBox
blog.

Figure 2-12:
White space
on the Con-
tently blog.

Deploying Interactive Content

Before moving on from the topic of attention, I want to touch on the development of interactive content. It's a relatively new content type that can really grab your prospects' attention. This content type is becoming popular because it's easy to create with some new tools. It's popular with customers because you don't have to require an email address.

Some examples of this type of content are

✔ Interactive infographics

✔ Quizzes and assessments

✔ Interactive white papers

✔ Advanced calculators

✔ Polls

✔ Interactive videos

✔ Interactive shopping catalogs

You gain several benefits from using this type of content, but I specifically want to highlight two key points here:

✔ **Higher potential to develop a long-term customer:** When prospects make an investment in your content by answering questions or providing their own content, this content becomes their asset. They may return to your site often and possibly purchase something.

✔ **Knowledge about your audience:** When prospects answer questions, fill in a quiz, or take an assessment, they are providing information about themselves. This information is given to you freely, so they don't feel coerced.

Recently, several companies have come online to help you create this type of interactive content. Here are some examples:

✔ **Ceros (**`http://ceros.com`; see Figure 2-13**):** This company's platform helps you create interactives for formats including infographics, lookbooks (a collection of photos showing different aspects of something), and microsites.

✔ **SnapApp (**`http://snapapp.com`; see Figure 2-14**):** SnapApp helps you create ten different types of interactive content, including contests, quizzes, and infographics.

✔ **Ion Interactive (**`http://www.ioninteractive.com`; see Figure 2-15**):** This company specifically targets content marketers and provides support or services to create interactive content.

Figure 2-13:
Ceros.

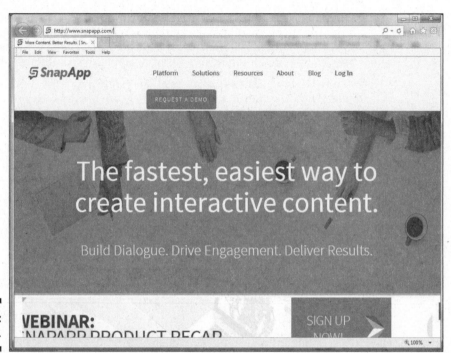

Figure 2-14:
SnapApp.

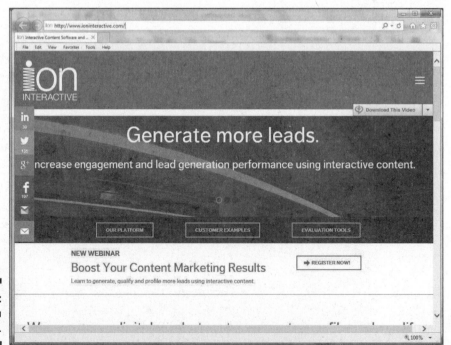

Figure 2-15:
Ion
Interactive.

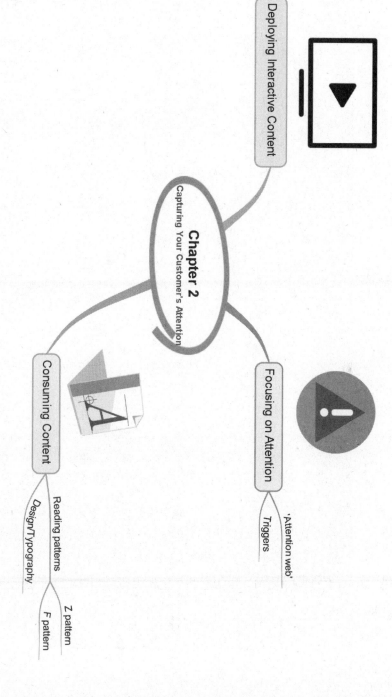

Deploying Interactive Content

Chapter 2
Capturing Your Customer's Attention

Consuming Content

Focusing on Attention

Design/Typography

Reading patterns

Z pattern

F pattern

Triggers

'Attention web'

iMindMap
www.thinkbuzan.com

Chapter 3

Understanding Your Business Model and Brand

● ●

In This Chapter

▶ Discovering the "Jobs To Be Done" concept

▶ Understanding what drives revenue

▶ Uncovering what your brand means

▶ Recognizing brand goals

● ●

*Y*ou may be asking yourself why a book about content marketing strategy has a chapter about business models and brands. There's a good reason for that. You can't really begin to determine your content marketing strategy until you determine how your company generates revenue and retains loyal customers. After you understand that, you'll know what your customers find valuable in terms of products and content. You'll be able to deliver the kind of content that keeps your customers engaged and buying.

Oddly enough, some companies don't really understand the business they're in. That may sound counterintuitive, but it's true. Your company could be one of them. I speak to C-level managers who fully understand what their product does, but not what "job" (or jobs) it does for their customers. If you don't know what job your customers are hiring your product to do, you won't fully understand what your customers want.

In this chapter, you look at what you need to know about your own business model and how to present your brand effectively. You'll thank me later.

Separating Your Business Model from Your Brand

This section starts by defining two important concepts: business model and brand. After looking at the meaning of each of these concepts, you'll find it easier to effectively address each one.

- ✔ **Your business model:** Your business model describes how you make money. This concept is inward facing, meaning that you look inside your company to see what drives your revenue. You consider operations, suppliers, and all the things that go into delivering a sound product.

- ✔ **Your brand:** Your brand is what your company means to your customers. Regardless of how you make your money, your brand is defined by the connections it makes in the minds of your customers. You take into account things like customer data, retention, and buying habits to determine what your brand stands for. You can declare what your brand means to your customers, but you can't make them believe it. They tell *you*. On social media, this message is amplified a hundred-fold.

Here's an example of how a business model and a brand go hand in hand. Apple (http://apple.com) makes its money by selling electronic gadgets that help us do things, such as communicate with the world in myriad ways. Apple's current mission statement reads as follows: "Apple designs Macs, the best personal computers in the world, along with OS X, iLife, iWork and professional software. Apple leads the digital music revolution with its iPods and iTunes online store. Apple has reinvented the mobile phone with its revolutionary iPhone and App store, and is defining the future of mobile media and computing devices with iPad."

When you buy an Apple product, you find that it employs cutting-edge design and performs well. This helps you see the value of purchasing other Apple products, like an iPad or a MacBook Air. Why? Because they work seamlessly together. Furthermore, you see the value of using the iTunes store to buy apps that work with your products. Apple would be a successful company by virtue of the products it creates. But by making its products work together in their own "ecosystem," Apple has created a strong business model that makes it the world's most valuable brand, according to Forbes (http://www.forbes.com/companies/apple/). Almost no one disagrees.

So what does the Apple brand mean? To understand that, you have to look at Apple customers. They are extremely loyal and see themselves as belonging to a world-wide community of people who think differently. They have a relationship with the company that can't easily be damaged. They stand in long lines to wait for newly released products, hoping to be able to snag the latest model.

Apple clearly understands the role its products play in the life of its customers. Do you understand your company's role? This understanding is critical to being a successful company. If you don't understand the brand value of your company, you will have weak content marketing efforts.

Understanding the business you're in

To understand the role your products play in the life of your customers, you need to grasp the concept of Jobs To Be Done (JTBD). It was developed by Clayton Christensen, who is well-known for his theories on corporate innovation and disruption. As his website explains, "Customers rarely make buying decisions around what the 'average' customer in their category may do — but they often buy things because they find themselves with a problem they would like to solve."

Christensen illustrates how companies can find the solution to the JTBD problem by detailing how he dealt with this problem for a fast-food company. After analyzing its customers' demographics and asking them about their favorite milkshake ingredients, the marketing department of a fast-food company still couldn't figure out how to increase milkshake sales. The company asked Christensen to help. He and his team proceeded to determine what customers "hired" the milkshakes to do with extensive interviews. (You can find more details at `http://hbswk.hbs.edu/item/6496.html`).

Christiansen's team found that customers all had a similar purpose for buying a milkshake. They had long, boring commutes to work. On their commute, they wanted

✔ Something interesting to do with their free hand as they drove

✔ Something that would help them stave off hunger until 12 p.m., when they could eat lunch

These are the jobs they hired their milkshake to do. So, they bought a milkshake to serve as both entertainment and sustenance.

You can see that by framing the problem this way, the fast-food marketers could come up with unique solutions to satisfy their customer. They needed to provide a product that would do the right jobs.

With this information in hand, the fast-food company proceeded to

✔ **Create thicker milkshakes:** The company needed to offer shakes that took longer to finish so that they would last during the entire commute.

✔ **Develop more interesting milkshakes:** The company added pieces of fruit to the shake that provided a chewing experience along with the fluid.

The milkshake was already perfect for a customer's free hand, so that aspect wasn't changed.

Christiansen's marketing team also uncovered some information about what parents wanted in a milkshake product for their kids. Parents wanted to buy their kids a milkshake as a treat during the day. This called for thinner children's milkshakes that wouldn't take too long to finish. So the fast-food company needed both thicker and thinner milkshakes on its menu.

You can see that by following the "what job is the product hired to do" line of exploration, the marketers arrived at very different solutions than they would have using a classic demographic analysis.

Christensen classifies the reasons for customers to buy as your *brand purpose*. He recommends naming your product after that purpose so that customers will know that your product meets their needs.

Mark W. Johnson (Clayton Christensen's business partner) says that "you know an innovation is disruptive when a new population has access to products and services that previously were only affordable for the few or the wealthy" (`http://blogs.wsj.com/accelerators/2015/01/23/weekend-read-disruption-is-not-about-slaying-giants-but-about-serving-new-customers/`).

Your offering to the customer should disrupt the status quo. For example, your product could do the job in a new way, as Airbnb (`http://airbnb.com`) does by offering local homes to travelers who don't want a hotel experience. Or it could be more convenient but not necessarily less expensive, such as Uber (`http://uber.com`), which is a service that quickly provides a taxi when and where it's needed.

Looking at some popular online business models

The Internet has spawned a host of business models that couldn't have existed before its inception. The following sections describe some of the most popular ones that don't require a bricks-and-mortar store to support it.

Affiliate model

Affiliates are people who agree to sell a product (or service) online for a fee. The key to creating a successful affiliate business involves developing an audience interested in a particular topic and then finding and recommending products you think they will like. The less work that you put in on the effort, the less likely you will be able to sustain a business that relies on people trusting your recommendations. Affiliates can also promote one specific product and provide content that supports and enhances it.

An example of a market in which you can find affiliate products is ClickBank (`http://www.clickbank.com`), shown in Figure 3-1. Vendors put their products on display and list their accompanying fee for a sale.

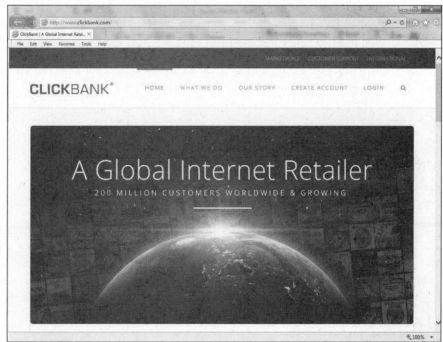

Figure 3-1:
ClickBank
offers
affiliate
products.

Membership model

A membership model has two characteristics. To run it, you have to

- ✓ Charge a monthly (or annual) fee
- ✓ Supply content that keeps your members interested

The content you supply can be informal, or you can organize into specific courses. One successful example of this type of site is Lynda.com (`http://lynda.com`), shown in Figure 3-2. This site has recently been purchased by LinkedIn and has different business courses in a variety of formats, with video being the most popular.

Peer-to-peer e-commerce site model (a community of makers or freelancers)

This model allows people with similar skills to access a business framework to display and sell their goods or services. This framework allows people to avoid having to set up their own shopping carts and customer-service mechanisms.

A successful example of this model is Etsy (`http://etsy.com`), shown in Figure 3-3. Etsy has thousands of vendors who hand-make their goods.

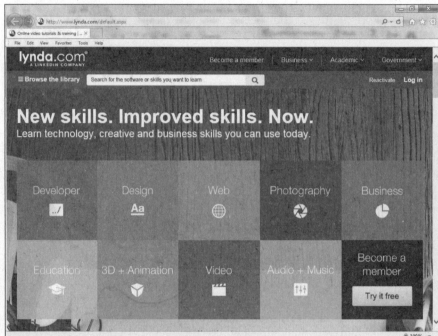

Figure 3-2:
Lynda.com supplies course content under the membership model.

Online retail model

I'm sure you're quite familiar with this model. A vendor offers goods available online and ships them to a buyer. The vendor may also have a group of vendors who supply his goods, which he then ships. One good example of this model is 1-800-FLOWERS.COM (`http://1800flowers.com`) shown in Figure 3-4, which provides flowers for all occasions. Before this type of vendor existed, you had to go to a florist and order flowers, which in turn had to be sent or referred to a local vendor.

One variation on the retail model is the "Long-tail" model introduced by Chris Anderson in his book *The Long Tail: Why the Future Of Business Is Selling Less of More* (Hyperion). The long tail refers to a niche audience that buys many products with low volume. For example, Ebay vendors sell a large number of different products to very niche audiences. A china vendor can have many different patterns of vintage plates, teacups, bowls, and other similar items and sell them to people who collect one specific pattern. The model works because the niche audience continues to buy for its specific collection.

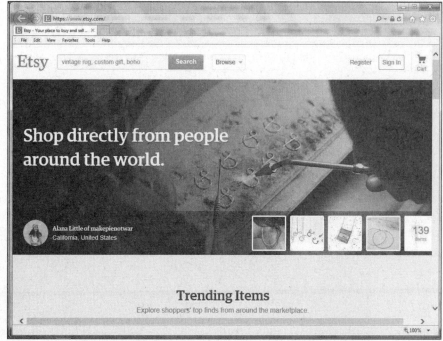

Figure 3-3:
Etsy is a thriving example of the peer-to-peer e-commerce site model.

Figure 3-4:
The online retailer 1-800-FLOWERS.COM.

Service model

This online version of the service model is becoming very popular because it allows time-starved customers to order something they want and get it delivered quickly without having to leave their house. One example of this is Seamless (`https://www.seamless.com`), as shown in Figure 3-5. It's your local take-out/pickup restaurant on a grand scale. You go to the site, put in your zip code, and choose food from local vendors. It's all handled from one site. Then you have it delivered or you can get it yourself. Rather than have one option, you can choose from a variety of local options.

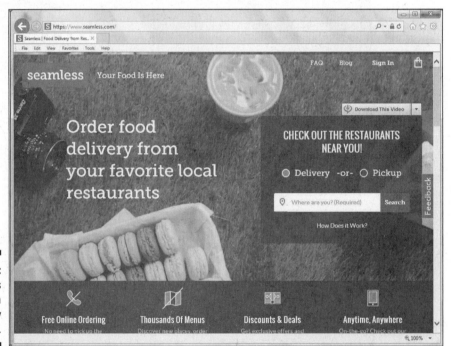

Figure 3-5: Seamless provides a food-delivery service.

Subscription model

The subscription model is not new, but the advent of the web has driven it to much greater heights. With this model, you join a site that offers ongoing access to something you want, and you typically pay a monthly or annual fee. One well-known example of this model is Netflix (`http://netflix.com`), shown in Figure 3-6. You can access the site's content as long as you remain a member.

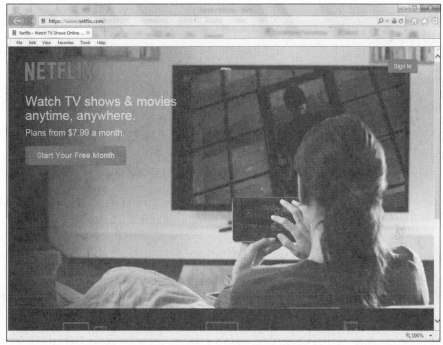

Figure 3-6:
You pay a monthly fee to access all the content on Netflix.

Considering the freemium model

Another business model worth noting is the *freemium* model, which is used for online software products. Companies who use this model provide a free version of their software with the expectation that some customers will want to pay for a premium version. Some business owners are leery of this model because it involves a risk that doesn't apply to a standard retail model. Instead of having customers pay as they go, you need to have the strong conviction that some customers will upgrade.

You should consider a freemium model if you are convinced that

- ✔ **Your product is integral to a business process.** Tools that make it easy for a user to do tasks that are part of her daily routine have a good chance of succeeding. Examples of such tasks are storing and sharing files. Dropbox (http://Dropbox.com), shown in Figure 3-7, gives you a free account and charges for additional storage space.

- ✔ **Your paying customers will be able to support the nonpaying ones.** In this case, a good example is LinkedIn (http://linkedin.com), shown in Figure 3-8, which provides a variety of career search services in addition to a free networking service.

Figure 3-7:
Dropbox offers a freemium service for storing and sharing files.

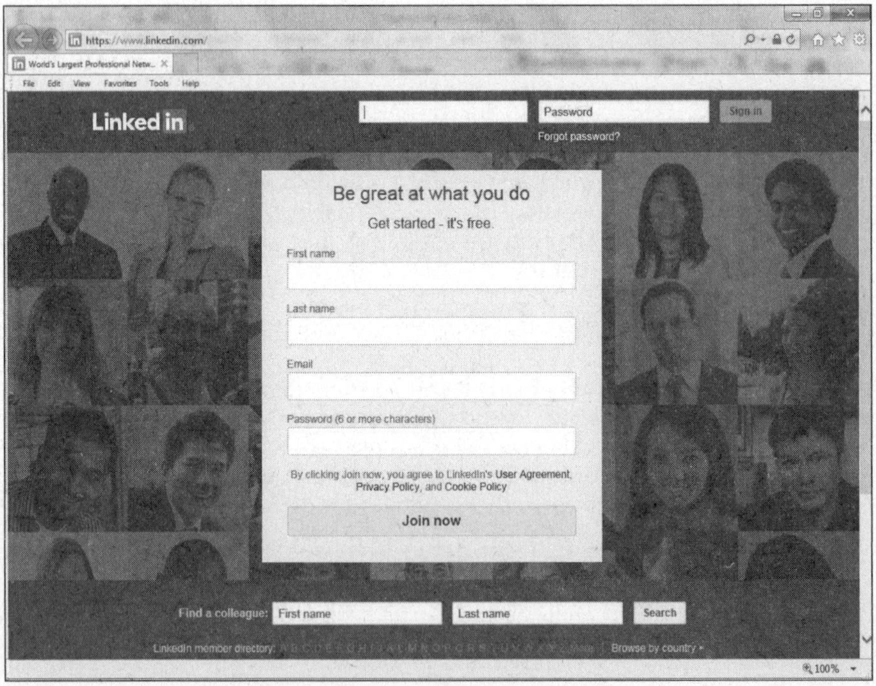

Figure 3-8:
LinkedIn offers free and paid services.

✔ **You can provide quality customer service to all customers, not just the premium owners.** An example of this is Evernote, the information storing and organizing platform (see Figure 3-9). The Executive Chairman of Evernote, (`http://evernote.com`) Phil Libin, has been quoted as saying, "The easiest way to get one million people paying is to get one billion people using" (Fast Company). From the very beginning, he was prepared to give everyone who used Evernote a quality experience. Currently the company offers a free version, a Plus version, and a Premium version.

Figure 3-9:
Be sure to add value to customers' lives with your free services, as Evernote strives to do.

What about free trials?

When you think of free, you can't overlook free trials. Companies use this tactic to entice customers to try and then buy. A recent success story using this tactic is Beats Music, the subscription streaming music service (purchased in May of 2015 by Apple and now called Apple Music). Unlike other services, such as Spotify and Pandora, Beats doesn't have a free version; members pay $9.99 a month.

According to Bloomberg Business, Apple Music (Beats) was able to turn seven out of ten free trial users into paying customers without a free version.

Analyzing Your Business Model

Because of the availability of online tools, you have a great advantage when analyzing your business model. All sorts of visual software tools are available to help you figure things out. The most popular of all the business model tools is the one presented by Alex Osterwalder and Yves Pigneur in their book *Business Model Generation*. (Full disclosure: I am one of 470 people from 45 countries who made a very small contribution to the book.) The tool is called the Business Model Canvas, from Strategyzer (see Figure 3-10). To analyze your business model, you use a visual "canvas" to lay out all the components that make up your business. What makes the tool so powerful is that it prompts you to look at each part of your business and see how it works with the other parts to bring in revenue. To learn more about the business model canvas, you can go to `https://strategyzer.com/canvas?_ga=1.164112764.256400004.1437491350`.

Figure 3-10: The Business Model Canvas from Strategyzer.

Here's a brief look at the components you need to document on the canvas:

- **Customer Segments:** List the clearly defined niches you serve.

- **Value Propositions:** This term refers to what you provide to customers to solve their problems. What are the specific products and services you offer — the value you promise to exchange with your customers for their payment?

- ✔ **Channels:** List the communication (social platforms and so on), distribution, and sales channels you use to reach customers.

- ✔ **Customer Relationships:** Describe what you do to maintain an ongoing relationship with each of the customer segments you serve.

- ✔ **Revenue Streams:** List the ways you make money based on the products and services you offer.

- ✔ **Key Resources:** Identify the resources you must have to run the business.

- ✔ **Key Activities:** Name the actions you must perform to run the business.

- ✔ **Key Partnerships:** Includes the vendors and partners you need to run the business.

- ✔ **Cost Structure:** Includes all the money you need to spend (expenditures) to run your business.

Businesses can have more than one business model at a time. In today's marketplace, startups and small business owners in particular find having several revenue streams desirable.

Discovering Your Brand

At company headquarters, your brand is looked at and understood in a certain way. Often, it can be mixed up with the product itself. But your brand and your product are two distinct things. The product is created by your company. But your brand is created in the mind of your customer. It is what customers feel when they use your product, including whether they perceive that your brand is authentic. Because prospects can't make a face-to-face determination about your company's truthfulness and ethics, they rely on your content. An authentic brand is one that seems truthful, transparent, and cares about its customers' satisfaction.

Want to know what Interbrand (http://www.bestglobalbrands.com/2014/ranking) says are the top five global brands in 2014? They are (1) Apple; (2) Google; (3) Coca-Cola; (4) IBM; and (5) Microsoft. Not too surprisingly, four out of the five are technology companies. They are cited for their ability to innovate and adopt change to become more agile.

Benefitting from attention to your brand

Marty Neumeier, a recognized branding expert, says that a brand is "a person's gut feeling, because brands are defined by individuals, not companies, markets, or the public." As much as people like to think that they choose brands for logical reasons, all the research on brand choice says that they operate on emotions. It is these emotions that you need to identify and respond to.

According to Regalix (http://www.regalix.com), an innovation consultancy, in 2015, 94 percent of marketers using social media say that one of their key objectives is to increase brand awareness.

Branding is so important because it does the following:

- **Helps you differentiate yourself from your competition.** For example, several tablets are on the market, but in 2014, Apple held the majority share at 32.5 percent.

- **Can live on while specific products may be phased out.** The good will that comes with loving a brand isn't easily destroyed.

- **Helps customers talk about a brand to their friends and family.** You want the social media army to actively recruit others.

- **Creates loyal customers.** Loyal customers are "money in the bank."

- **Is an asset.** Although it seems intangible, brands have equity. Brand names help products get into retail stores and attract attention.

- **Creates value for employees.** Popular brands make their employees proud and encourage employee retention.

Want to know how to recognize a loyal customer? According to Robert Passikoff, founder of Brand Keys (http://brandkeys.com/about), a branding consultancy, loyal customers are six times more likely to: "(1) Engage with your brand; (2) Pay attention to your marketing and advertising messages; (3)Think better of you; (4) Buy (and re-buy) your products or services; (5) Resist competitive appeals (attribute, benefit or dollar-based); (6) Recommend your product or service to others; (7) Invest in your company (if it's publicly traded); and (8) Give your product or service the benefit of the doubt in uncertain situations." Doesn't that sound like the customer you want to retain?

Is this the Apple Store?

An example of a company that didn't understand its brand was J.C. Penney. In its successful past, J.C. Penney was perceived as a well-priced store where families would stock up on their clothes for the year. Unfortunately, it lagged behind the times and competitors overtook it. In 2011, in an attempt to reinvent its brand, Penney's hired Ron Johnson, a former Target and Apple executive, to spin some magic in Penney's retail stores. Johnson's goal was to make the stores more like Apple retail stores. His attempt to revitalize the brand failed, and he was ousted in 2013. Several reasons were cited for his failure, but the main complaint from customers and management alike was that he just didn't understand the brand.

Try as you might, you don't really influence what customers experience when they use your product. You may want them to feel really excited, but the customer might reply with a yawn. Unless you can refresh the brand in some significant way, it is locked in customers' minds in a particular way.

According to Loyalty360 (`http://loyalty360.org`), 72 percent of U.S. customers drop a brand if they have had three bad customer service experiences. Brand loyalty is great, but you can't count on mistreating your customers and hoping they forget.

Knowing your current brand reality

Critical to understanding how to increase brand value is to understand what your customers think about your brand today. This is something you don't want to be guessing about. You can't improve something unless you establish a baseline.

So what can you do to create a twenty-first century brand that delights customers and encourages growth? In 2013, Roxana Strohmenger, Tracy Stokes, and Chelsea Hammond at Forrester Research, created what they call the TRUE Brand Compass Framework (`http://blogs.forrester.com/ roxana_strohmenger/13-07-15 calculating_brand_resonance_ introducing_forresters_true_brand_compass_framework`).

What makes a brand TRUE? It should be:

- *Trusted:* Is transparent with its customers, including showing its flaws
- *Remarkable:* Gets people talking about the brand
- *Unmistakable:* Creates a category of one (no one competes with it)
- *Essential:* Is irreplaceable in your customers' lives

These measures can be a recipe for evaluating what your current brand reality is and how you can redirect your actions. The following table provides some questions you can ask yourself:

Measure	*Questions to Ask*
Trusted	Do our customers think of us as trustworthy and transparent? What evidence do we have of that? What are we doing to reinforce our brand's authenticity?
Remarkable	Do our customers find us worth discussing with their friends? What evidence do we have of that? What are we doing to make it easy for customers to tell about their great experiences with us?

Measure	Questions to Ask
Unmistakable	How well do we differentiate ourselves from the competition? What evidence do we have of that? Can we list our competitors and describe the ways we are different?
Essential	Do we have a place in our customer's everyday life? What evidence do we have of that? What can we do to make our products become part of a customer habit?

Earlier in the chapter, I describe multiple business models for you to be aware of. But what about managing multiple brands? You can see that managing multiple brands is a very complex problem. A major company like Proctor and Gamble has multiple brands and successfully manages all of them. If you are a small business, you need to think carefully before you spread your resources too thinly to support more than one brand.

Solidifying the Look of the Brand

So far in this chapter, I've delved into issues surrounding what your customers and employees *think* about your brand. Now it's time to look at what they *see*. Chances are, when you visualize a brand, you either see the product in your mind, like the iconic Coke bottle, or a logo, like the Nike swoosh. A great deal of time and effort goes into establishing the look of the brand, and companies don't always get it right.

Considering design components

Design and color play a tremendously important role in the branding of a company. Every year, companies spend millions of dollars to update and refresh their brand. Here are the design elements that distinguish a brand:

- **Tagline:** A tagline can help your potential customer understand the essence of your brand. Think American Express's tagline "Don't leave home without it." American Express wants its customers to feel that their credit card is essential to their everyday life.

- **Design:** Design of online properties is a critical component of branding because it can convey a sense of modernity (good) or irrelevancy (not good!). Also key nowadays is a design that allows mobile devices to display the design correctly on their smaller screens.

- **Logo:** As you see in the sidebar about logos, a logo can be critical to a brand. But don't think that it must be complex. Actually, simpler is often better. Consider the IBM logo (`http://ibm.com`), shown in Figure 3-11. It's nothing fancy, but it has stood the test of time.

Can an inexpensive logo succeed?

To answer the question in the heading, if you're the iconic hot lips logo used by the Rolling Stones, it can. That logo has been in service for almost fifty years and counting. Major brands create logos with great care and buckets of money. If you're a small business of any kind, your funds are generally restricted to paying vendors and meeting payroll with very little left over to pay yourself. But does the lack of funds matter? Could an inexpensive logo be just as good or better? That depends on how well your designer can capture the essence of the brand.

In 1969, Mick Jagger went to the London's Royal College of Art and asked a fledgling artist, 24-year-old John Pasche, to create some visuals for his band. Rather than use Jagger's suggestion of a Hindu idol, he went with his own instincts. He chose what he felt was the most outstanding feature of the man in front of him — "the size of Jagger's lips and mouth" (`http://www.adweek.com/news/advertising-branding/how-mick-jaggers-mouth-became-rolling-stones-legendary-logo-165928`).

Pasche got £50 ($77) for his efforts, and the rest, as they say, is history. So don't be discouraged if you can't afford an expensive, focus-grouped logo. You might be better off.

Figure 3-11:
The IBM
logo is
simple but
classic.

- ✔ **Icon/avatar:** This is the little design that you see in the upper left of a browser page or on a website. Because the icon or avatar is viewed so often, it makes a lasting impression. Don't overlook its importance.

- ✔ **Graphics and photos:** We know that visuals communicate ideas that we can't express in words. Your graphics are very important, so stay away from stiff stock photos and clip art.

- ✔ **Fonts:** Fonts are the lifeblood of brands, but people don't think about them. They just accept the feeling they convey. If you think of iconic fonts, you'll arguably find none more iconic than Disney's (`http://disney.com`). No company would dare use something remotely similar for fear of confusing its customers.

- ✔ **Color:** Color sets the mood for brands. Very few brands have done a better job of pairing a color with the idea of luxury than Tiffany and its little blue box (`http://tiffany.com`).

Figure 3-12:
The iconic
Disney font.

Using a digital asset management tool

Digital asset management (DAM) companies provide a tool to help you manage your brand assets online. DAMs provide a central repository for company assets such as documents, photos, and videos. If you have a small shop, you may not need a system like this. But if you have multiple assets and multiple locations, using a tool like this can be a productive way to help your employees manage their work.

WebDAM (`http://www.webdam.com/`), shown in Figure 3-13, is a well-known digital asset management company. It has a cloud-based system that makes it easy for your employees to manage your brand assets from anywhere.

Figure 3-13:
WebDAM.

IntelligenceBank helps companies manage digital assets (see Figure 3-14). The company, which is noted for its pleasing visual interface, provides a calendar and planner (http://www.intelligencebank.com/).

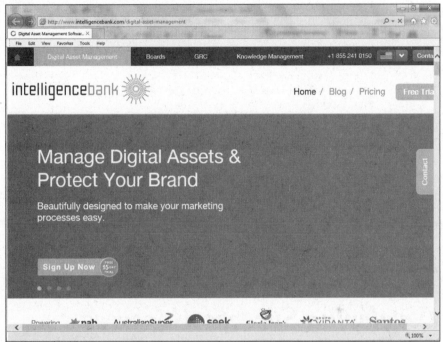

Figure 3-14: Intelligence-Bank.

If you're looking for major brand assets like logos needed for blog posts and other content, you can probably find them at Find Guidelines on the Web (http://findguidelin.es), shown in Figure 3-15. This is a portal site run by Arno Di Nunzio, whose purpose for the site is "to ease the life of us graphic designers by creating the largest collection of brand guidelines in one convenient central location, with just the right amount of functionalities" (http://findguidelin.es/about/). It's a great resource. Rather than have to go to each site individually, you can find the assets you need in one place.

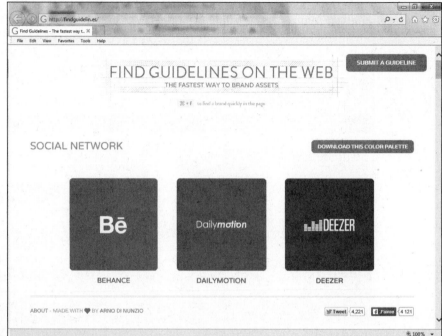

Developing Success Measures for Your Brand

Management expert Peter Drucker famously said, "What gets measured gets done." In the case of branding, you are dealing with a set of measurements about your brand from which you must extract conclusions. The measures that you use to evaluate your brand are tied to customer perceptions and the actions you take to fortify them.

Unlike measuring the number of followers or the amount of Likes you get, these measures are a bit more complex. (I cover those types of measures in Chapter 15.) You have to determine whether the actions you take support, advance, and enhance your brand.

Brand measurement can be a bit complex. Part V of this book looks at the fifth of the Five Cs (see Chapter 1 for a list of the Five Cs). I call the fifth one Check-Back Analysis. This term refers to the notion that for every measure you look at, you should look back to evaluate the data you collected and possibly revise it. With all the data available, you should mine it for information that will actually increase the likelihood of success.

If you are new to content marketing, it makes sense to develop some gross brand measures that you know are available and can be evaluated. Following are some possible measures to choose from. Many measures are available; these are just suggestions:

- ✔ **General company measures:** Market share; ROI; gross revenue

- ✔ **Brand awareness:** Reach; engagement with social media

- ✔ **Brand loyalty:** Retention; frequency of purchases

Using the brand worksheet, which you can download at `www.dummies.com/extras/contentmarketingstrategies`, select what you will measure and how. You can review those measurements in Chapter 20.

Producing Engaging Branded Content

I promised we'd get to the part about branded content after looking at business models and branding. So here we are. You want to know how to create content that solidifies your brand awareness. After you have all your brand elements in place, you need to communicate them at every customer touchpoint.

Marc Blanchard, Executive Creative Director at Creative Agency Havas Worldwide (`http://ny.havasworldwide.com/`) proposed a great framework to help analyze brand engagement. I use this framework to figure out how to develop custom content for brand engagement. (To see Blanchard's full analysis, go to `https://quarkstone.wordpress.com/2012/09/17/brand-engagement-in-the-networked-world/`. And for a more in-depth look at content creation for the buyer's journey, see Chapter 8). The model prompts the following questions:

- ✔ **Exposure:** What kind of content would you like potential customers to see when they meet your brand?

    Unfortunately, you can't control how a prospect first sees your brand. With all the social platforms, landing pages, and messaging tools available, you just hope they find you. But you should give some thought to the possible touchpoints. You can look at a few basic venues to determine what your customers will see. Those venues are Google search results, your main website, and your brand pages on all the social platforms. Make sure that all the platforms are cohesively branded and convey the standards that you hold for your brand.

    Content suggestions: The content you create for brand exposure should introduce your potential customer to the solutions you offer. Develop content like webinars, e-books, and thought-leader posts that clearly present the value of your product or service. Demonstrate that you have a community of satisfied customers that you would like prospective customers to join.

✔ **Response:** What customer emotion does your content trigger?

What do you want your prospects to feel after they learn about you? Determine what content you need to create to get your prospect moving in your direction and away from your competitors.

Content suggestions: Offerings such as comparison charts, demos, and free trials help customers invest time and effort in you.

✔ **Experience:** How do you help customers convince themselves that the experience you have makes you an expert?

You know that your customers will make an emotional decision about you and convince themselves that it was a rational one. Make sure to provide anything customers might need to feed both the emotional and rational sides.(See Chapter 12 for more details about customer motivation.)

Content suggestions: Convincing content can be testimonials that speak to people's emotional side as well as data sheets with features and benefits that assuage the needs of the logical side.

✔ **Outcome:** What action do they take?

You have an intended outcome in mind. Make sure that it's clear to your prospects what you want them to do next. Although you wish otherwise, you may not get them to buy without taking smaller steps first to get to know you.

Content suggestions: Create things like free lead generators (information in exchange for something) and free newsletter subscriptions to get them to give you an email address or perform another action, such as attend a webinar.

Monitor how well the content performs, and increase your use of ones that make a difference.

Check out the next page for a mind map of this chapter's content, and download a color version at www.dummies.com/contentmarketingstrategies.

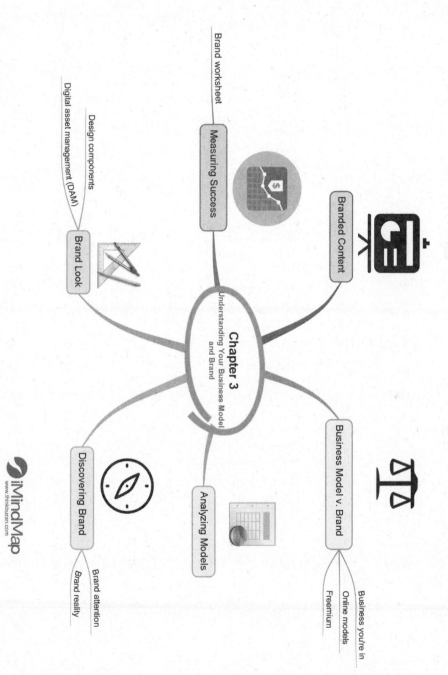

Chapter 4

Facilitating Buy-In from Your Team

. . . .

In This Chapter

▶ Preparing leaders to sponsor the project

▶ Ensuring everyone understands content marketing concepts

▶ Developing a reporting plan

. . . .

*I*f content marketing is such a powerful strategy, why don't most company executives quickly embrace it? To understand that, you need to look at the issues that impact the average manager. You also need to know why even your savviest colleagues are hesitant to jump in with both feet.

Content marketing does not require a complicated strategy, but it strikes fear in the hearts of many executives. Unlike marketing collateral, which is produced once and shared many times, content marketing requires the ongoing production of new content with no end in sight. It causes managers to think like publishers — which is not something they are used to doing. They know they are on unfamiliar ground and are reluctant to commit vast sums to funding new content initiatives. They feel comfortable producing their company's product; they don't like having to add "publisher" to their title.

In this chapter, you consider the issues surrounding buy-in for content marketing projects. Even if you have great ideas, you need to know how to persuade others to join you. This chapter deals with some of the emotional factors that people face when they are asked to work on new initiatives. Be prepared to deal with both the logical concerns and the fear that new projects bring up.

Presenting the Big Picture

The nature of marketing has changed in the social media era. Unless your company has already realigned itself to put the customer at the center of all the marketing you do, you may have a bigger lift than you expected.

When you prepare to implement a new content marketing strategy program, you can be faced with altering the organizational chart. That is not an insignificant undertaking.

You might have multiple department silos and inadequate governance that makes implementing a content marketing strategy even more complicated. In addition, you are potentially impacting a significant piece of the marketing budget. According to the Content Marketing Institute, "the average B2B organization spends 28% of its marketing budget on content, and the average B2C organization spends 25%" (http://contentmarketinginstitute. com/2015/03/buy-in-conversation-content-marketing/).

Identifying your audiences

To get a clear idea of how to approach buy-in, you should focus on three audiences, who are as follows:

- ✓ **Your internal project customers:** Your internal staff is critical to your success. Your staff needs to buy into your vision and embrace the idea of change. In this group, you may have people ensconced in their own comfort zones who will be upended by your plan. You'll also have others who simply think your idea is a bad one because they aren't in charge of it.

Without internal buy-in, your project will fail. You can't afford to ignore anyone's concerns. Do a very thorough search to identify all your stakeholders. One of the key ways to fail is to exclude a stakeholder. Err on the side of caution and contact anyone who may need to be involved. People can always decline your invitation.

An article written by Jackie Lohrey of Demand Media called, "The Importance Of Identifying Stakeholders In A Project" (http:// smallbusiness.chron.com/importance-identifying- stakeholders-project-74730.html) helpfully delineates three levels of stakeholder involvement that you should be aware of. They are as follows:

- ✓ **Direct stakeholders:** These are the people who will actively work on the project and the department staff who will enact the plan.

- ✓ **Outcome stakeholders:** People whose work is affected by the results of the project, including departments such as customer service who will deal with customers affected by your plan.

- ✓ **Influencers:** People who have influence over the project itself. These are the top executives who can stop your project from happening.

When you understand the hierarchy of your stakeholders, you can more effectively manage their participation. You may want to meet them in their respective groups rather than as part of the whole so that you can give them extra attention.

✔ **Your targeted customers:** Customers need to be at the center of your marketing universe. The further your organization is from that ideal, the harder it will be to implement your plan. Management will continually need to be convinced that what you are proposing will develop a stronger relationship with the customer.

✔ **Your vendors and other outside colleagues:** Don't forget that your company doesn't operate in a vacuum. You have suppliers that rely on your business, business partners who provide financial backing, and others who help you succeed. Make sure to include them in your thinking when you are working on buy-in. You need their support.

You may be introducing more than a new initiative when you begin your project. You could be fundamentally changing the way your company does business. If this is the case, a clear-eyed view of the situation is needed before you begin. For more on this topic, see Chapter 2.

Using the Five-Prong Approach (FPA) to collect buy-in information

You've heard a great deal about content marketing as a strategy. You're also aware of the fact that the ROI can be difficult to pin down. So how can you convince your managers to spend valuable marketing dollars implementing a strategy without a definite return?

One effective way to collect information to get buy-in is to use what I call the Five-Prong Approach (FPA). The FPA includes five types of content that will help persuade your audience.

You can download a copy of the FPA worksheet here: www.dummies.com/extras/contentmarketingstrategies.

This presentation isn't the plan itself. The plan is a significant document that needs to be carefully studied. This is the high-level presentation that you create to get buy-in to move forward and then flesh out the plan further with stakeholders. After you have made this presentation and, you hope, secured buy-in, you have to schedule meetings with the specific stakeholders who will weigh in on their particular areas of responsibility.

So what are the five content items that make up the presentation? Here they are in order:

- **Definitions of concepts that underpin your project:** You need to identify and explain the concepts you are discussing. Never assume they are understood by everyone. Present your definitions at the start of your presentation. Also at this time, ask anyone who is unclear about a term you use to speak up during your talk.

  Even when people claim they understand what a concept means, that understanding may differ from your definition in some way. You want everyone agreeing to the same thing, so make sure to provide your own definition for anything that is new or open to interpretation.

  Example: Begin by defining the concepts that you believe are crucial to understanding the project. In this example, let's define how two terms differ: Content Marketing Strategy and Content Strategy. It's important to note to all involved that you have to deal with both content marketing strategy and content marketing to do a thorough job. (In Chapter 2, I discuss the issues surrounding your business model and how content marketing fits in.) Here are the definitions.

  Content Marketing Strategy vs. Content Strategy: A content marketing strategy will serve your customers by providing them with the information they need to use our products and love our brand. A content strategy details how specific content will be created and distributed to customers.

- **Statistics and proof that others have succeeded with similar initiatives:** Proof is critical when you are facing a group of executives. These people need evidence in the form of data so that they can convince themselves that your plan can work. More important, they want to be able to convince their upper management, if need be.

  Example: For example, you might want to create two graphics that depict the following statistics that help prove your case:

  Graphic 1: According to DemandMetric, "[c]ontent marketing costs 62 percent less and generates roughly three times as many leads as traditional marketing (http://www.demandmetric.com/ content/content-marketing-infographic).

  Graphic 2: A study done by Kapost and Eloqua as reported by the Content Marketing Institute found that "[c]ontent marketing costs 31 percent less than paid search for medium-sized businesses and 41% less for larger organizations (http:// contentmarketinginstitute.com/2015/03/buy-in- conversation-content-marketing/).

✔ **A story about how it worked:** Find a story about another company (in the same industry, if possible) that has succeeded using the strategy you recommend. Make sure to call out major revenue successes when applicable.

Example: Here's a story about how Xerox was struggling with two important marketing problems in 2013:

- Xerox couldn't differentiate itself from their competitors. Most marketers believe that a large company like Xerox would have no problem standing out from the crowd, but in today's attention-grabbing marketplace, no one can be complacent. The company needed to reset the conversation with executives to focus on how it solved problems for real customers, not just repeat the generic "We solve problems." Many of its competitors were making the same claims, and buyers had a hard time investigating the differences.

- Xerox also needed to bypass the gatekeepers who prevented the company from reaching the C-level audience it was targeting with its marketing collateral. The audience would toss out anything that looked like an ad.

To solve these problems, Xerox partnered with Forbes to create a magazine called "The Chief Optimist." It contained information about how Xerox was working with particular customers and solving problems, and it had tips from executives. Because the companies packaged this offering as a magazine, gatekeepers didn't toss it when sorting administrative mail. Also, they created a digital version that included video, which they announced via email.

How did it work out? According to Jeannine Rossignol, VP-marketing communications at Xerox, "The 'Get Optimistic' campaign has led to more than 1,500 sales appointments that have generated more than $1 billion in a pipeline with a 12-to-18-month sales cycle" (`http://adage.com/article/btob/xerox-custom-magazine-past-admin-gatekeepers/290019/`).

A slide with that quote on it would get any manager's attention.

Obviously, not every company has the resources that Xerox does. But the model holds. If you provide premium content to your targeted market, you will get your customers' attention.

Try to include more than one success story to indicate that one example was not an anomaly.

✔ **Visuals:** You need compelling images to add color and break up all the text. In the upcoming example, I show you how to depict your proof as graphics. You should also include any other visuals that tell the story.

Example: How about supporting visuals in a well-designed magazine? In Figure 4-1, you see the cover of the Xerox magazine. A magazine with interesting visuals will help you make your point.

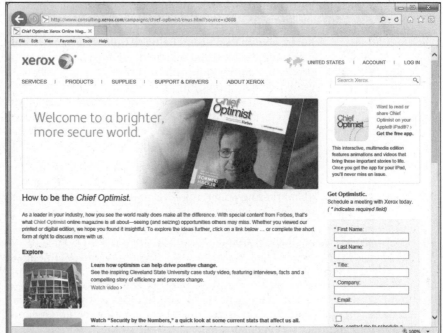

Figure 4-1:
Xerox's
Chief
Optimist
magazine.

✔ **Time to listen:** At the end of the presentation, stop and let your audience know that you have slated time to listen to everyone's concerns and opinions. Make it clear that you expect to hear from everyone before coming to any consensus on next steps.

By using the Five-Prong Approach, you share your most persuasive information as well as uncover objections to the preliminary plans.

Engaging the Leadership Team and Identifying Roles

Throughout your project, you want to focus on keeping upper management engaged. You can make your plan easier to shepherd by understanding how the best leaders approach change.

According to the Project Management Institute's "In-depth Report on Enabling Organizational Change through Strategic Initiatives" (http://www.pmi.org/~/media/PDF/Publications/Enabling-Change-Through-Strategic-Initiatives.ashx), highly effective leaders do the following:

- Focus on well-defined milestones and metrics
- Ensure that their senior managers are committed to the change
- Take ownership and expect accountability
- Use standardized project management practices
- Expect that the executives who sponsor the project are actively engaged

With these criteria in mind, read on to discover the kinds of questions you need to answer as your quest for management buy-in continues.

Understanding what leaders want to know

Be aware of the fact that the managers who have to sign off on your initiative may be just as fearful about losing their status or their job as everyone else on the project. For this reason, be proactive and answer the questions that keep managers up at night:

- **How can you demonstrate that the plan will be successful?** Managers want to know that you have thought the project through and are prepared to make it a success. If they feel that you are ill-prepared to take the project to its conclusion, you will know that immediately. You need to lay out the pros and cons and discuss how to deal with possible failures. Of course, you can't foresee everything that will happen, but you can plan for the ups and downs that go into a typical initiative. Your manager wants to know that you are aware of things that could go wrong and have thought about how to mitigate them.

- **What metrics will you use?** It's important for leaders to know that you have consulted with IT and other departments about which measures will be the most predictive of success. I go into the selection of metrics in more detail in Chapter 15.

- **How long will it take before we see results?** Managers hate risk. Can you do an experimental project that takes a short time and demonstrates positive results?

- **What are the budget implications?** Can your experimental pilot program use a small budget instead of moving into a big upfront expenditure?

✔ **How will this help us overtake the competition?** You must be able to answer questions about the competition. Be clear what your competitors are doing. Do they already have a program like this in place? Are they likely to use it to take your customers away?

✔ **What else can you do to ensure success?** Try to present more than one alternative pilot plan that you can implement in the event that the first one doesn't succeed. Show your manager that you have a plan B.

✔ **What happens if we don't go forward with this project?** One of the key points that every manager wants to know is what happens if the company doesn't move forward with the project. Will there be consequences that the manager is unaware of? Aside from what the competition is doing, you want to present any trends you see. Demonstrating that your company will be left behind can help promote buy-in.

Understanding how roles will work

After you have made sure that you have looked at all the issues that may arise from implementing the project, you need to spell out the specific roles that each person needs to play. Although those roles may be obvious to you, they're not always obvious or viewed in the same way by other team members.

Let stakeholders know what's expected of them. Ask them what they need to complete their roles. Your greatest expense will most likely be your staff allocation. Create teams of stakeholders and work together with each group to spell out roles and responsibilities.

Communicating the Essentials to Everyone

One of the key items in the list of buy-in items is a plan to keep everyone aware of the project's progress and status. Keeping the leaders apprised of the progress is not enough. If all the participating stakeholders are not aware of how the project is going, they will lose interest, or if problems arise, they might actively sabotage the outcome.

It can come as a great surprise to project leaders to find that members of their team are against the success of the project. The only way to grapple with this possibility from the beginning is to be aware of the politics and the goals of each stakeholder. You need to be aware of the following:

- ✔ **Does anyone stand to lose status or power?** This is a significant question to consider. People often forget that a motivating factor for almost everyone on the project is to not lose face or disrupt their comfortable routine.

- ✔ **Have you left out people who need to know, or have you assumed that everyone has gotten the word?** People who are not kept informed can feel slighted. It's better to let as many people know as possible.

- ✔ **How does the Information Technology department fit into the mix?** You know that this group can make or break the project. If you have a tiny project, then maybe it's not a big issue. But if you have any technology that must be integrated, start with your technicians first.

Expecting resistance to change

When preparing to persuade your colleagues to join you in this great content marketing adventure, you should be aware that people have a natural resistance to change. This should come as no surprise to you, as you likely feel the same way when a person or circumstance forces a change in your daily routine.

The reason that you're so open to and excited about the prospect of adding a content marketing project is that you've spent a good deal of time collecting evidence, thinking through the issues, and generally persuading yourself that it's worth the effort. Your colleagues have had no such indoctrination. You are approaching them in the state you were in before you signed on to this initiative. The problem is that you don't remember any skepticism or questions you might have had at the beginning.

It's important that you take yourself back to that state of mind when content marketing was new and somewhat frightening. Did you ask yourself questions like "How can we generate content when we're so short-handed?" or "What the heck are we going to write about on a consistent basis?" Those are the kinds of questions everyone, including senior management, will be asking themselves at the start.

For more about what motivates people to do a good job, you may want to refer to Daniel H. Pink's book *Drive: The Surprising Truth about What Motivates Us* (Riverhead). In it, he uncovers the fact that we are not motivated by money to do a good job. The desire to direct our own lives and give back to others is what really moves us. Understanding this idea can help you persuade your colleagues to participate.

Establishing results that will be shared

With a lot of attention being focused on the use of big data to make marketing decisions, people are beginning to understand how powerful mining their company's data can be. Looking at ways to use their own data to develop practical insights is becoming more mainstream.

When embarking on a content marketing project, regular reporting of findings can help ease the mind of nervous execs who are counting on a positive outcome. In Chapter 15 we look at choosing metrics for your initiative. Here we are focusing on the promise of regular reporting so that everyone will be apprised of the project's progress. Each department has different goals that are important to them. When developing a reporting plan you want to assure stakeholders that they will be kept informed.

Check out the next page for a mind map of this chapter's content, and download a color version at www.dummies.com/contentmarketingstrategies.

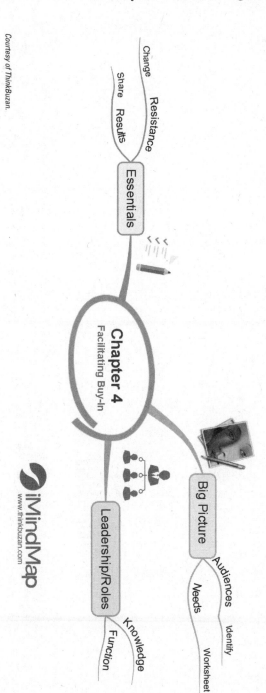

Courtesy of ThinkBuzan.

Chapter 5

Putting Your Content Marketing Plan and Presentation Together

In This Chapter

▶ Reviewing resources

▶ Breaking down silos

▶ Developing a timeline

▶ Presenting your plan

*Y*our content strategy plan is made up of many moving parts, all of which are covered in this book. Regardless of the size of your company, you have to prepare a plan that shows how all the pieces fit together.

In this chapter, you see what goes into the overall plan and what you can do to ensure that your company gets on the path to success. You discover how reorganizing may facilitate the content process, and you consider the culmination of all your hard work: preparing your plan.

In case you're wondering why the documentation of your overall plan is in Part I of the book, it's because I believe that it helps to see what you will be doing with all the checklists, models, and worksheets I ask you to create. If you do the work as you go along, you'll be ready to come back here and document your plan to get signoff.

Reorganizing for Success

As you create your plan, keep an issue in mind that holds many companies back from successfully implementing their content strategies. It's the problem of silos — that is, a group or department in an organization that is focused on its goals and doesn't know what the rest of the organization is doing. Many companies today are rigidly organized, which almost ensures that your content plans will be hampered.

Before technology had such a major effect on business, it made sense to create individual departments that operated independently of one another. With the advent of social networks and integrated systems, this way of organizing makes less sense. I'm sure that if you work in a silo structure, you often feel constrained and in the dark about much that is happening from day to day.

According to the 2015 Marketing Budgets Report done by the Econsultancy in partnership with the Oracle Marketing Cloud, shown in Figure 5-1, 71 percent of marketers surveyed agree that "they are focusing on breaking down internal silos to better coordinate and integrate marketing efforts" (`https://blogs.oracle.com/marketingcloud/new-2015-marketing-budget-benchmarks`). I hope that your organization is one of them.

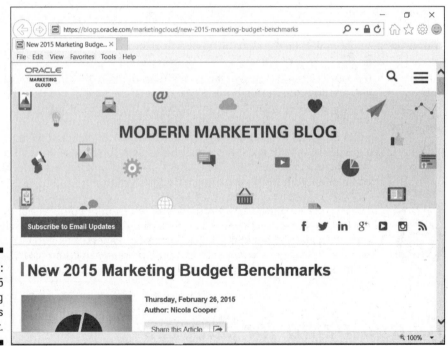

Figure 5-1:
The 2015
Marketing
Budgets
Report.

Busting silos

Nearly everyone agrees that implementing a content marketing strategy requires a willingness to innovate and change. The key is to make the need for changes obvious to all involved. The first step to rethinking silos involves looking at current bottlenecks. If you were to create a flow chart that follows your content process from beginning to end, you would see that several impediments arise along the way.

A helpful way to look at silos is suggested by Colleen Jones from Content Science (`http://review.content-science.com/2014/02/5-types-of-content-silos-to-break-down/`; see Figure 5-2). Jones recommends breaking down silos into five types so that you can more easily recognize them. See how many you have experienced.

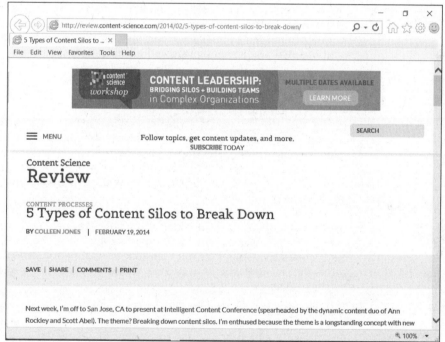

Figure 5-2:
Content
Science.

The silos are organized by

✔ **Department:** This is probably the most common silo you will encounter. Each department has its own goals, messages, and metrics. When trying to implement content plans, you are hampered by the lack of cohesion and the duplication of effort.

✔ **Channel:** This silo is composed of different channels competing against one another for the customer's attention. You may have a mobile group who communicates messages that are different from your retail group.

✔ **Discipline:** This silo pits the subject matter experts against the content strategy planners. This issue is especially common when you have technical or other complex data that needs to be explained. The subject matter experts develop content independent of strategy, making everyone's job more difficult.

✔ **Customer/user phase:** This silo impacts the buyer's journey and creates confusion for the customer. When you create content for a user phase, you also need to consider how it could be repurposed for other phases. By limiting your content creation to one user phase, you are wasting time and money.

✔ **Feature:** You probably recognize this one. Product features are championed by different groups with conflicting messages. This is an honest mistake, but detrimental nonetheless. Product managers need to work together to ensure a cohesive experience for the customer, who doesn't want to speak to different groups about the same issues.

Advocating change

I'm sure you recognized most if not all of these silo types. As you read about them, you may clearly see why they should be reorganized. But people fear change. It's a natural response to facing the unknown, especially at work. When you try to suggest this reorganization, you will probably find that some of your colleagues will

✔ **Ignore your ideas:** I'm sure this is not a new experience for you. We all have ideas that other people find unworkable. But in the case of silos, it's particularly damaging. You aren't faced with people who disagree with you. You are faced with people who ignore your ideas and conduct business as usual.

✔ **Tell you why it won't work:** This tactic is a little more palatable. People argue about why your idea won't work. They may actually believe what they say or are merely reacting to the fear of change.

✔ **Actively work against you:** Needless to say, this is the most disturbing response. It's one thing to argue with a colleague. It's quite another to have someone sabotage your plans.

Of course the outcome depends on what your executive team wants to do. You can make the case and hope that the team makes the right decision. Your colleagues will have to go along. (For more about resistance to change, see Chapter 4.)

Identifying the Components of Your Content Marketing Plan

You company's content is everywhere. If you could create your plan from scratch, you would be able to do everything effectively and efficiently. Unfortunately, creating from scratch is rarely the case. You have to deal with legacy items and the way things were done before.

In some cases, building from legacies can be a good thing. But more likely, you have to develop new ways to overcome internal obstacles to get to your goals. The next section looks at the resource items that you must address in your plan.

 As you consider all the components of your plan, you might propose a trial plan to show proof of concept. This trial plan gives the executive team the ability to say yes to a small plan that isn't seen as a big risk.

Documenting needed resources

When you present your content marketing plan, be aware that management will be keenly focused on required resources. For this reason, you want to carefully map out and present your resource section. Here's what this section includes:

- ✔ **Budget:** You know that this is the most important aspect of your plan. Many content marketers complain about the fact that they lack the proper budget to do what they need to do. The key to getting the budget you need is to present a case that shows how the project will ultimately tie back to revenue generation.

  According to Michael Sebastian in Ad Age (`http://adage.com/article/digital/content-marketing-remains-a-fraction-budgets/296059/`), a 2015 survey about content marketing tactics was given to 601 marketers by Contently (`http://contently.com`). They found that that 34 percent of respondents cited the lack of budget as their chief frustration. This should come as no surprise because 52 percent of them said that less than 25 percent of their budget is devoted to content.

- ✔ **Staff:** The success of content marketing strategies can depend on the way the content team is configured. If you are proposing a reorganization, as discussed previously, your costs may be difficult to pin down for this presentation.

If costs are hard to pin down, explain how a dedicated team would work together. You may also be proposing that you outsource your content writing, which requires a separate budget. (For more on dedicated writing teams, see Chapter 13.)

✔ **Systems and procedures:** This part of the presentation depends on what systems you already have in-house. You may already have a customer relationship management system (CRM). You may be proposing a content management system (CMS). Obviously, you want to lay out the purpose of any new system you propose and show how it integrates with what you're using now. (I cover systems and procedures in Chapter 13.)

Measuring success

To make your presentation meaningful, you want to choose a few metrics that can indicate success. If you're just getting started analyzing your metrics, I recommend that you refer to the infographic called Content Marketing Metrics that's shown in Figure 5-3. Created by Pawan Deshpande, the CEO of Curata, the original infographic can be found here: `http://www.curata.com/blog/content-marketing-measurement-29-essential-metrics-infographic/?mkt_tok=3RkMMJWWfF9wsRoiuKvNZKXonjHpfsX56eskXqa%2FlMI%2F0ER3fOvrPUfGjI4CT8JnI%2BSLDwEYGJlv6SgFSbDBMah21LgFWxk%3D.`

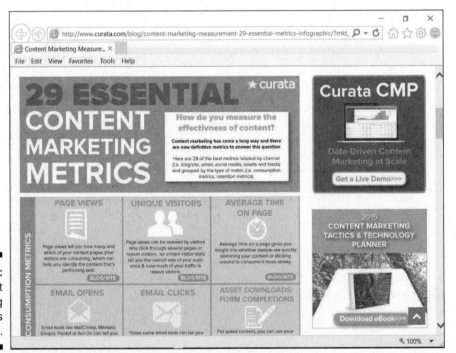

Figure 5-3:
The Content Marketing Metrics infographic.

This infographic lists what Deshpande cites as the essential metrics used to measure content effectiveness by category. Look at the ones that make the most sense for your proposal, and speak to your webmaster about which ones she can provide for your project trial.

Establishing the timeline

The timeline for your project is another important factor. It lets your audience know how big a commitment needs to make. Creating a visual timeline that adds some interest is also helpful.

Don't forget to create a timeline for your trial plan, too. It will help make the case that a short experiment is worth trying.

Here are some tools to help you create your timeline:

- ✔ **Timeglider** (`http://timeglider.com`): See Figure 5-4. This tool helps you create visually rich timelines. You may opt for something more basic for business, but these are eye catching.

- ✔ **TimeRime** (`http://www.timerime.com/en/`): See Figure 5-5. This is another tool that allows you to create visually interesting timelines for project planning.

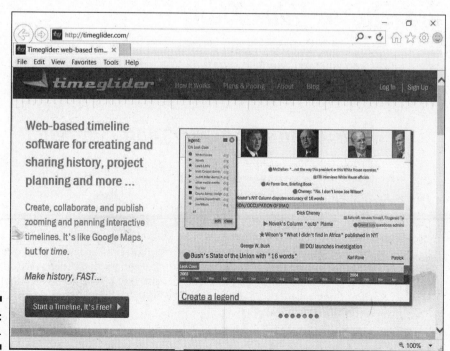

Figure 5-4: Timeglider.

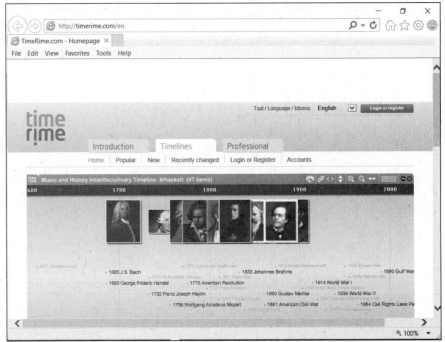

Figure 5-5:
TimeRime.

Presenting Your Plan

Now is your chance to make a real impact on your organization. If your plan is implemented, you know you will be able to increase revenue, improve customer satisfaction, and develop loyalty.

Revisiting the Five-Prong Approach

In Chapter 4, I introduce the Five-Prong Approach (FPA) and provide an FPA worksheet for you to use to facilitate buy-in.

(You can download the Five-Prong Approach worksheet at `www.dummies.com/extras/contentmarketingstrategies`).

This section describes putting together a full content marketing plan with all the pieces completed. If you haven't collected all the content listed in this section, refer to Chapter 4 and get preliminary buy-in to collect the material using the aforementioned worksheet and the example outlined in Chapter 4.

On the worksheet, you are asked to compile information that will support your plan. After doing that, you can put the content that you gathered into action along with the items identified in the "Documenting needed resources" section, earlier in this chapter. To recap, they are as follows:

- **Concepts:** Include definitions for any unfamiliar concepts.

- **Statistics and proof:** Include visuals of statistics including diagrams and charts. These can go a long way toward making the presentation more interesting. Here are some tools to consider:

  - **SmartDraw** (http://smartdraw.com)**:** See Figure 5-6. SmartDraw has a lot of different templates you can use to create your own visuals.

  - **ChartGizmo** (http://chartgizmo.com)**:** See Figure 5-7. You can create interesting charts using this very easy-to-use tool.

  - **Cacoo** (https://cacoo.com)**:** See Figure 5-8. This is another easy tool, and it lets you create diagrams and collaborate effectively with your team.

  - **Creately** (https://creately.com)**:** See Figure 5-9. This tool allows you to create a variety of diagrams, including flow charts, Gantt charts, and mock-ups.

Figure 5-6: SmartDraw.

Figure 5-7:
ChartGizmo.

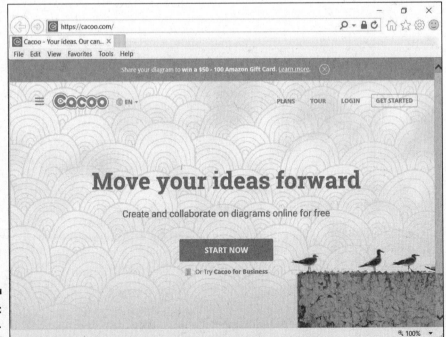

Figure 5-8:
Cacoo.

Figure 5-9:
Creately.

- ✔ **Story:** For ideas about story presentation, see Chapter 12. You need to make sure that your business story is front and center when you talk about content creation.

- ✔ **Visuals:** Aside from creating specific diagrams and charts, you may want to use some royalty-free images. If so, check out a Google image search or use a free site like Pixabay (`https://Pixabay.com`), shown in Figure 5-10. It's a great general site where you can find almost any image you need.

Putting It All Together: Your Presentation

Here's where all your previous hard work pays off. You are ready to put together the plan that you will use to move forward with content marketing. In the past, pockets of content have been created throughout the organization, but now it's time to get a formal plan working that brings all that content together.

Use the following sections as a framework for presenting your content marketing plan to company executives and staff.

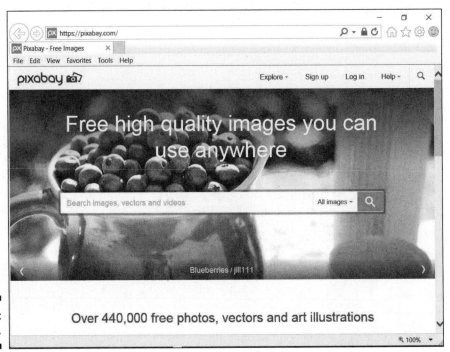

Figure 5-10: Pixabay.

Introduction

Set the stage by telling a story about why the plan is crucial to the success of the company. A good beginning might be a story about how the competition is using content marketing to their great advantage, or how your company lost out on a big deal because your content was lacking. You want to get your audience's attention, so the opening must have an emotional component. Also let your audience know that you will be proposing a trial plan at the end that will mitigate risk and provide proof of concept.

Goals/Mission

You looked at your business model and brand in Chapter 2, along with your goals and mission in Chapter 1. Now it's time to show executives how the plan ties back to the overall business goals of the company. If your plan doesn't integrate with larger goals, you have no chance of getting approval. You may want to show a visual of your business model canvas (see Chapter 3) and the work you've done to analyze the business landscape.

Business story/message

Your audience will be more likely to see the value of the plan when you show its members how your business story and messages drive your content plan. Give your audience examples of content that will be created based on your company story.

Content marketing strategy

As you know, your content marketing strategy is informed by the following: your personas; the buyer's journey; your content strategy; and your promotion plans. Although you can't go into depth about each of these, show your audience the visuals of the persona worksheet, buyer's journey, and channel plan.

Resources

As mentioned earlier in the chapter, your resource section is key to determining how much of a risk your management perceives the project to be. Plug the information I recommend, (like measures and timelines) into each of the sections: budget, staff, and systems. Make sure to reiterate that you will propose a trial plan at the end.

Success measures

Present the success measures that you recommend and briefly explain why you chose them. Your list will expand and change based on what you are creating. You just want to propose a few that are basic and will indicate immediate success or failure.

Timeline

Show the visual timeline you created and discuss how it could be modified based on resources allocated.

Next steps and your trial plan

In your next-steps discussion, talk about how you will provide more in-depth information to anyone who wants to receive it. Then be prepared to listen to questions and concerns.

Next, present your trial plan, which should include such things as the following:

- Mini goal for the project. A mini goal is a short-term goal that can demonstrate the potential effectiveness of the project.
- Resources needed
- Timeline
- Success measures

When you've completed your presentation, congratulate yourself on the hard work you put into getting here. No matter the outcome, you've proposed a plan that can help your company succeed with content marketing.

Check out the next page for a mind map of this chapter's content, and download a color version at www.dummies.com/contentmarketingstrategies.

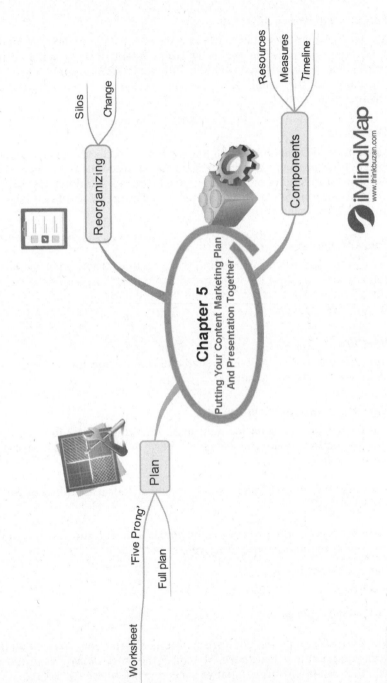

Courtesy of ThinkBuzan.

Part II
Uncovering the Customer Experience

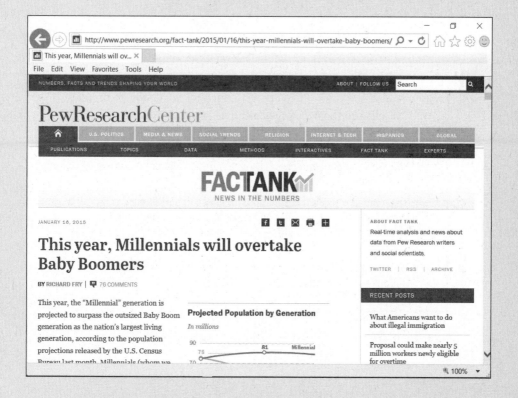

Want some guidelines to assist you in properly documenting your buyer's journey? Go to www.dummies.com/extras/contentmarketingstrategies.

In this part . . .

- ✔ Collecting and analyzing customer data can present some challenges. In this part, you see how to avoid the most common mistakes.

- ✔ You need to define the characteristics of your audience. I show you how using personas.

- ✔ You need to provide the right content for each part of the buyer's journey. I give you a model to help you to determine the kind of content that should be available for each phase of the journey.

- ✔ Your content can enable your salespeople to make the buyer's journey more effective.

Chapter 6

Dipping into Customer Data

Are you drowning in data but don't have enough useful information? Most companies today are encountering big data problems. (*Big data* is the term used to describe all the analytical information collected from digital content.) A book on content marketing strategies would not be complete without a discussion of data. But before you look at specific content measurements, you need to understand the impact technology has had on data and the opportunities and problems it presents. In today's marketplace, data plays a key role in every part of your online business and is critical to your content marketing success.

The good news is that both small and large companies can collect the data they need to make smart decisions. The bad news is that so much data gets collected that making sense of it can be hard. In this chapter, you look at the types of data that are available to you to gather, and the problems you may run into when trying to harness their value.

Understanding Big Data

To expand on the brief definition of *big data* from the introduction, it's really a massive digital collection of structured and unstructured data. (I define both types a little later in this chapter.)

Thanks to technology, we have reams of customer data available from our customer relationship management systems (CRMs), and even more is being collected on social media platforms and generated by users in the form of ratings and reviews.

The first instance of the use of the phrase *big data* was said to have been used in a paper written by the National Aeronautics and Space Administration (NASA) in 1997.

Big data is a valuable commodity for content marketing. It lets you see data patterns that you may have missed and allows you to make predictions about the content your customers want. But you need to ask yourself a question before you launch a big data effort. That is, what are the business goals for the data you are collecting? As discussed in Chapter 3, your content needs to tie in to your overall business goals — and your big data effort needs to tie in as well. You want to be sure that the questions you want your data to answer are crucial to the success of the business itself.

Big data collection and analysis can be expensive. Your company will quickly sour on the effort if it doesn't deliver on its promise to increase revenue and satisfy customers.

Looking at different kinds of big data

In the last 50 years, we've always been able to extract some form of data for marketing efforts. You could get such things as a customer list with locations or a list of purchases by amount. So why is data collection an issue now?

The answer is that we have more data now than ever before. We get data from smartphones, social networks, Internet sites, and factories with data sensors on machinery, and more. We assume that all of it must be useful — we just aren't sure how to harness its value.

To understand some of the basic concepts that underlie big data, you can start by looking at the kind of data you can extract. Table 6-1 shows the model that IBM follows.

Table 6-1		Types of Data
Data Types	*Description*	*Examples*
Descriptive	"Who" data	Geo-demographics, attributes, characteristics
Behavioral	"What" data	Transactions, payments history, and orders
Interaction	"How" data	Emails, web clicks, chat transcripts
Attitudinal	"Why" data	Market research, social media

You can look further at how to understand the who, what, how, and why designations by looking at descriptive data, behavioral data interaction data, and attitudinal data as follows:

- **Descriptive data:** This is your "who" data. You analyze it to find out who your customers are.

- **Behavioral data:** This is your "what" data. You analyze it to find out what interactions your customer has had with your company.

- **Interaction data:** This is your "how" data. You analyze it to find out how your customers interact with your company. It helps you understand their reasoning for interacting with your brand.

- **Attitudinal data:** This is your "why" data. It tells you why your customers are interested in your brand.

Looking at problems with big data

Aside from the types of messages that can be extracted from big data, you also need to recognize that you are dealing with two different categories of data — structured and unstructured. Structured data has been around a long time, but unstructured data has become available with the advent of social media. Here's how they differ from one another:

- **Structured data:** In previous years, all the data that companies collected was structured. The data fit into neat categories and could be presented on a spreadsheet. For example, think about a list of customer deliveries. Each cell in the database had predictable information — location, date of delivery, and so on. Computers were programmed to collect this data, and everything was very straightforward. When data scientists received this data, they knew what to expect and how it would be analyzed. This is still true.

- **Unstructured data:** With the advent of social networks and user-generated content, you now have a mountain of data that isn't structured. You have reviews, comments, and ratings. You also have a variety of formats — photos, live streaming data, and video. This data is more complex and requires different ways of analyzing and extracting meaning from it.

In addition to the structure, businesses have other problems to confront. Marketers have dubbed these problems "the Four *V*s" of big data.

The problems are related to the following:

- ✓ **Volume:** Information scientists believe that 90 percent of the world's data has been created in the last few years. Dealing with all of it in an effective way has been difficult for both large and small companies.

- ✓ **Variety:** We have cellphones, tablets, computers, networks, and even watches that generate data. As I've mentioned, some is structured and some is not. None of it fits into a neat little package that can be easily analyzed.

- ✓ **Velocity:** Data is coming at us at an incredible rate. Not only are there vast amounts of it, but the problems are compounded by how fast new data is created.

- ✓ **Veracity:** Can the data be trusted? Do managers want to stake their reputations on the fact that all the data that is flowing in is accurate? Common sense suggests that not everything collected can be used to predict customer behavior. How do you separate the wheat from the chaff?

According to an article by Paul Theriot, president of Alesco Group of Companies, a data management services company, a McKinsey analysis found that ". . . companies that put data at the center of their marketing and sales decisions improve their marketing return on investment (ROI) by 15 to 20%" (http://www.dmnews.com/dataanalytics/when-big-data-and-small-data-work-together/article/335012/).

Uncovering the Role Big Data Plays in Content Marketing

When you think about your content, you probably focus on what topic to write about and where you will distribute it. Those are important questions. The way you answer those questions, and many others, is by analyzing your data. When content marketing was in its infancy, many companies flew by the seat of their pants. They believed that they instinctively knew what kind of information their customers wanted.

They proceeded to send out steady streams of content, only to find that much of it was greeted without enthusiasm. That's when managers decided that big data really did matter. Now they know that they need to use data to tell them how to beat the competition and get customers' attention. There's no time to waste sending out content that doesn't hit its mark.

Improving your content marketing

So, as a content marketer, you want to know how using big data will improve your content marketing efforts. You should be happy to know that it enhances your effort in several ways. It helps you:

✔ **Be more effective against your competition.** By analyzing a variety of data, you can understand your competitors in ways that you couldn't before. (See Chapter 8 for ways to analyze customer data.) This understanding helps you create content with quality that surpasses that of your competition.

✔ **Find new ways to compete.** New data may allow you to find and explore new business models and niches. This exploration helps you create content that expands your customer base and creates new revenue streams.

✔ **Zero in on your targeted audience.** With more data telling you about channels, you know how and where to communicate with your customers. You can create the content that customers value and distribute it to the places they will look.

✔ **Interact with your community.** By knowing where your customers congregate, you can create a community of like-minded people who will help guide your content marketing efforts by providing feedback.

✔ **Analyze your wins and losses.** By quickly showing you what tactics are succeeding and failing, you can make revisions to content that improve website traffic and customer satisfaction.

Using real-time content

Obviously, the desire by marketers to provide customers with exciting real-time content is strong. It's a way to capture attention. The key to using this content effectively is to keep your customers at the center of all your efforts.

Throughout the book, I focus on the idea of creating content that speaks to specific personas on their customer journey. Don't get sidetracked by providing real-time content that doesn't speak directly to *your* customers.

Customers have grown used to having their smartphones and other devices with them so that they can communicate as needed. Companies should expand their content messages as much as possible to take advantage of real-time content. (See Chapter 12 for details about content types.) But creating real-time content doesn't limit you to clever tweets during the Super

Bowl, (although Oreo made great use of Twitter then: `http://www.wired.com/2013/02/oreo-twitter-super-bowl`). Here are some other ideas that can expand your real-time reach:

- ✔ **Newsjacking:** Newsjacking is defined as the art of using news stories and celebrities to create timely content for your customers. I'm sure you've seen content with titles like "What [insert rock star name] can teach you about [insert concept]." The trick with this content is to actually make the information valuable, as opposed to just using a celebrity name to get attention.

  Some marketers argue that getting attention is what newsjacking is about, but your audience will tire of it if you keep providing content attached to famous names and events that's just not useful.

- ✔ **Conducting Twitter chats:** Don't only rely on tweets. Twitter chats are available in real time to all interested parties. You may be able to interest new users in your company by appealing to them from this channel. In addition, the transcript (content) will be available to them after the live chat.

- ✔ **Hosting Google Hangouts:** Developing a webinar (an online seminar) for Google Hangouts is a quick and easy way to target customers on Google, the web's most popular search platform. It also lets you create content that can be viewed later.

Discovering the Internet of Things

Are you curious about the Internet of Things (IoT) and how it relates to data? You're going to hear more about the IoT as time goes on. The IoT is a network of items that communicate their data to people and things without the need for human interaction. Included are such things as sensors in machines, appliances, and electronics.

Reviewing IoT market size

Technology writer Walt Mossberg of Re/code, shown in Figure 6-1, describes the IoT as "a whole constellation of inanimate objects [that] is being designed with built-in wireless connectivity so that they can be monitored, controlled, and linked over the Internet via a mobile app." Mossberg says that users can install these objects in the home "without changing wiring or hiring a professional" (`http://recode.net/2014/01/28/smartthings-automates-your-house-via-sensors-app/`).

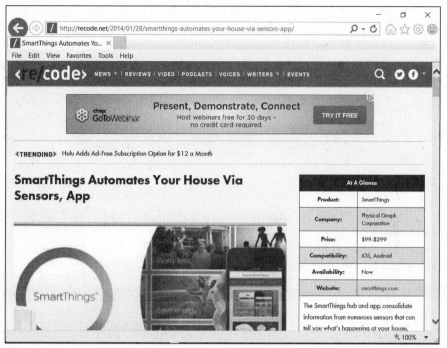

Figure 6-1:
Re/code.

What are examples of how the IoT benefits both business and consumers?

- ✔ **Business:** In the enterprise space, your factory floor can have machines that tell your managers when they need maintenance or need to have parts replaced.

- ✔ **Consumer:** As a consumer, you can be alerted when someone comes to your front door or when your appliance is out of warranty.

So how big a market will the IoT be? eMarketer, a digital marketing research firm shown in Figure 6-2, reported that figures by International Data Corporation (IDC) put IoT worldwide sales at $660 billion. IDC projects sales in 2020 to be at $1.70 trillion (http://www.emarketer.com/Article/Marketers-Put-Internet-of-Things-Data-Usemdashand-Works/1012824). Does that get your attention?

In addition, Intel projects that in 2020, there will be two billion objects in the IoT (see Intel's infographic, shown in Figure 6-3 and found at http://www.intel.com/content/www/us/en/internet-of-things/infographics/guide-to-iot.html).

Clearly, you should not ignore this trend. What you need to know is how it will impact your customers.

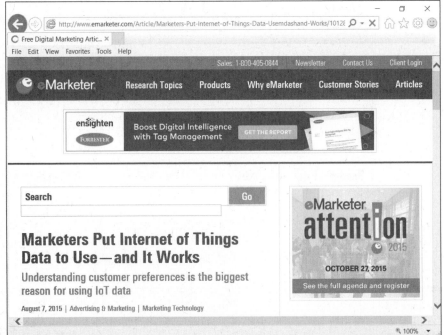

Figure 6-2:
eMarketer's
report on
IoT sales
projections
from IDC.

Figure 6-3:
The Intel
infographic
on IoT.

Impacting content marketing

To help you understand how the IoT will affect your customer's experience, here's an example to consider. Your customer can receive your content in a myriad of places. She is no longer confined to gadgets such as her laptop and iPhone. For example, her refrigerator can alert her to problems with food temperature. This capability affects your touchpoints (points of contact between the customer and the company) and the customer journey, and requires you to develop new messages for customer consumption based on the device customers are coming from.

Following are some specific ways in which the IoT impacts content marketing and the customer experience. In March of 2015, Altimeter produced an excellent report called "Customer Experience in the Internet of Things: Five Ways Brands Can Use Sensors to Build Better Customer Relationships" by Jessica Groopman (`http://www.altimetergroup.com/2015/03/new-research-customer-experience-in-the-internet-of-things`; see Figure 6-4). This report discusses a variety of ways the customer can be affected by the IoT, including providing support and rewards. Four in particular have a direct impact on content marketing.

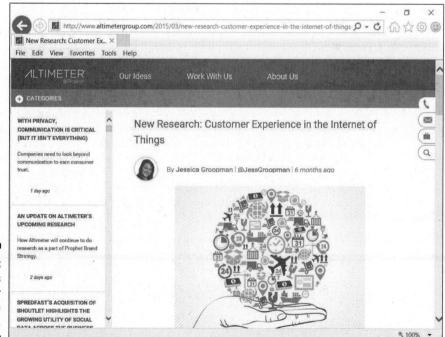

Figure 6-4: Altimeter's Customer Experience Report.

Following are ways to provide consumers with information and affect their decision-making:

- **Environment and proximity data**: You can send consumers your product messages based on factors like location, weather, and product interaction. Retailers, for example, can send targeted messages about what to wear or eat to beat the heat.

- **Location-based information:** Another way to use location data is to determine the customer's proximity to the product itself. Companies can guide shoppers to find nearby products and to choose the specific product when they are in the retail store itself.

- **Monitoring data:** The product can monitor and send a variety of data from the device itself. An example is a health device that reports current heart rate to the user.

- **Breaking news:** Companies can alert users to important announcements and emergencies right from their devices in real time. Such alerts provide a public service as well as benefits to the user.

It's magic

A great example of a company utilizing the IoT with big data to impact the customer experience was reported by Conner Forrest on ZDNet (http://www.zdnet.com/article/ten-examples-of-iot-and-big-data-working-well-together).

Disney created a wristband called MagicBand for use at Disney World. It has an RFID (radio frequency ID) chip inside it and connects a visitor and his family to all the services at Disney World. After you check in with your MagicBand, much of the annoyance associated with traveling and getting around is alleviated.

You can enter the park, make restaurant reservations, track your luggage, and make purchases. All your activities are recorded for you by your MagicBand. In addition, it provides people with experiences personalized just for them.

Disney made a considerable investment in developing the technology. It's one of the first forays that Disney has made in the IoT, but the company is betting that customers will be delighted by the seamless customer experience and will return often.

Visualizing Big Data

One of the ways in which companies are coping with the influx of big data is to create visual displays that help them make sense of the data. For example, you've probably seen infographics that attempt to simplify the data. You can also use tools to create dashboards, mock-ups, and simulations.

So how do you decide whether your data would lend itself to one of these visualization types? One way is to ask yourself the purpose of your visualization. Jim Stikeleather laid out three reasons to visualize data in his article "When Data Visualization Works — and When It Doesn't" for the Harvard Business Review in 2013 (https://hbr.org/2013/03/when-data-visualization-works-and/).

Stikeleather recommends data visualization for

- ✔ **Confirmation:** If your purpose is to confirm your assumptions, you want to display visuals (possibly on a dashboard) that help you determine whether you are correct. Visualization also helps you to look at how your present model works and whether you need to make changes.

- ✔ **Education:** If your goal is to educate, you can take one of two routes: simply report on your findings, or gather new insights about what you are seeing.

- ✔ **Exploration:** If your purpose is to explore new relationships and processes, you should create visuals to predict and manage the data.

Use this list as a guideline when you are deciding whether visualization will enhance your data. After you understand your purpose for creating visuals, you can help others understand your findings.

Check out the next page for a mind map of this chapter's content, and download a color version at www.dummies.com/contentmarketingstrategies.

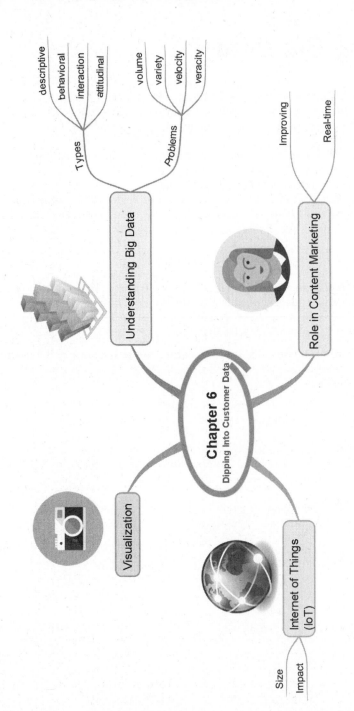

Understanding Big Data

Types
- descriptive
- behavioral
- interaction
- attitudinal

Problems
- volume
- variety
- velocity
- veracity

Role in Content Marketing
- Improving
- Real-time

Chapter 6
Dipping Into Customer Data

Visualization

Internet of Things (IoT)
- Size
- Impact

iMindMap
www.thinkbuzan.com

Courtesy of ThinkBuzan.

Chapter 7

Discovering Buyer Personas

. . . .

In This Chapter

▶ Understanding how personas enhance marketing efforts

▶ Uncovering data types to investigate

▶ Collecting the right information

. . . .

*N*othing is more important for you as a content marketer than understanding your customers. Without such understanding, you can't develop content or make your product indispensable. Enter the use of buyer personas. Marketers have a love-hate relationship with them. They know that they need to create and use them, but they find personas difficult to develop.

Creating personas can be tricky. You can't treat them like lifeless customer profiles that are created once and pulled out only for quarterly meetings. Buyer personas represent who your customers are. You have to understand who they are and what they care about. When you create persona documents, you should realize that they change as your company does.

In this chapter, you look at how to develop personas that play a critical role in your content marketing efforts. You also see how to avoid making common mistakes.

Reviewing Persona Development

The persona concept is not a new one. It was first mentioned by Alan Cooper in his 1999 book *The Inmates Are Running the Asylum* (SAMS). In the book, Cooper talks about how one needs to discover customer personas rather than create them from untested assumptions. When you create a persona, you are mixing your own customer data with your understanding of the marketplace to represent your ideal buyer. This is key because if you make assumptions without having real data to back them up, you risk derailing your content marketing efforts.

If you're like many marketers, the concept of personas makes you uneasy. Chief among the reasons for this uneasiness is that personas aren't easy to create or maintain. Your customer constantly changes her opinions, likes, and behaviors. You therefore have to keep abreast of her needs and wishes.

According to a 2015 joint study done by Quantcast and Forbes, 54 percent of companies agree that for audience targeting, identifying the proper personas is their biggest challenge (`https://www.quantcast.com/blog/how-brand-marketers-are-reaching-the-right-audience-a-forbes-insights-report`; Figure 7-1). So you're not alone in your quest to get personas done right. They are complex and can't be tossed off quickly.

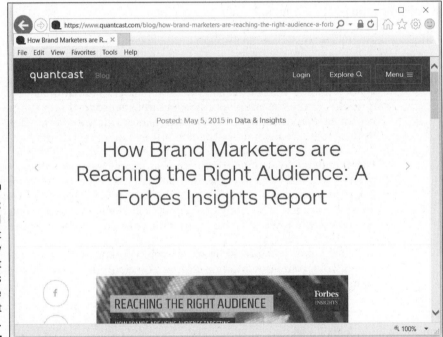

Figure 7-1: You can find the joint study by Quantcast and Forbes on the Quantcast blog.

You can't sell to everyone, of course, so understanding your niche is crucial before you create your personas. You've probably heard the term *niche* used all the time, but what does it actually mean? Your niche is the special corner of the marketplace that is interested in your products and services. When you understand your niche, you help your company reach its most interested buyers.

It's important to recognize that customer profiles and personas are not the same thing. You can easily create a standard customer profile and think that the job is done. A customer profile will get you only so far, however. You can know a person's age or gender but still not know what truly entices that person to buy your product. To know that, you need to dig deeper.

There is some controversy of late about the value of personas for content marketing. Some marketers argue that your creativity is stifled because you are essentially using cookie-cutter descriptions. That's exactly why I propose that you look at the bigger picture of your marketplace and the potential to find new niches and customers. This effort won't be wasted.

Understanding how persona creation improves content

The work of developing personas involves a combination of art and science. You need hard data to justify your conclusions. You also need a sense of how that data translates into customer emotions and actions. If you have a poorly constructed set of personas, you may do more harm than good.

The first question you may have as a content marketer is whether your content benefits from using buyer personas. Does it really matter if you haven't developed personas for your teams to focus on? The good news is that developing personas greatly improves the content you create. Read on to see how.

When you use personas, you can:

- ✔ **Tap into feelings and emotions in your copy.** After you understand how your buyers want to feel when they use your product, you can evoke those feelings with your content.

- ✔ **Use buying triggers in emails and real-time messaging.** If you know your personas' buying triggers, you send your emails and messages at the right time to interest buyers. You can also make sure that the same content is on your website and anywhere else where your buyers find you.

- ✔ **Directly address problems they are experiencing.** Solving problems for your customers is key to revenue generation. Your content, in all appropriate formats, should focus on problem solving.

- ✔ **Use influencers to persuade them.** Obviously, knowing who your customers respect and listen to is an important piece of the content puzzle. You want to include influencer endorsements in your content when possible.

Want a great way to find out which influencers resonate with your content? Try a tool called Onalytica (http://www.onalytica.com), shown in Figure 7-2. It lets you upload a file or add a link to your content and then sends back a roster of influencers who would be interested in that content. It's also great for finding influencers and new Twitter followers. Onalytica has lots of interesting uses and is free to try.

✔ **Rank content priorities.** Personas can tell you what is most important to your customers. This is helpful when you have to create an editorial calendar that reflects true customer interest. Some content topics can be categorized as "nice to have" and others a "top priority."

✔ **Speak to life goals that customers care about.** Personas tell you what life goals drive customer behavior. If your product can be linked to those goals, you will have attention-getting content.

✔ **Focus on what your customers want instead of what they say they want.** When you understand persona motivations, you can focus your content on what they really care about rather than what customers say they want. Customers don't always know what they want until they see it. By focusing on content that fits buyer personas, you won't waste time.

Figure 7-2:
Onalytica.

I've worked with client teams who initially laughed at the notion of creating personas that they call "imaginary friends." Their attitude changes when they realize that personas keep them laser focused on real customer needs. It helps prevent them from wandering off when someone suggests a tactic that doesn't relate to the people they want to serve.

Taking action to understand your customers

One of the main reasons that personas are hard to create is that you just can't sit quietly in your office and look at data. You need to take action to gather everything you want to know.

Here are some actions you need to take:

- **Meet actual customers on a regular basis.** Customer feedback is crucial. You need to know what they think, how they view your company, and how and why they use your products. Meeting real customers can be frightening to some. You don't want to say anything that might upset them. But if you can be regularly in touch with some of your clients, you can learn almost everything you need to know about how to make your products better.

- **Dig for special data.** You need to look at the data that is currently being collected by your company. Unfortunately, you may not find what you need. For this reason, you must be proactive and request the type of data that you require. Don't assume that it doesn't exist. The more likely scenario is that no one has ever requested it before.

- **Look at content consumption.** One key piece of data for every piece of content that you own is what the prospect has done with it. For example, if it's a video, was it watched to the end? More than once? Was it forwarded to a colleague? When you see how the content was consumed, you can get a better handle on whether it hit the mark and how interested the prospect is in receiving more.

- **Review sentiment analysis.** What is sentiment data? It's user-generated content about your company and its services. This is also called opinion mining. You can set up a formal system to analyze this data, or if you are working on a smaller scale, you can look at actual customer comments.

  For example, you may have lots of comments about your customer service on Twitter. If you see that the majority are complaints about how long your company takes to get back to customers, the sentiment is negative. On social platforms, not all publicity is good publicity.

✔ **Do what you ask your customers to do.** This should be a hard-and-fast rule. You may think it's only tangentially related to content creation, but if so, think again. You and your team should use your websites, landing pages, and blogs in the exact way you ask your customers to use them.

Although this seems like common sense, you'd be surprised at how little most content marketers know about the actual workings of their own sites. For example, if something is hard to understand, you want to add content right in that spot online that makes it easier. If you haven't used the site, you don't know what you need to add to make it better.

✔ **Make sure that content creators know your keywords, and keep content creators updated about any revisions you make.** It's important that all your content creators know what keywords you are using. It helps them shape the content they create and makes them aware of what you are trying to accomplish. Also make sure to keep them abreast of changes. This may seem like a small detail, but it will help them generate new ideas suited to your audience.

✔ **Make support people and sales your front line for feedback.** When you get your customer service people and sales reps to give you constant feedback, you are giving yourself a competitive advantage. You want to continually create content that solves problems. By knowing what people are struggling with and by providing answers, you are directly affecting customer satisfaction.

✔ **Talk to all your company stakeholders.** The last thing you want to do is miss out on the wisdom that other departments can provide about your customers. Engage them and let them know what you're doing. You will also establish some good will around the company by seeking out others' advice.

Collecting Information

What types of data should you mine to gather information for your personas? The list goes well beyond the usual prescription to conduct one-on-one interviews. If you take the time to collect different types of data (see the upcoming Table 7-1), you gain the added insight you need to serve your customers.

Finding different data types

Table 7-1 shows some recommended types of data that you should seek out when creating your personas.

Table 7-1	Data for Persona Development	
Data Type	*Examples*	*Suggested Places to Find It*
Demographic/ socioeconomic	Age, gender, education, income, standing in the community	Customer surveys, government data, Quantcast, comScore, Nielsen, Experian Simmons
Psychographic	Habits, values, hobbies	One-on-one interviews, social media platforms, customer surveys, buying patterns, forums, blog comments, Google analytics
Trend information	Popular culture	TrendSpottr, Trend Hunter, BuzzSumo, Magazines, Online news sites, TV shows, Google trends, Customer surveys
Questions/pain points	Questions customers are asking/jargon they are using	Quora, Yahoo Answers, Stack Exchange, Wiki answers, blog comments, Internal customer support, Google Analytics, customer events, conferences, sales team and other internal departments
Social media content	Twitter, Facebook, others	Social Mention, Google Alerts, TweetReach, IceRocket
Internal customer records	Buying patterns, product usage	Internal company reports, CRM systems
Search	Keywords	Google Analytics, Google Autocomplete, Ubersuggest
Gated content	Lead generators	Top-ten lists, tool lists, e-books, PDFs

Table 7-1 contains a reference, in the last row, to gated content. That is content that requires an email address in exchange for viewing it. This type of content is being used for a variety of content. According to MarketingCharts, shown in Figure 7-3, data from KoMarketing, Huff Industrial Marketing, and BuyerZone indicated that customers are willing to complete a form to get the following type of gated content (http://www.marketingcharts.com/online/b2b-vendor-websites-whats-important-and-whats-lacking-53697/):

- Trial offers
- Product demos
- Product evaluations
- Research
- Brochures and data sheets

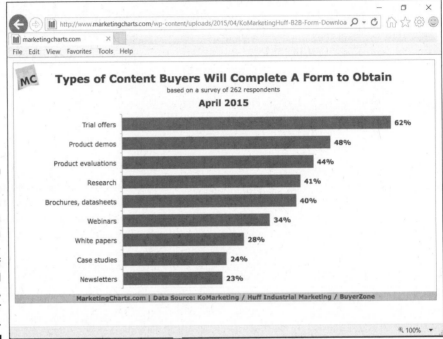

Figure 7-3:
Market-
ingCharts
Data from
KoMarket-
ing, Huff
Industrial
Marketing,
and Buyer
Zone.

To find persona information on some of the top brands, you can search YouGovProfiles (`https://yougov.co.uk/profiler#`). If you think that your company has a similar type of user, you may learn some interesting things.

Deploying listening tools

Smart content marketers know that listening to their customers is crucial. That's why good listening tools are available online. A *listening tool* is a tool that helps you find out what your customers are saying online about you and your brand. For example, if someone mentions your brand in a tweet, you want to know about it. These tools help you find those mentions and comments. Here are a few tools that will help you stay in touch with what your customers are talking about:

✔ **Social Mention** (`http://www.socialmention.com`): Shown in Figure 7-4, this is a great, free, real-time tool that monitors the web and social media. You type in your topic and you get back information on sentiment, top keywords, top users, top hashtags, and sources of content.

- ✔ **Google Alerts** (`http://alerts.google.com`)**:** This tool, shown in Figure 7-5, is very easy to use. Put in the names or product brands you are interested in, and you'll be notified when they show up.

- ✔ **TweetReach** (`https://tweetreach.com`)**:** This tool helps you monitor everything happening on Twitter related to your search (see Figure 7-6). It includes your topics, hashtags, competitors, and accounts.

- ✔ **IceRocket** (`http://www.icerocket.com`)**:** Shown in Figure 7-7, this is a great free tool that you can use to monitor your topics on both blogs and Twitter in real time.

- ✔ **Quora** (`http://quora.com`)**:** This is a different kind of listening tool (see Figure 7-8). Use it to see what people are asking about your topic. I like it because it gives me a good perspective on how people approach a topic and what really concerns them. You will also find interesting answers to these questions from other users.

Figure 7-4: Social Mention.

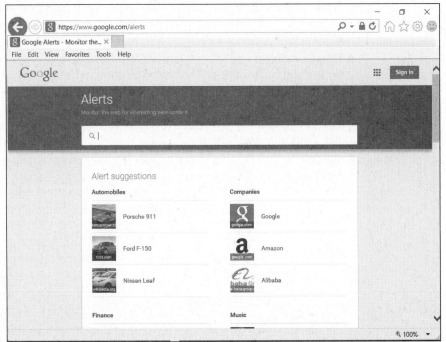

Figure 7-5:
Google
Alerts.

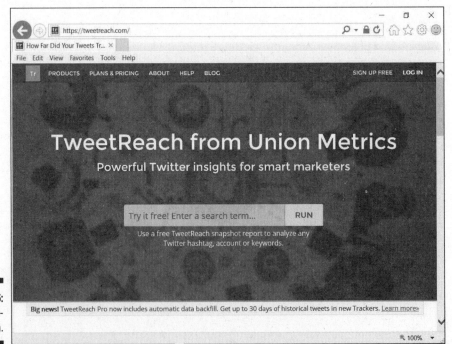

Figure 7-6:
Tweet-
Reach.

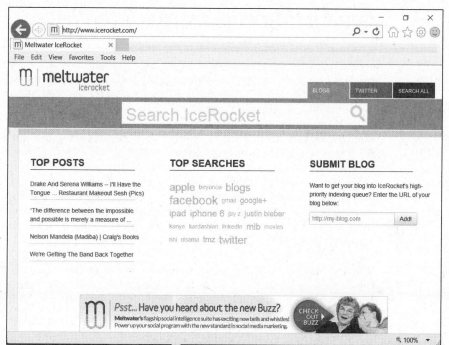

Figure 7-7:
IceRocket.

Figure 7-8:
Quora.

Conducting one-on-one interviews

Interviews with your customers can be the cornerstone of great persona creation. If your company has the time and inclination to approve this activity, don't hesitate to jump in. Meeting and asking your customers for their thoughts and opinions will help solidify your understanding of how your products are bought and used.

The wrinkle in your plans may come from other departments, such as sales. Sales may welcome an opportunity to introduce you to customers — or that department may be less than enthusiastic. If you are in a small company without a sales force, this may not be an issue. Marketing and management may be one and the same. Obviously, the best thing to do is to follow the guidelines your company sets. If you are prohibited from interviewing customers directly, you can still create personas that can be useful by using some of the tools listed previously in Table 7-1.

When you are conducting an interview with your customers, you want to ask them questions that will put them at ease and capitalize on their experience with buying and using your product. Make sure to probe for the meaning behind the answers.

You also want to make sure that you collect all the pertinent demographic data such as age, job title, income, and other information. You can then move on to questions that pertain to your products. Of course, your specific questions relate to whether you're speaking to a B2B customer or a B2C customer. Typically, you will want to know your customers' questions about the following:

- ✔ Life goals and personal motivators
- ✔ Goals for using the product
- ✔ Things they don't like about the product or your company
- ✔ People who influence their buying behavior
- ✔ Triggers that cause them to buy
- ✔ Where they consume their information and how they find new products
- ✔ What other products they tried before choosing yours

Make sure to capture real customer quotes so that you can add them to your persona documents. This helps give the staff using the documents the feeling that your personas represent how real customers think.

Key to the development of your personas is to look at behavior patterns. It's just as helpful to know what your personas don't like or wouldn't do as it is to know what they would.

Documenting your personas

The way you present your personas will go a long way toward getting internal acceptance. If you have a receptive audience, you can use a typical template that includes a name, a picture, and details.

You can download a persona worksheet to help you create this template at www.dummies.com/extras/contentmarketingstrategies.

If you have a skeptical audience that resists the idea of using personas, you may want to start with a document that doesn't use the word *persona* and gives a generic style title and no picture. For example, you call it a customer profile and give it a name that reflects their characteristics, such as Anxious Parent. This would not be your preferred method, but getting acceptance is key to moving forward.

You may find my advice to move slowly with personas somewhat surprising because you don't see the negative aspects. Unfortunately, some people strongly resist using personas. You'll know pretty quickly if you are dealing with this kind of audience.

If you are just getting started documenting your personas, you may want to start with a helpful tool like Make My Persona from HubSpot (shown in Figure 7-9), which walks you through the process. You can find this tool at http://makemypersona.com/?utm_campaign=Make%20My%20Persona&utm_source=Blog%20-%20Persona%20Tools.

Avoiding Common Mistakes

As mentioned previously, creating personas is not easy. There are several mistakes that you and your team can make along the way. Here are six common ones I have encountered when companies create their buyer personas:

- ✓ **Mistaking themselves for the customer.** This may have happened to you. You begin telling your manager or colleague about a solution to your customer's problem. You have researched the data and the marketplace and believe that this information should be added to your persona. Your manager shoots down your idea because he doesn't believe that you are right.

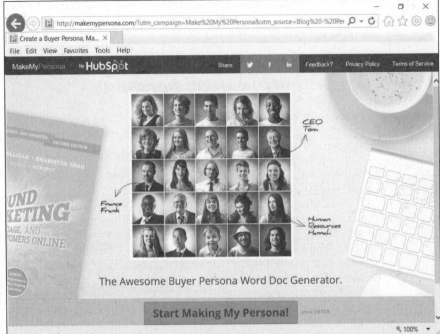

The Awesome Buyer Persona Word Doc Generator.

Start Making My Persona! (PRESS ENTER)

Figure 7-9:
HubSpot's
Make My
Persona
tool.

He bases his opinion on the fact that it's not how he thinks about the problem. He forgets that he's not the customer. This is a very common problem. People who work closely with products begin to think that they are the customers. In reality, they would never be a purchaser of the product.

✔ **Listening to what someone's relative thinks is a good idea.** This happens frequently. Someone's relative has a strong feeling about something, and your colleague is swayed by their opinion and wants to make it part of the persona. But I assure you that "favorite" features should not be based on what your colleague's cousin likes.

✔ **Forgetting to collect data about the customers who didn't complete their purchase.** You can often learn just as much from customers who didn't complete the purchase of your product as you can from those who did. You need to know why your customers abandoned their shopping cart in mid-buy. This is extremely helpful because you want to know where you are falling short and what you can do to plug that leak. This data should be included in persona information.

✔ **Thinking that understanding the features and benefits that personas prefer is the whole picture.** Most product managers love their products. That's a good thing. But customers unknowingly want you to appeal to their emotions. When you don't understand how the product makes them feel, you miss out on an opportunity to grab their imagination and create a customer for life.

✔ **Not understanding what entertains your customer.** You spend time collecting information, but you don't find out what your customer finds entertaining. If you know more about this, you can create great content pieces that will engage your prospects. You also need to know where they consume information and in what format.

✔ **Ignoring what people don't like about your product.** Obviously, you focus on what they do like so that you can appeal to prospect. But you also want to know what they don't like so that you can fix it and retain customers.

According to Adele Revella, the founder of Buyer Persona Institute (`http://buyerpersonainstitute.com`), a study from ITSMA says that 44 percent of marketers surveyed say that they have personas but 85 percent of them don't believe they are using them effectively (`http://www.itsma.com/research/increasing-relevance-with-buyer-personas-and-b2i-marketing/`). It's important that you take the time to integrate your buyer personas into your content marketing efforts.

Looking at How Generations Differ

Every generation puts its definitive stamp on society. In this section, you look at two groups that have a major impact on your content marketing efforts — millennials and Generation C.

Understanding millennials

According to a Pew Research Center study, shown in Figure 7-10, 2015 was the year that millennials became the largest generational group in the United States, surpassing baby boomers (`http://www.pewresearch.org/fact-tank/2015/01/16/this-year-millennials-will-overtake-baby-boomers/`). Millennials are defined as those who were ages 18 to 34 in 2015. The oldest millennial was born in 1981.

Much has been reported about how millennials differ in their attitude toward marketing and technology. They have grown up with digital gadgets and are not intimidated by them. They can easily spot hype and are resistant to it in marketing messages. They like to be asked to participate by companies and are more likely to take the advice of another millennial they don't know rather than be influenced by a popular brand.

According to a 2014 article in the *Wall Street Journal*, millennials spend an average of 18 hours using media per day. This includes playing video games, checking email, and watching live TV — much of which is done simultaneously (`http://blogs.wsj.com/digits/2014/03/13/data-point-how-many-hours-do-millennials-eat-up-a-day/`).

Figure 7-10:
Pew
Research
Center
study.

In an attempt to understand how millennials view content, NewsCred conducted an important study called "The Millennial Mind: How Content Drives Brand Loyalty" (`http://newscred.com/assets/downloads/guide/ NewsCred_Millennial_Mind.pdf`; see Figure 7-11).

Here are some of the study's key findings:

- A majority of the millennials surveyed favor content that is tailored to their age, location, and cultural interests.

- Thirty percent don't read content unless it educates or entertains them.

- Forty-one percent abandon content that is too long.

- Seventy percent share content that makes them laugh.

- Google and Facebook are the top platforms they use to find content.

- Fifty percent share content about a cause they believe in.

- More than 50 percent prefer to engage with brands on their company websites or social media.

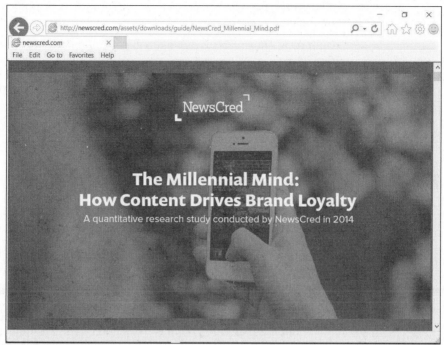

Figure 7-11:
The
NewsCred
Millennial
study.

So what does this mean for your content efforts if you are targeting millennials? Obviously, they are a discerning group. They want the content they engage with to be age appropriate and to have some intrinsic value. They won't normally sit through long content, but you can catch their attention when you discuss their favorite causes. One interesting finding is that they will engage brands on their websites, not just on social media networks. This is an opportunity for you to beef up content on your website.

Meeting Gen C

An offshoot of the millennials is a group called Gen C. Unlike millennials, Gen C is not really a generation in the true sense of the term, but rather a construct made up of people who live their lives connected to their devices. They could be from any age group, but they have distinct characteristics. Sixty-five percent of them are under 35 but the rest are spread among the other generations.

Google identifies Gen C as consumers who care about the following:

- ✔ **Creation:** They like the act of creating content — taking pictures, giving their opinions, and sharing them online.

- ✔ **Curation:** They like gathering others' interesting ideas, photos, and articles and sharing them with their friends.

✔ **Connection:** They want to stay connected, and 76 percent watch YouTube videos every day.

✔ **Community:** They want to belong to groups that do things they support and admire.

Surprisingly, Gen C'ers interact directly with brands. If you are a content marketer, you want to make sure that you engage these prospects by asking them to participate and take action.

Identifying a Prospect's Emotions

The shift in control from marketers to prospects has created a strong need for content marketers to figure out what a prospect needs at every stage of the buyer's journey. (See Chapter 8 for more about the buyer's journey.) One of the things that is central to your investigation of buyer personas is how your customers feel when they buy and use your products. It's imperative to use emotional language in your content — that is, language that evokes feelings.

We all know that our moods and emotions impact our buying habits. People joke about shopping — dubbed *retail therapy* — as a way to soothe them-selves. That's proof that customers are influenced by their feelings. Both B2B customers and B2C customers are influenced by emotions even though busi-ness buyers would like to think otherwise. An awareness of emotions that affect your buyers can help you seek them out in your customers.

Here are some common emotions that influence buyers:

✔ **Fear:** You want to know what concerns and fears your customer may have so that when you write your content, you can show how your prod-uct would impact that fear. Will it help alleviate it? That's a great motiva-tor to buy.

✔ **Guilt:** Customers don't always buy your product for positive reasons. Sometimes it will be bought to assuage someone or make up for the lack of something. Your content could highlight that emotion.

✔ **Concerns about status:** Of course, this is a big motivator. If you are selling a luxury product, you want to make sure that you tap into the notion that the purchase of your product will elevate a buyer's status. Conversely, if you are aiming at a frugal buyer, you want to ensure that your content targets that mentality.

✔ **Desire to mitigate risk:** Whenever someone makes a purchase, they worry about taking a bad risk. If the product cost is small, the concern is lower, but it's always there. If you can mitigate that risk in some way, such as by adding a money-back guarantee to your content, you can help your customer say yes.

✔ **Desire for instant gratification:** If this motivation is present, your content should focus on it. Every marketer loves an impulse buyer.

✔ **Fear of Missing Out (FOMO):** This is a relatively new addition (or addiction). People who are plugged into their devices have a fear that if they are not paying attention to online activity 24/7, they are missing out on what's happening. They want to know about the latest products, trends, events, and gossip. They want to know what their friends are doing and how they themselves compare. To capitalize on this phenomenon, your marketing can provoke users to feel that they have to have your product or risk being left behind.

Keeping Up with Trends

Keeping your eye on trends is an important part of a content marketer's job. You want to know what your customers are seeing, hearing, and thinking about in the wider culture. Sometimes trends come in with a huge flourish. Other times, they sneak up on you. Keeping yourself in touch with popular culture helps you know what your customers might want next or what they will reject.

Here are a few sources in addition to the listening tools discussed earlier in the chapter, in "Deploying listening tools," to help you plug in to what's happening around you:

✔ **Google Trends** (`https://www.google.com/trends`): This is a free tool that lets you know what's popular on Google, which is a sure way to know what people are interested in. Here's a look at the term Content Marketing (`https://www.google.com/trends/explore#q=content%20marketing`). As you can see the trend spikes upward starting in 2011, as shown in Figure 7-12.

✔ **Trendspottr** (`http://trendspottr.com`): Shown in Figure 7-13, this tool allows you to create alerts for the topics you care about. It's a real-time tool that keeps you on top of trends by monitoring web content, including that of Facebook and Twitter.

✔ **Trend Hunter** (`http://www.trendhunter.com`): Shown in Figure 7-14, Trend Hunter is a community of people who report on the latest trends. The site has lots of interesting information on what's trending and why.

✔ **BuzzSumo Trends:** BuzzSumo has added a trends section to its search capabilities, as shown in Figure 7-15. It shows you content that is trending for major topics or the specific topics you set up. To create your own trend search, go to `https://app.buzzsumo.com/trending` and set up the topic of your choice. You can see what's trending in 2, 4, 8, 12, or 24 hours.

If you want to learn about how to uncover trends, check out *Non-Obvious: How To Think Different, Curate Ideas & Predict The Future,* by Rohit Bhargava (Ideapress Publishing, 2015).

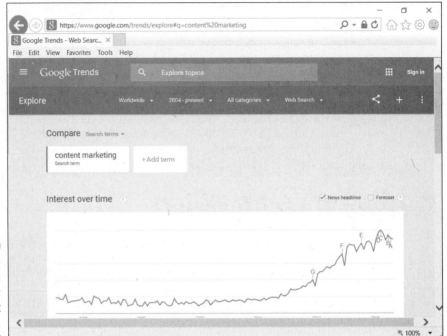

Figure 7-12:
Google
Trends for
Content
Marketing.

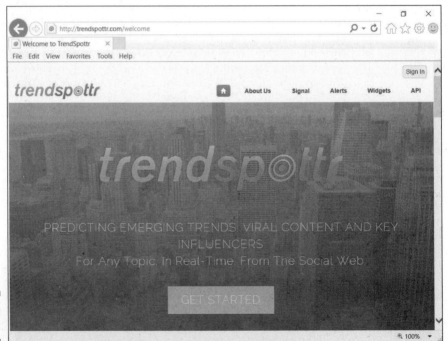

Figure 7-13:
Trendspottr.

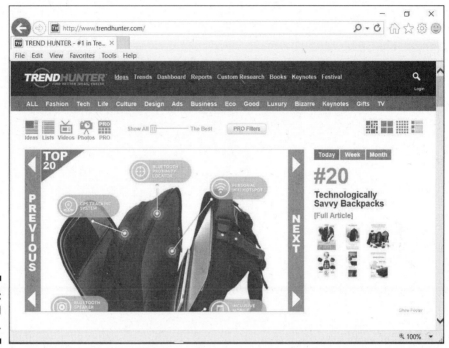

Figure 7-14:
Trend
Hunter.

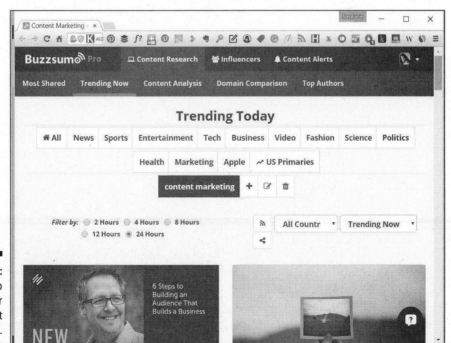

Figure 7-15:
BuzzSumo
Trends for
Content
Marketing.

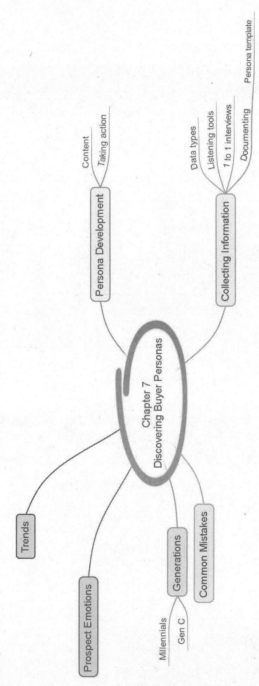

Chapter 7
Discovering Buyer Personas

Persona Development
Content
Taking action

Collecting Information
Data types
Listening tools
1 to 1 interviews
Documenting
Persona template

Trends

Prospect Emotions

Generations
Millennials
Gen C

Common Mistakes

Courtesy of ThinkBuzan.

Chapter 8

Taking the Buyer's Journey

In This Chapter

▶ Understanding the buyer's mindset

▶ Unearthing your touchpoints

▶ Using an omni-channel approach

▶ Creating the right content to influence a purchase

The guidelines for the best customer experience continually change. The only aspect that remains constant is that buyers are empowered and define their own journeys, and you need to accommodate them. Some customers like to check prices on mobile devices in retail stores; others spend hours online collecting information before making a decision. Your job is to make sure that your customer has all the information she needs to choose your product without becoming confused or annoyed.

As you begin to create your customer journey, understand that no book or article can tell you how to map *your* buyers' exact journey — so don't be frustrated. Your customers are unique and will take the journey that makes sense to them. You can look at what your customers are doing now and extrapolate from that. However, you can't ensure that they will take the path you choose for them. In addition, your business is unique and has its own unique way of delivering your products and services. That's a good thing. But it makes defining the optimal experience for your customers harder.

In Chapter 7, you take the first step in mapping your customer journey by creating personas. In this chapter, you integrate those personas into the customer journey. You look at the ins and outs of mapping that journey and see what content is required for each of the touchpoints along the way.

Touchpoints, also called contact points, are the places where customers interact with a brand while researching, learning, and entertaining themselves. These contact points are where you need to observe what the customer does and thinks. You can't treat a touchpoint as an isolated moment in time. You need to understand the context and what the customer wants to achieve.

In this chapter, I give you the concepts and tools you need to create a customer journey map. But the real effort begins when you take the time to look at every step in your customer's nonlinear path and analyze the content you need to provide. It won't happen overnight, but if you take the time to do a thorough job, the effort will be well worth it.

Harnessing the Customer Experience

In today's marketplace, buyers want to be able to explore information on all their devices from any location. They explore retail stores, the web, print and broadcast outlets, customer events, and so on, and all in a nonlinear process. What you need to do is to anticipate the potential contact points and provide content for each one.

But even more important than a focus on touchpoints alone is an understanding of the journey your customers take. You need to walk in their shoes to understand their behavior and what they need. This is where your personas come into play. Of course, mapping the journey using a host of procedures, systems, personas, and touchpoints can be complex. But the payoff is worth it.

According to an article called "The Truth About The Customer Experience" in the *Harvard Business Review,* Alex Rawson, Ewan Duncan, and Conor Jones from McKinsey found that a focus on the buyer journey is "30% to 40% more strongly correlated with customer satisfaction than performance on touchpoints" (https://hbr.org/2013/09/the-truth-about-customer-experience). This is a key finding. If you focus only on individual touchpoints but miss the bigger picture of the customer journey, you'll find the mistake costly.

Looking at the customer experience from both sides

When you and your team meet to discuss the ways you are going to interact with your audience, you believe that you know where to engage them. Or do you? The Economist Intelligence Unit, sponsored by Panasonic, did an interesting worldwide survey in 2014 called "Creating a Seamless Customer Experience."

The survey's goal was to show how both senior executive and customer groups viewed service delivery to customers (http://www.economistinsights.com/sites/default/files/Creating%20a%20seamless%20customer%20experience.pdf).

A customer group was shown a list and asked, "Thinking of the ideal customer experience, which of the following elements are most important to you?" The top five elements chosen were as follows:

- ✔ Fast response to inquiries and complaints
- ✔ A simple purchasing process
- ✔ Ability to track orders in real time
- ✔ Clarity and simplicity of product information across channels
- ✔ The ability to interact with the company via multiple channels 24/7

As you can see, the customers wanted fast, simple, always-on interactions. No friction, no delay.

Nothing listed here is an unreasonable request for a twenty-first-century company. If your company were rated on these criteria, how well would it do?

The same survey asked the executive group and the customer group similar questions. It asked executives, "Which of the following channels does your organization currently use to interact with customers (companies)?" It asked the customer group, "Which of the following channels do you use to learn about and compare products?"

I'm sure you are anticipating what they found. The executives focused on a few channels that were popular with customers, but for the most part, the differences between the channels executives thought were important and those that customers chose as important were significant. I chose the five channels that were the most at odds to report here. They include:

- **Search engines:** Twenty-five percent of executives say their company uses search engines to interact with their customers; 69 percent of the customers say they use this channel.

  Missed content opportunity: Search engines are most often used in the early stages of the customer journey. If customers are searching and your content is not optimized for search engines, you won't even be on their radar screen.

- **Friends and family**: Zero percent of executives say their company communicates with customers through their family and friends; 51 percent of customers say they consult family and friends.

  Missed content opportunity: Obviously, this is a big misstep. Recommendations from trusted friends and family are a big factor when deciding to make a purchase. These executives have made no attempt to reach the customer's influencers on social networks.

✔ **Independent websites:** Nineteen percent of executives say they use independent websites to interact with customers; 46 percent of customers say they use these sites.

Missed content opportunity: This mistake is a hard one to understand when you think about all the guest posting and cross promotions available to most content marketers.

✔ **Email:** Sixty-seven percent of executives say they use email to interact with customers; 38 percent of customers say they use this channel.

Missed content opportunity: This one requires some understanding of what kind of emails executives are referring to. If executives use personalized emails to send targeted content to buyers, they have a good chance of getting the buyers' attention. Obviously, buyers would have given their email address with the expectation that they would receive emails. If the executives are sending what we would consider spam, that is, content that was neither requested nor desired, these emails would rank very low among customers.

✔ **Phone:** Fifty-five percent of executives say they use the phone to interact with customers; 24 percent of customers say they use this channel.

Missed content opportunity: Obviously, this is a tactic that should most often be used in the later stages of a customer journey and only if the buyer has given permission. Cold calling (that is, without permission) just doesn't fit with content marketing tactics.

Benefitting from an omni-channel approach

One key benefit of mapping out your buyer's journey is that it helps you understand where to put your greatest effort. So how do you go about putting your plan together? Start with an omni-channel mindset. This means that you have to think of all the different customer touchpoints as one integrated journey. No more multi-channel approach; instead, all the channels are connected.

A multi-channel experience is not the same as an omni-channel experience. You likely already have a presence on several channels. But if the customer experience on all these channels is not consistent and integrated, you are not an omni-channel marketer.

Content marketers make the common mistake of thinking about their customer's journey as a discrete set of linear steps. For example, marketers create a content plan for their social media channels and another for their website. (See Chapter 14 for details about channel plans.) They forget that consumers are jumping from one channel to another, from different locations and on different devices. They aren't giving any thought as to how they fit together. That's your job.

According to a study done by Neustar and Multichannel Merchant, depicted in their infographic at `https://www.neustar.biz/resources/infographics/optimize-omnichannel-marketing-infographic`, 70 percent of companies surveyed said that omni-channel strategies are important or very important/critical to their companies.

This is rewarding

Want to hear how one savvy marketer is using omni-channel marketing to the fullest? Jason Trout on the Multichannel Merchant blog reports on how Starbucks is getting it right (`http://multichannelmerchant.com/must-reads/5-excellent-examples-omnichannel-retailing-done-right-14052014/`).

Starbucks has created a rewards app, shown in the following figure, that uses omni-channel

marketing to its fullest potential. When a user downloads the Starbucks app, he can use it to find stores, redeem reward points, and purchase in-store coffee. The user can also view his account from his phone or the web, and it is updated automatically on all his channels. Starbucks understands that helping users buy coffee and get rewards is a smart way to keep the revenue (and the coffee) flowing.

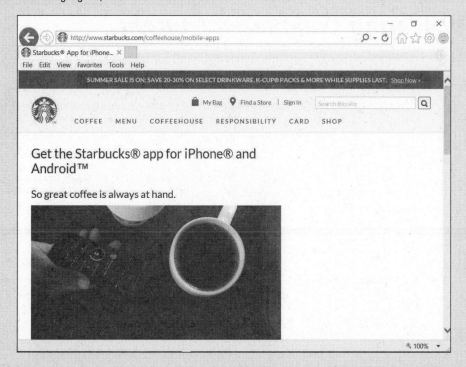

You need to provide prospects with a frictionless journey that doesn't require an online road map to traverse. If buyers want to look at your Facebook page on their mobile, or look at your website in your bricks and mortar store, you need to make sure they are viewing a consistent message that ties all their activity together.

I'm sure this makes sense to you because that's how you buy products, regardless of whether you're making a B2B purchase or buying a sofa for your home. In fact, Google reports that during the 2014 holiday, mobile shopping clicks were more prevalent than those on the desktop. When shoppers decide to buy, it doesn't matter to them where they are or which channel they use.

Here's an example: Imagine that your customers are looking at your website and see something they are considering purchasing. They want to look at it in your store to make sure that it is exactly what they want. When they walk into your store, you can trigger a discount coupon on their smartphone. Then they can buy using that coupon. When they return home, they can check your website to look at the shipping arrangements. If you don't have a bricks-and-mortar store, your customer will still want to shop where and when it's convenient for them, so you have to create a buyer's journey that supports their path.

Uncovering Commercial Intent

Given all the concepts you have to deal with for the customer journey, you probably don't want to hear about keywords, too. But it's important to understand how they fit in when you're constructing your buyer's journey. When you think about your keywords, you probably choose ones that provide your users with the information they are looking for. Before you do that, however, you should consider the ones you need when focusing on the customer journey.

The keywords that people use tell you their intent, that is, what they are trying to accomplish. When you create your keyword list, you should consider buyers' *commercial intent*. That means that you want to focus on keywords people use when they intend to buy things.

Here's how this works. People undertake basically three types of searches:

- ✔ **Informational searches:** This is the type of search users perform when they are primarily looking for information. Their searches contain such words as "how do I" or "where can I." For example, the results of a Google search for "how do I create content" is shown in Figure 8-1.

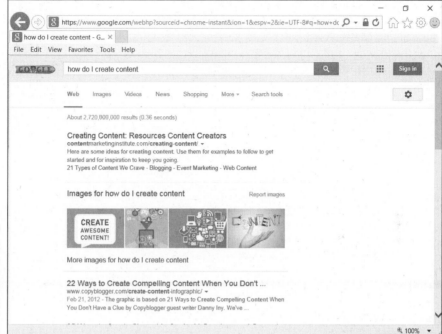

Figure 8-1:
Google
results for
"how do
I create
content."

✔ **Navigational searches:** Users conduct this kind of search when they know exactly what they are looking for. For example, if they want to read articles on Ian Cleary's blog, they type in **razorsocial**, as shown in Figure 8-2.

✔ **Transactional searches:** User intent here is to buy something. This is the type of keyword that you want to focus on. You want to ensure that the people who want to buy can find you.

Along with words such as *buy*, the category of product appears. For example, you see searches such as "buy organic baby food online" or "ship organic baby food." The results for a search on Google for "buy organic baby food online" are shown in Figure 8-3.

Make sure to use transactional keywords when constructing your content for your customer journey.

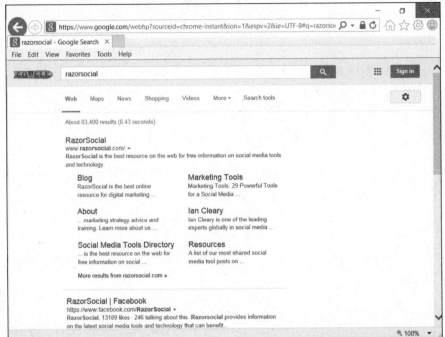

Figure 8-2:
RazorSocial.

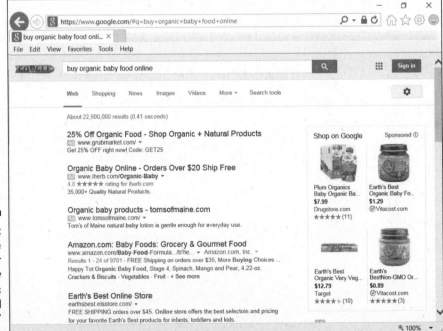

Figure 8-3:
Google
results for
"buy
organic
baby food
online."

Want to buy it now?

In an interesting contrast, Instagram and Pinterest both rolled out their new buying mechanisms at the same time in 2015. Adweek's Christopher Heine reported on the different way they approached harnessing their customers' buying intent (`http://www.adweek.com/news/technology/instagram-offers-big-data-pinterest-has-purchase-intent-165168`). One chose to sell directly from its site; the other chose to use ads to target customers.

Pinterest added a Buyable Pins button that allows users to search by price and buy the items that interest them. Users can purchase directly from major retailers such as Macy's and Nordstrom right on Pinterest. Pinterest is capitalizing on the fact that a great many Pinterest users go on to buy the items they pin.

In a different take on buyer's intent, Instagram is creating an ad business that will allow advertisers to target ads based on Facebook profiles. (Facebook bought Instagram in 2012.) Facebook is capitalizing on its big data asset.

Defending Against Competitors

Closely following your competitor's efforts is key to understanding what your prospects will encounter in their research. If you know that your competitors have provided comparison charts and data sheets, you should do so, too. You want to make sure to do a good job of demonstrating how choosing you is the better option. You need to cover all aspects of the buyer's journey to win the sale.

Researching competitors

You've spent time learning about what your competitors are doing. But you can't effectively compete if you don't know what your customers know about your competitors. You want to know what they do well and how they fall short. Your job is to surpass their marketing efforts and win the sale.

Your most effective way of winning the sale is to look at your competitors through your customer's eyes. Your customers don't care how much your competitors spend on advertising, syndication, and content creation. All they know is how well their needs are met.

In the past, doing competitive analysis was a costly endeavor. Corporate spies, focus groups, and lots of wining and dining of staff went into getting information. Nowadays, you can do a host of things online to understand your competitors' strategy. The information is digital and ready to be scooped up.

Here are some things you can do:

✔ **Analyze your competitors' website.** I'm sure your staff looks at your competition's media properties on a regular basis. Your staff probably knows more than a company's customers do when the competitor redesigns the website or changes product features.

✔ You don't want to overdo this analysis. Keeping *too* close a watch on competitors can prevent you from focusing on your actual customer's desires.

One mistake that I've seen companies make is to try to clone their competitor's site design and approach everything in a similar way. They do this in the mistaken belief that the customer will choose them because their product is simply better. Unfortunately, that's not how people think. They take into account the whole brand experience. Someone may pick your competitor for reasons that have nothing to do with the actual functioning of the product. Remember to tell your customer what's unique about your brand.

To look at actual data about your competitors, you can check out tools like these:

- *SimilarWeb (*`http://www.similarweb.com`*):* See Figure 8-4. You can put in competitor domains and see traffic statistics, referring sites, bounce rate, and more.

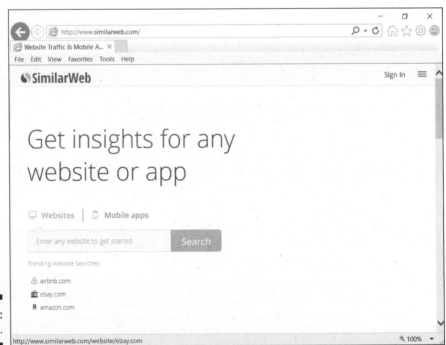

Figure 8-4:
SimilarWeb.

- *Ahrefs* (https://ahrefs.com): See Figure 8-5. I like this tool because it not only has lots of great data but also lists the top ten competitors for the domain you enter. Put in your competitor's domain and see what you find.

✔ **See what their customers say on social media platforms.** You can do this at both a high level and a granular level. You can look directly at competitors' social media sites to see what their customers are saying. Then you can use data analysis tools to compare your sites.

✔ **Analyze their content offerings:** See the next section for how to analyze competitors' content. (You can also use SEMrush and MozBar, again in the next section, to get competitive data.)

✔ **Download their product specifications and online resources:** Obviously, you can go to a company's website and download anything that any user can.

The key to doing a good job with competitive research is to focus on what your customers care about. Next, you consider how to analyze competitive content so that you can improve your own.

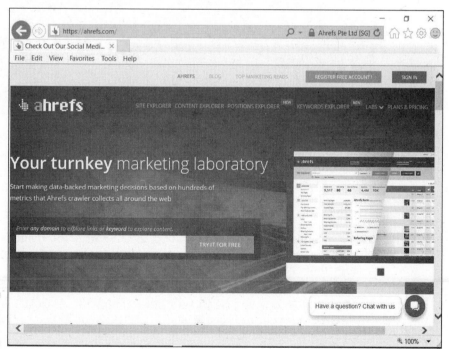

Figure 8-5: Ahrefs.

Analyzing your competitor's content

To understand what your competitors are offering, you need a reliable way to analyze their content. In his article "An Epic Guide To Creating Epic Content," (`http://robwormley.com/how-to-create-epic-content`; see Figure 8-6), Rob Wormley recommends three effective tools that you can use to learn about your competitor's content.

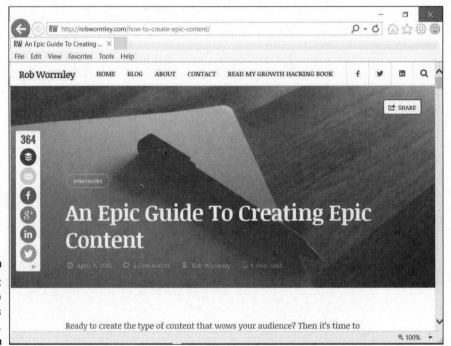

Figure 8-6: Rob Wormley's blog.

The tools are

- ✔ **BuzzSumo:** Go to BuzzSumo (`http://buzzsumo.com`) and type in your competitor's domain. You see a list of the most popular posts for the date range that you specify. Analyze as many as you need to make a solid determination of what content is resonating with that audience.

- ✔ **MozBar:** To see the title and meta description for the post, use the MozBar for your browser, as shown in Figure 8-7 (`https://moz.com/tools/seo-toolbar`).

- ✔ **SEMrush:** To see the top keywords that the content ranks for your competitor, go to SEMrush (`http://semrush.com`), shown in Figure 8-8. Put in the URL and click the Positions link to see the Organic Search Positions chart. You can also see a lot of other key information.

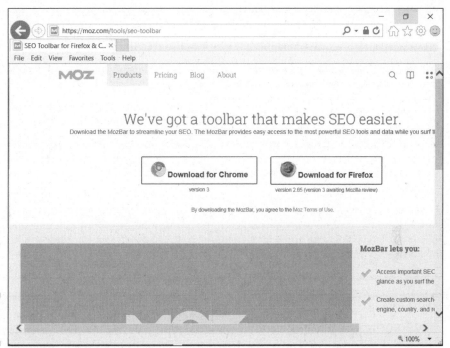

Figure 8-7:
MozBar.

Figure 8-8:
SEMrush.

Would you recommend me?

Finding exactly the right measures to determine how well you are doing against your competitors can be difficult. You have so many measures to consider. One quick way to see how your company is doing is to use the Net Promoter Score (http://www.netpromoter. com/why-net-promoter/know) to measure your customer's overall experience with your company.

To deploy it, you survey your customers using a 1–10 scale. You ask them, "How likely are you to recommend our brand to a friend or colleague?" Then you score it as follows:

- ✔ Promoters (score 9–10): People who love your brand

- ✔ Passives (score 7–8): People who are neutral and could move to the competition

- ✔ Detractors (score 0–6): People who are unhappy with your brand and could damage it with negative comments

Subtract the detractor score from the promoter score and you get a number from –100 to +100. Based on this score, you can evaluate what immediate actions you need to take.

Go through and evaluate the content for completeness and novelty. This evaluation should give you a good start on analyzing your competitor's content. After you have evaluated your top competitors, evaluate your own content to compare it. You can use the compare function in the settings in BuzzSumo in Tools ⇨ domain vs. domain.

Identifying the Stages of the Buyer's Journey

To reach your prospects, you need to understand what content they need to purchase your product. Rather than send out generic content and hope for the best, you need to create content that targets the buying stages your prospects pass through.

Understanding the buying process and journey map

The typical buying process is divided into three stages: awareness, consideration, and decision. I have added two more, purchase satisfaction and ongoing use, because I believe that your content job is never really done. If you don't support your customers, you will lose them.

Here are the five stages of the buyer's journey:

- ✔ **Awareness:** The prospect acknowledges a problem and begins to research a solution.

- ✔ **Consideration:** The prospect looks at options and competitors and narrows down her choices.

- ✔ **Decision:** The prospect chooses your product and looks at your specific buying details to determine customer support, shipping, and any other follow-up.

- ✔ **Satisfaction (post purchase):** Buyers want to feel that they made the right choice, and they want information that confirms that choice. This information can include usage tips and other ways to use the purchase that they didn't know about.

- ✔ **Ongoing use:** Buyers want to feel supported in their continued use of the product and may become advocates if their relationship with the seller is nurtured correctly.

So now that you know the stages that buyers pass through, you need to figure out where they go to get the information they need. For this purpose, you create a journey map.

Journey maps come in all sizes and styles. You can make them highly detailed or just cover the basics. What most journey maps lack is the marriage of your personas with your expected journey.

As the buyer's journey has evolved, marketers have been realizing that creating generic content for prospects in each stage is a waste of time and money. You need to speak to your specific buyer. The customer is expecting something more personalized, geared to her tastes and sensibility. You have done the hard work of creating personas (or see Chapter 7 if you haven't). Now it's time to use them.

Perhaps when you first got started marketing your content, you created a bunch of blog articles that you thought your audience would like. Many times, you guessed wrong, and your traffic numbers indicated that. Then you got a bit savvier and started to look at what content actually drove engagement, whereupon you created more of that kind of content. By creating personas, you took the next step in giving your audience the content they really need. Now, by applying those personas to the customer journey, you are accelerating the buying process.

If you're just getting started with developing your map, I recommend that you go slowly. The main work is to identify each stage, pair it with a persona, and then lay out all the touchpoints.

Benefitting from the journey map

If you wonder whether creating a journey map is worth the time and effort, think about the fact that it keeps you and your organization focused on the specific needs of your customer. That's critical. Some other key benefits of journey maps are that they

- ✔ **Help you determine what your priorities should be.** You know that you will never meet every customer need, create every piece of desirable content, or always make the sale. There's just an overwhelming amount of work that needs to be done. But you *are* going to try. To get a handle on your priorities, a journey map shows you the actions that will have the most impact on the customer experience.

- ✔ **Get everyone on the same page.** A visual map lets everyone know what the goals are and why they exist. Everyone can see how everything fits together, and team members can agree or disagree right up front so that buy-in can be established.

- ✔ **Let you see where your customer experience is broken.** An interesting thing can happen as you map your customer's journey. You can see where your path breaks down. If you don't have sufficient content for each stage, that lack will become apparent and you can remedy it.

- ✔ **Show you what each department needs to do to collaborate effectively with one another.** A visual map of the customer journey helps staff members move out of their silos and collaborate effectively. It's hard to stay isolated when you know what the rest of the team is trying to accomplish.

- ✔ **Help you determine the content needed for each stage of the journey.** Obviously, you need to match content to each point in the journey. I show you how in the next section.

So, what are the key items you want on your journey map?

- ✔ **Buyer's stage/goal:** I list the possible stages that your customer may go through in the section "Understanding the buying process and journey map," earlier in this chapter. You can add those to your map if they fit your products. Also include the specific goal statement for your product or service.

- ✔ **Persona:** If you followed along in Chapter 7, which covers creating personas, you have them ready to go. If you haven't created your personas yet, doing so is important because you need to identify on the map the persona you're targeting.

    When you complete your persona research, you should be able to note what special concerns and needs your persona has right on your map.

- ✔ **Touchpoints:** See the next section to determine how to apply touchpoints to the map.

Make sure to identify all the stakeholders who are part of the process to ensure that you do a thorough job of mapping everything.

Focusing on content for each part of the journey

As mentioned previously, beginning your journey map is a complex undertaking. Because this is a book about content marketing, I want to go one step further and show you how to add content to the journey map. I list some possible choices in the upcoming Table 8-1 for you to choose from.

Table 8-1		Content for the Customer Journey	
Buyer Stages	*Personas*	*Potential Touchpoints*	*Suggested Content Types by Stage*
1. Awareness: Identifies a problem and does a broad search	Example: Jane Brown	Search engines on mobile and computer; brand websites; blogs; landing pages, social media platforms, ads, influencers	WOM, e-books, reports, photos, infographics, blogs, articles, recommendations, video, influencer content, testimonials, PR
2. Consideration: Narrows options and looks at specific products and pricing	Personas	Brand websites; blogs; landing pages, social media, rating and review sites, ads, influencers, email	Product tour, demos, free trials, free samples, interviews, testimonials, pr, webinars, videos, white papers, case studies, pricing, webinars, recommendations
3. Decision: Makes final comparisons and chooses your product	Personas	Customer service on social media and website or in store, mobile, salesperson, email	Product specifications sheets, buyer's guides, comparison charts, webinars, a look at the checkout process, shipping info, payment options, online customer support options
4. Satisfaction: Felt immediately after purchase	Personas	Customer service, social media, website, mobile, email	email follow-up, tech support, community, social media, webinars, online training

(continued)

Table 8-1 *(continued)*

Buyer Stages	Personas	Potential Touchpoints	Suggested Content Types by Stage
5. Ongoing Use: Uses product and could become a potential advocate	Personas	Customer service, social media, website, mobile, email	Free tips, online training, conferences, webinars, video, support, in-person meetings

---

To create a journey map with content, follow these steps:

1. **Choose the buyer stage.**

2. **List the specific persona you are targeting.**

3. **List the touchpoints by thinking through the path you think this persona would take.**

4. **List the type of content you need to create to support that path.**

Another helpful way to understand how your prospect thinks about content in each stage of his buying journey was presented by Mathew Sweezey from Salesforce in Pardot's 2013 State of Demand Generation Consumer Survey (`http://www.slideshare.net/pardot/sshare-2013-demand-report`), shown in Figure 8-9.

The report states that when a prospect begins his search for product information, he thinks about the following:

✔ In the first phase (noted previously in this chapter as the awareness stage), he considers himself and how to do his job better. He looks at content such as blogs, articles, and industry blogs.

✔ In the second phase of his research (noted previously in this chapter as the consideration stage), he looks for social proof — that is, how others benefited. This includes content like case studies, interviews, and videos.

✔ In the final phase (noted previously in this chapter as the decision stage), he looks at content about your company to help him decide whether you are the right choice. This includes content such as buyers' guides, comparisons, and sales sheets.

As you're creating your content, think about whether customers are thinking about how the product impacts them (what they think), social proof (what others say), or you (what you say).

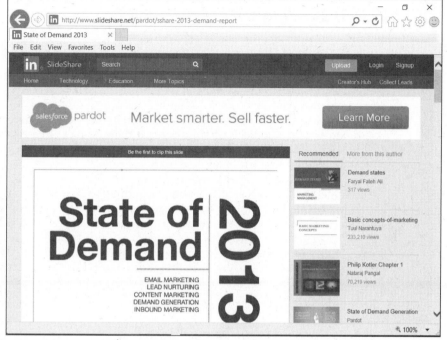

Figure 8-9:
Pardot 2013
State of
Demand
Generation
Consumer
Survey.

Ask the experts

Daniel Newman of Broadsuite reported in Forbes on a study by Nielsen that was designed to figure out which type of content had the most impact in each of the buying stages (http://www.forbes.com/sites/danielnewman/2014/04/10/the-role-of-influence-in-the-new-buyers-journey/). Nielsen tested three categories of content: (1) expert third-party content (influencers and subject matter experts); (2) branded content (marketing content); and (3) user-generated content (reviews, ratings, and so on). The study found that expert content won in all the buying stages.

This is an important finding. It doesn't negate the need for all the content types listed in Table 8-1, earlier in the chapter. It does tell you that you need to pay special attention to your earned media, as I discuss in Chapter 16. People want to reassure themselves that they are making the best decision and will look for experts to confirm it.

Personalizing Your Content

Forbes Magazine named personalization one of the top trends for 2015 and said that "Personalization is not a trend. It is a marketing tsunami." Are you ready for the onslaught? Can you provide the type of personalized experience that your customers expect?

Personalizing content is a tricky business. Customers want to have a personalized experience but also want to feel that their privacy is being respected. This is a fine line to walk. But walk it you will, because consumers no longer tolerate content that isn't matched to their needs.

This statement is not an exaggeration, according to Janrain, a company that uses proprietary technology to help companies find new users on social media (see Figure 8-10). Janrain performed a study called the "2013 Online Personal Experience Study"(`http://janrain.com/about/newsroom/press-releases/online-consumers-fed-up-with-irrelevant-content-on-favorite-websites-according-to-janrain-study`).

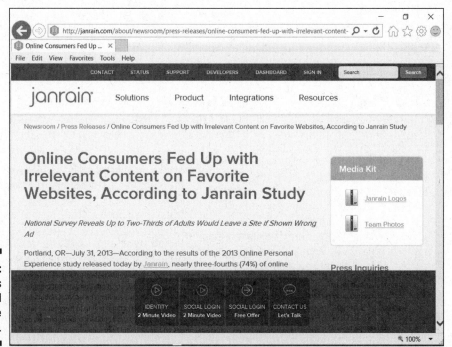

Figure 8-10: Janrain's Personal Experience Study.

The study asked respondents how they would respond to content that wasn't relevant to them. What did Janrain find? Seventy-five percent of the respondents said that they would leave a website if they were shown ads or content that didn't align with their interests. Fifty-seven percent said they would be willing to give some personal information if it was used responsibly for their benefit. Additional findings indicated that consumers are unwavering in their desire to see content personalized for them and wouldn't hesitate to leave a site that didn't cater to their needs.

Larry Drebes, CEO of Janrain, said that "[c]onsumers have reached the tipping point when it comes to being shown content that isn't relevant to them. It's a wake-up call for brands to fix this problem or risk losing customers and prospects." As you can see, your customers will only get more insistent about personalized content.

If you work for a company that doesn't use personalization technology, that's not surprising. According to a study done by Econsultancy and Monetate, a company that provides personalization services to organizations, more than half (56 percent) of companies don't use it on their websites. In fact, 72 percent of the respondents said they know it's important but that they "don't know how to do it" (`http://info.monetate.com/CROnlinePersonalisationUS_Research.html?utm_source=M-W-Blog&utm_campaign=R-Personlisation`).

So if you're interested in getting started with personalization, what should you consider?

- ✔ **Your organization's state of readiness:** Is your organization prepared to do the work and allocate the budget necessary to do a good job of personalizing your owned media? Does management believe it's a good idea?

- ✔ **The strength of your personas:** Do you have confidence that you can use your personas as the framework for your personalization efforts? If you don't have personas or have given them short shrift, you're not ready to put a personalization program into practice.

- ✔ **Your data collection efforts:** Do you have a customer relationship management (CRM) system or other data collection management tools to ensure that you have the data you need? Will you be able to assess the effectiveness of your efforts?

- ✔ **Your email capabilities:** Can you send out personalized emails with your current system and track the results?

- ✔ **Your mobile messaging efforts:** Will you be able to reach consumers with your offers via their mobile devices?

Check out the next page for a mind map of this chapter's content, and download a color version at `www.dummies.com/contentmarketingstrategies`.

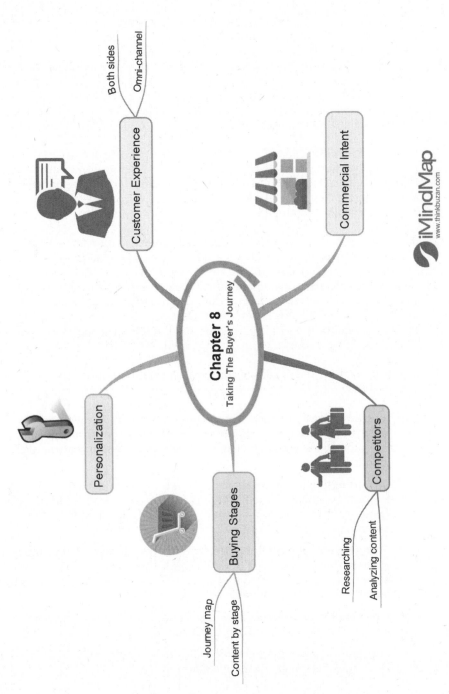

Chapter 9

Embracing Sales Enablement

• •

In This Chapter

▶ Learning where your company fits on the maturity scale

▶ Considering the evolving role of sales reps

▶ Accommodating the needs of salespeople

▶ Improving the sales coaching process

• •

Sales Enablement (SE) is a relatively new term (circa 2010) that focuses on the processes, tools, and techniques companies use to increase the effectiveness of their salesforce and includes marketing automation, digital asset management, CRM systems, and social media monitoring tools.

Of course, the idea of creating sales content to improve sales is not new. Companies have struggled with getting their products into the hands of their customers for centuries. In the early 1900s, the Jell-O Company had its salespeople distribute free Jell-O recipe cookbooks to customers to show how to use Jell-O with their favorite dishes. It is recorded that more than 15 million cookbooks were distributed in some years and the sales of Jell-O doubled over time.

What is new is the use of the web to assist salespeople in getting the right information to the customer at the right time from anywhere in the world. In this chapter, we look at the adoption of SE and the ways in which you can deploy it to help your sales reps to hit a home run every time.

Discovering Sales Enablement

When you look at the world of SE, you quickly discover that it means different things to different companies. And some companies take an informal approach whereas others set up rigorous systems that impact every part of their organization. It depends on the size and needs of each company.

The definition of SE that I think fits the largest possible audience was Doug Winter's definition in the Business Journals. He writes, ". . . sales enablement is the ability, by any sales rep, to systematically deliver a personalized, one-on-one customer experience" (`http://www.bizjournals.com/ bizjournals/how-to/marketing/2014/06/what-is-sales-enablementand-why-should-we-care.html?page=all`). Just as in the Jell-0 selling days, salespeople need to deliver targeted sales information right into the hands of the buyers. Today, companies reach those buyers via their mobile phones, tablets, or laptops. But the problem remains the same: "One size fits all" never does. The key to effective selling is the ability to present a personalized experience directly to each buyer.

So what essential elements must be present to make an SE system effective? Although several features make up a world-class system, three components are critical:

- ✔ **Data analytics:** These analytics collect and use data to make decisions about what the customer wants so that the sales cycle can be completed quickly. Your SE system must give you the ability to see what customers download, look at, and ask about so that you know what they care about.

- ✔ **A CRM system:** This system provides integration with current customer information to help speed the sales response at each point during the buyer's journey.

- ✔ **A cloud-based content database:** Both sales reps and customers need to have the latest content and product updates available to them from anywhere. Trust me: Your competitors will.

Gaining a competitive advantage

Managers who are presented with the concept of SE need to be convinced that making the effort to implement a new strategy is worth the time and money that's required. Will it actually improve the win rate? Can it provide a competitive advantage? Answering these questions is key.

So what are the reasons to implement a sales enablement strategy? Some benefits include:

- ✔ Making sales reps more responsive to the specific needs of the customer, giving the company a competitive advantage

- ✔ Increasing demand by strategically deploying the type of content that potential customers are looking for before engaging a salesperson

- ✔ Speeding up the time to complete a sale by answering all the questions customers have whenever they have them

- ✔ Keeping all the salespeople up-to-date and aware of changes to products and services

✔ Assisting sales coaches to meet the individual needs of all sales reps by analyzing their data

✔ Helping reps gain traction early in their tenure by giving them access to the training they require when and where they need it

I'm sure you agree that these are very desirable outcomes of a sales enablement system. Any manager would love to be able to show results like these to his company's executives. Unfortunately, making them happen takes a lot of strategizing and experimenting, which I go into in depth in Chapter 8.

Evaluating your current status

To begin considering your own SE, it is helpful to determine where your organization stands on the SE continuum. Demand Metric, a marketing and research firm (see Figure 9-1), uses a model it developed called the "Sales Enablement Maturity Model." You can download it here (http://www.demandmetric.com/content/sales-enablement-maturity-model).

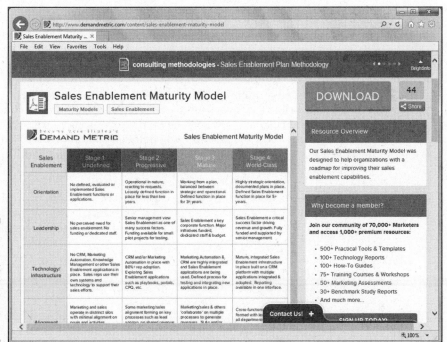

Figure 9-1: The Sales Enablement Maturity Model by Demand Metric.

Look at the descriptions of the stages of maturity to determine where your company is right now. Note that the relationship of sales to marketing is an important component. Table 9-1 describes the levels.

Table 9-1	The Stages of Maturity in Sales Enablement Strategy
Maturity Level	*What's Happening*
Undefined	No sales enablement activity or perceived need. No structure or operational tools in place. Sales and marketing departments are siloed with no collaboration. Win rate is less than ten percent.
	(When a company is organized into silos, it means that each department is independent and does not know what the other departments are doing. There is no collaboration.)
Progressive	You're in the early days of a loose system (fewer than two years). Requests are made for sales enablement function. Some light response has been received. Sales and marketing departments are aware of each other's activities and have some coordination. Win rate is 10 to 20 percent.
Mature	A system has been in place for more than three years. A budget and staff are allocated. There is integration of both automation and a CRM system. Sales and marketing have mutual goals. Win rate is 20 percent.
World Class	The system has been in place for more than five years. A strategic plan is in place, and sales and marketing work hand in hand with shared revenue responsibilities. Win rate is more than 25 percent.

Do you recognize your company in one of these descriptions? You're unlikely to be at the world-class level. Don't feel frustrated; so few companies are. It's a slow process. You can, however, move the process forward by identifying your company's stage of maturity to help focus your efforts and learn what is possible. You also want to consider what goes into making your organization world class in SE.

Tamara Schenk is Research Director of the MHI Research Institute. Her blog is shown in Figure 9-2 (`http://blog.tamaraschenk.com/`). In her SlideShare presentation, she says that four pillars drive world-class sales enablement (`http://bit.ly/1JeWFG7`).

Consider whether your company can implement these pillars. The four sales enablement success pillars are as follows:

✔ **Design:** Have the customer at the core of your strategy. We know that in today's marketplace you need the customer at the center of all your marketing efforts. This includes the design of all your owned media like websites and blogs. If your website is hard to navigate or find something, then you need a redesign. Customers are not as forgiving about this as they were when the web was new. Their expectations are high, and you need to meet them.

Figure 9-2:
Tamara
Schenk's
blog.

- ✔ **Scope:** Integrate frontline sales managers. This means that your frontline sales managers need to have a way to get feedback from every customer-facing employee. They need to know what's going on in real time.

- ✔ **Foundation:** Have a foundation in sales operations. All your sales content and training need to support the sales structure as a whole. This framework will ensure that your salesforce gets the right type of training when salespeople need it.

- ✔ **Collaboration:** Collaborate to integrate your company services. If you have siloed departments, you know that you are preventing people from doing their best work. Interaction and shared responsibilities make your teams successful.

Understanding the new role of sales reps

The role of the sales rep continues to evolve. All the positive value that the web provides also brings with it some obvious negatives — with the main one being that the salesperson is no longer in control of the sales process. In contrast to previous years, salespeople don't control the narrative these days.

According to SiriusDecisions (https://www.siriusdecisions.com), a research and consulting company, salespeople typically come into the conversation when the buyer has completed more than half of the buying process. (I discuss the buyer's journey in depth in Chapter 8.)

This means that being proactive and catching the buyer earlier in the cycle would be an excellent way to decrease the time it takes to complete the sales cycle. That's what a real SE system can help you do. It helps you empower the salesperson to find those buyers who are searching your solutions and related topics.

Today's purchasing teams are larger and spread out across departments. Salespeople rarely get to sit across from the ultimate decision maker. By providing cloud-based content to anyone in the company who is interested, reps can help speed up the buying cycle.

In his book *The Frugalnomics Survival Guide* (Alinean Press), sales expert Tom Pisello defines our current selling environment as a place where corporate "buyers have become more empowered, skeptical and economic-focused" and expect to know the monetary value of a company's solution before making a decision. I'm sure your sales reps would agree.

Mobility is another one of the critical factors that an SE system must have to accommodate the changing role of sales reps. First and foremost, a mobile SE system provides the content that customers want anytime, and anywhere. But it also is a great boon to salespeople who can't tie themselves down to a desk in an office. Salespeople have been known to prepare for presentations on subways, in coffee shops, and at their kids' soccer games, so mobility is a must. You need to supply devices to present from the cloud.

The TechCrunch blog (http://techcrunch.com/2014/11/11/the-rise-of-the-sensornet-4-9bn-connected-things-in-2015-says-gartner) predicts that there will be 4.7 billion "things" connected to the Internet by the end of 2015. Shouldn't all your sales content be connected?

Training Your Salesforce

Every manager knows that a well-trained salesforce is the key to success. Yet many organizations fail to take the simplest actions to empower their salespeople, such as neglecting to make sales information easy to find and forgetting to update everyone when changes are made to sales software.

A 2015 Dell study indicated that 52 percent of Dell's salespeople believed that they didn't have access to the most current compliant content (`http://www.cmswire.com/customer-experience/weighing-the-merits-of-sales-enablement/`).

In addition, many companies still labor under the delusion that a typical "sales personality" exists that you must hire. In its blog, HubSpot reported that according to Dave Kurlan from Kurlan & Associates and founder of the Objective Management Group, several sales myths still exist among people who hire sales reps (`http://blog.hubspot.com/opinion/study-3-of-4-sales-reps-ineffective`). They include the following:

- **Your sales rep needs to be an extrovert.** Recent findings have shown that introverts can also make great salespeople. They tend to be empathetic and caring. You need to look among both types for your best reps.

- **Your hire should be a driven person.** This one assumes that your sales rep is driven in all areas of his or her life. In reality, you need to choose someone who is really motivated to be a great sales rep. Being driven in other areas doesn't translate into sales prowess.

- **It's preferable for your salesperson to be an athlete.** Do athletes win at everything they try? Clearly not. It's great if your sales reps have good training habits as long as they can translate those habits to sales performance. If not, they're irrelevant.

Do you still believe these myths? If so, it's time to shake them off and look carefully at the person you're going to hire for the skills that actually matter.

So what should your sales training include? You should consider three types of training:

- **Structured training sessions:** The classic sales training that you're likely most familiar with is structured training. Just as in any college course, structured training has a syllabus, and the salesperson is expected to learn in a specific sequence. Typically, a salesperson goes through this type of training when first joining the company. But using this kind of training alone is outmoded. By combining it with all the devices and technology available, companies create a much more valuable learning environment.

- **Learning on the go:** Cloud-based training is ideal for salespeople on the go. They can get whatever they need no matter where they are. They can send the right content for every step of the buyer's journey. (I cover content for the buyer's journey in Chapter 8.)

- **Interactive sales meetings:** Face-to-face sales meetings or video conferencing are still indispensable. That's because it's still important for members of a sales team to share their wisdom and trade success stories.

Coaching Your Reps to Become Winners

One of the key functions of an SE system is the use of sales coaches. But are all sales coaches created equal? Your experience tells you they're not. Some salespeople are born coaches who can spot and solve problems; others just can't cut it.

According to the blog InsightSquared, shown in Figure 9-3, Mark Roberge, the head of sales for HubSpot, says that the number-one asset for a sales rep is "coach-ability." He found that length of experience doesn't matter. What does matter is the rep's ability to learn from her coach and use that knowledge to transform her selling. In fact, Roberge found that more experience tended to make his sales reps less *moldable*, meaning that they became less able to see things in a different way (`http://www.insightsquared.com/2014/02/mark-roberge-and-the-experience-myth/`).

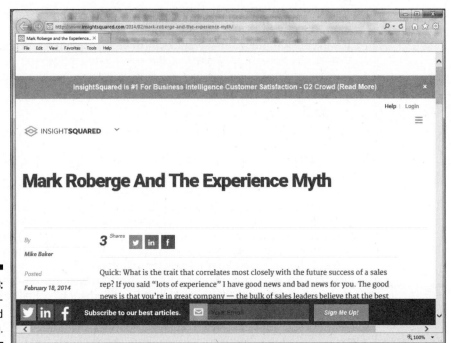

Figure 9-3: The Insight-Squared blog.

When evaluating your company's coaching capabilities, you want to consider these four aspects:

- ✔ **Determine whether your coaches are up to the task.** Typically, sales coaches come from the ranks of the salesforce. They get promoted upward based on the quality of the job they have done, not the one into which they are being promoted. The better the sales rep, the more likely he will be elevated to the status of manager or coach — his skills notwithstanding. For this reason, it's important to assess whether your coach can impart the skills necessary to train an effective salesperson.

- ✔ **Evaluate your coach's overall management skills.** This is a key component, although many companies overlook it. If the coach is a bad manager, she won't be able to spend the time doing the most important tasks. She needs to assess how much time she should spend with each sales rep to make a difference. If the coach can't manage her own time, she's likely to be an ineffective coach.

- ✔ **Assess whether you're giving your coaches the materials they need to be effective trainers.** As you know, training materials must be available to sales reps at all times. The key question becomes, do coaches have the training materials they need? If you ask your coaches to create training on the fly, you're hampering their ability to be efficient.

- ✔ **Look at the metrics used to evaluate a sales rep.** An SE system must have built-in metrics to help coaches determine what and when the rep is learning. Without these measures, coaches will have to guess what they have accomplished, or take their rep's word for it.

Checking Out Sales Enablement Blogs

Because sales enablement is a relatively new topic, you may not be aware of blogs that focus specifically on this topic. If you want to regularly follow SE, here are three major blogs that merit your attention:

- ✔ **Salesforce,** the premier provider of sales software in the industry. You can find a wealth of information about sales enablement at this link: `https://www.salesforce.com/blog/`

- ✔ **Forrester** (`http://blogs.forrester.com/sales_enablement`), shown in Figure 9-4. Forrester is a well-respected research and consulting firm that provides up-to-the minute information.

- ✔ **Association for Talent Development** (`https://www.td.org/Publications/Blogs/Sales-Enablement-Blog`), shown in Figure 9-5. The Association for Talent Development is a professional organization that supports sales trainers around the globe.

Figure 9-4:
The
Forrester
blog.

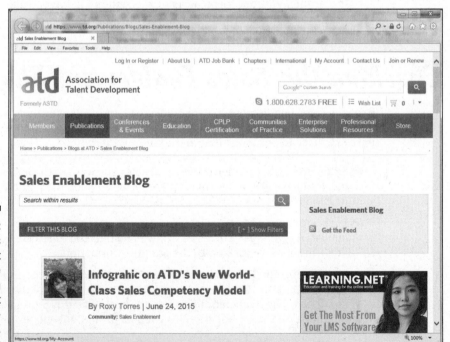

Figure 9-5:
The Sales
Enablement
blog of the
Association
for Talent
Develop-
ment.

Courtesy of ThinkBuzan.

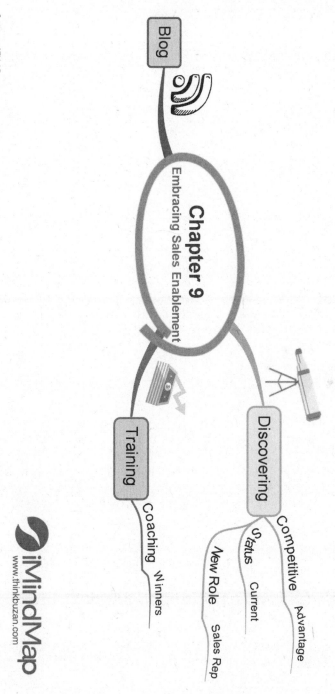

Blog

Chapter 9
Embracing Sales Enablement

Training

Coaching   Winners

Discovering

Competitive   Advantage

Status   Current

New Role   Sales Rep

iMindMap
www.thinkbuzan.com

Part III
Creating Actionable Content

Publishing content consistently is the secret to building your audience. Discover five tips for creating consistent marketing content at www.dummies.com/extras/ contentmarketingstrategies.

In this part . . .

✔ Developing a content plan is as important as documenting your content marketing strategy. Learn how to map out your content plan using a downloadable worksheet.

✔ You need to take advantage of all the content types available online. In this part, you look at several and find out how to include them in your content marketing efforts.

✔ Why do stories matter? See how to connect with your ideal audience using effective storytelling methods.

✔ Developing processes such as an editorial calendar and workflow systems is crucial to your success. See how using tools can simplify the process.

Chapter 10

Examining Your Content Plan

In This Chapter

▶ Knowing the value of your current content

▶ Understanding the needs of stakeholders

▶ Identifying gaps in content

*I*f you don't have a content plan in 2016, you are seriously jeopardizing your company's chances for success. Everyone from "boring" companies like machinery manufacturers to red-hot companies like BuzzFeed have one.

As you begin creating your content plan, you need to remember that your content marketing strategy is different from your content plan. A content marketing strategy determines how your company goals will be met by marketing your content. A content plan details specifically how your content will be created, managed, and distributed to meet the goals you identified in your content marketing strategy.

In this chapter, you look at the current state of your content and what it takes to put a content plan together. I also point you to a downloadable content audit worksheet to help you document your existing content. For more on your content marketing strategy, see Chapter 1.

Evaluating Your Content

Your content can be one of your company's greatest assets if you give it careful thought and attention. Some companies have been slow to get on the bandwagon, but they were quickly convinced when their competitors developed engaging content that attracted *their* customers.

If you're wondering whether custom content matters to your customers, ask the Chief Marketing Officer Council World Wide (`https://cmocouncil.org`), shown in Figure 10-1.

Figure 10-1:
Chief
Marketing
Officer
Council
World Wide.

This organization's research indicates that 78 percent of customers believe that companies that create custom content are interested in creating relationships with them. You engender goodwill by spending the time and money to create quality content.

Benefitting from a content plan

If your company has a content marketing strategy, you wonder if you need a content strategy as well. If you're skeptical as to why you should create a content plan, take a look at some ways it will benefit you. When you have a cohesive content plan, you can

- Increase brand awareness and brand loyalty by being in the right place with quality content

- More effectively evaluate content performance and revise as necessary

- Save time and money and avoid duplicating efforts

- Meet customer needs during every part of the buyer's journey

✔ Ensure that you deliver quality content that has been through an effective editorial process

✔ Deliver a consistent message on all your distribution channels

According to the infographic by Demand Metric, shown in Figure 10-2, "80 percent of people appreciate learning about a company through custom content and 60 percent are inspired to seek out a product after reading content about it." You can find the infographic at `http://www.demandmetric.com/content/content-marketing-infographic`.

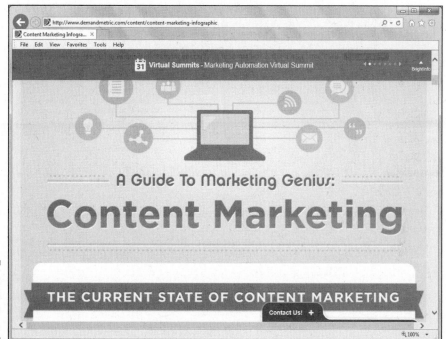

Figure 10-2:
Demand
Metric
Infographic.

If you now grasp the value of having a content plan, you probably want to know how to make your content superior to that of your competitors. First off, the name of the game is *quality*, not *quantity*.

Doug Kessler, creative director and cofounder of Velocity Partners (`http://www.velocitypartners.co.uk`), outlined some interesting ways to get noticed in his article "5 Ways to Stand Out in a Sea of Content." The article appears in the CMS Wire blog, shown in Figure 10-3 and found at `http://www.cmswire.com/digital-marketing/5-ways-to-stand-out-in-a-sea-of-content/`.

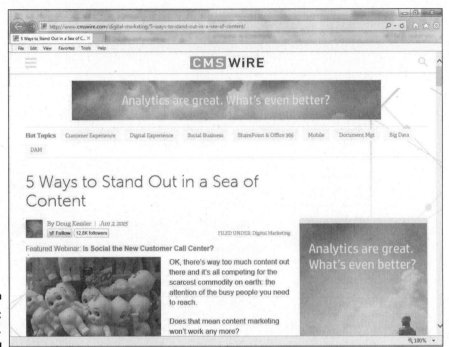

Figure 10-3:
CMS Wire.

Kessler suggests the following five tactics:

- **Stay in your sweet spot:** He defines your sweet spot as the overlap between your company's knowledge and the things your customers care about. If you stay in that area, you are sure to create quality content.

- **Use psychographic targeting:** Know what specifically resonates with your customers, and provide them with content that addresses their concerns.

- **Harness emotion, not just the facts:** As I describe in more detail in the later section called "Going Viral" you're most likely to get people to like and share your content when it evokes strong emotions.

- **Practice insane honesty:** This is an important concept. Kessler says that when you highlight your faults, people appreciate your honesty and are more likely to do business with you.

- **Create confident content:** This is content written by great writers who know their stuff and are convinced that what they have to share will be of value to you.

Also be sure to check out the Velocity Partners SlideShare called "Insane Honesty in Content Marketing" (`http://www.slideshare.net/dougkessler/insane-honesty-in-content-marketing`). It's a great example of the idea behind the saying "Total honesty is the best ruse ever invented."

Determining content maturity

Are you just getting started creating your content or is your company an old hand at it? Knowing where you stand is helpful when you begin creating your content plan. To determine your status, you can use a content maturity model. Todd Cameron has written an article about Kapost's "The Content Operation Maturity Model," shown in Figure 10-4 (`http://marketeer.kapost.com/content-operation-maturity-model/#axzz`). You can use it to assess where your company falls on the content maturity continuum between novice and practitioner.

Figure 10-4: The Kapost Content Operation Maturity Model.

Here are the status designations:

- **Novice:** This group is just getting started. Members may have siloed departments and don't have an established process to create content.
- **Practitioner:** If you fall into this group, you're starting to create processes and beginning to establish some visibility.
- **Intermediate:** This group is starting to establish a strategy and develop workflows.
- **Advanced:** If you are in this group, you're really moving forward. You are revenue focused and developing sound channel plans.
- **Expert:** This group has mastered content creation. You are doing everything right. You're optimizing your content and focusing on leads and revenue.

So where does your company fall on this continuum? Determine where you are now and what you need to do to get to the next level. Then let all the staff know your designation and what people can do as a team to move forward. This is a great way to motivate teams because they can see how collaboration will be rewarded.

Assessing Your Content

It's time to look at your content so that you can learn what needs to be added or revised going forward. To assess your content, you need to do several things in the following order:

- Talk to your stakeholders
- Conduct a content audit and determine whether you have gaps in your content
- Create visual maps of key sites

The following sections consider each of these actions in turn.

Interviewing your stakeholders

Internal stakeholders play a very important role in your content plan. Their importance is often overlooked because listening to them takes time and effort. They are the keepers of important information and understand the history behind the content that's been created.

One-on-one interviews are preferable, but you can do group interviews if you have very large groups of stakeholders.

Prepare interviewees by giving them the questions beforehand. You want them to be ready to give their perspective on the company's content and procedures. Making the effort to speak to them will help you

- ✔ Find out about sites, landing pages, and other pages that were created and forgotten
- ✔ Understand why particular sets of content were created and how they performed
- ✔ Discover content needs that aren't being met
- ✔ Learn about systems and procedures that are working well or need improvement
- ✔ Understand how internal stakeholders work together and what the challenges are in collaborating
- ✔ Get buy-in for your content plan when you have completed it

You can see that you will miss important insights if you avoid talking to all your stakeholders. Jump in and get it done. Your stakeholders will appreciate being consulted.

Conducting a content audit

Are you ready to conduct your content audit? It's the step in the process that tells you exactly what content you have. If you work for a large enterprise, pockets of content may or may not have been documented. If you work in a small business, you may have a full audit or none at all.

The key to doing an effective content audit is deciding beforehand how comprehensive in scope you will get. You can determine the scope based on your specific goals, the volume of content, and the resources you have to accomplish the task.

You download the content audit worksheet at `http://www.dummies.com/extras/contentmarketingstrategies`.

Ask yourself the following questions to clarify your thinking:

- ✔ **How do I define the goals of this project?** Is this project being done for an imminent campaign or does it have to encompass all your content? Make sure that you can articulate the goals you have for each project.

✔ **Are there specific priorities that I can apply?** Based on what you are trying to accomplish, can you limit your investigation to certain channels or types of content?

✔ **Will it help me to know about every piece of content that exists?** Decide how much depth you need to go to. Can you take a middle ground that collects representative content, or must it be all inclusive?

✔ **How deeply should I go into the specifications for each piece of content?** Do you want to take the time to document all characteristics for each piece of content? Do you want to know everything about a piece of content or can you be selective?

Now that you have determined the scope of your audit, take a look at what your content audit worksheet can include:

✔ **Title:** The exact title of the content piece. You may have several pieces with similar titles.

✔ **Location:** The URL where the content is located. It's very important to note this location when doing the audit. Don't duplicate efforts by requiring a producer to go and locate it every time it's needed.

✔ **Persona:** The persona name for whom you created this content.

✔ **Buyer's journey step:** The step in the buyer's journey for which you created this content, such as "Consideration." (See Chapter 8 for more on the buyer's journey.)

✔ **Format:** Describe the specific format the content is in. Is it an e-book, a blog post, something else? This information will help you determine how you can repurpose it.

✔ **Topic/keywords:** Put in the known keywords that were used and, if possible, the specific topic under which this content was categorized.

✔ **Call to action (CTA):** Identify the CTA for the content piece. Knowing the CTA is very useful when you are determining a content sequence, such as a link to a landing page.

✔ **Metrics:** List any metrics you have that let you know how well the content performed.

As mentioned previously, you might not choose to include all the preceding items. Modify this worksheet based on the type of content audit you're doing. You also have to determine whether you can collect some of the items in a reasonable amount of time. Make this worksheet work for you based on the job at hand.

It's important to use the content audit to help you determine the gaps in your content. You do this when you are putting your content plan together.

Visualizing Your Sites

When planning your content, consider visually mapping it to see the big picture. One way to do this is to create a map of your content ecosystem.

Mapping your content ecosystem

Your content ecosystem shows you how your content fits together. Your map can be as detailed as you like. You can document every site, social media account, and landing page you have, or you can list only the most important ones. It's up to you. The goal is to create an easy way to see how and where your content is distributed.

To create this kind of map, you can reference the PESO model in Chapter 16. An example of this kind of mind map template is shown in Figure 10-5. (You can also download this mind map — and see it in color — at www.dummies. com/extras/contentmarketingstrategies.)

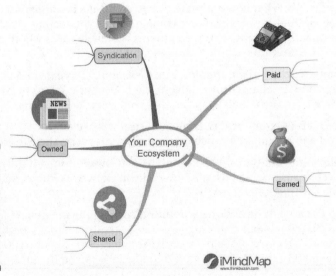

Figure 10-5: Suggested mind map for documenting your ecosystem.

As you can see in the figure, you can document your ecosystem by category:

- ✔ **Owned media:** List all your branded sites, including your website, blog, micro sites, and user-generated content (UGC).
- ✔ **Shared media:** Include your social platform accounts and any places you guest post, embed infographics, or upload slide shows.

✔ **Paid media:** Here you list media that you pay for, such as Facebook ads and traditional and native advertising.

✔ **Earned media:** Examples of earned media are influencer reviews, traditional PR, and media relations.

✔ **Syndication:** Add sites in this category if you are distributing your site via syndication.

A map of your content ecosystem helps you see the big picture of your content distribution. If you keep this updated, it can be a valuable tool for you and your team.

Picturing website content

Another map that you should consider creating is one of your website's and or blog's home page content and subpages. I've been doing this with clients for years and find that it serves several important content-related purposes.

Mapping your website in this way helps you do the following:

✔ **See exactly what content your company thinks is important.** By seeing what content is displayed on the main pages, you instantly see the content that is highlighted. You can then ask stakeholders whether they believe it reflects current business goals.

✔ **Compare maps of competitor websites.** You can create and compare maps of your competitors' sites to see how your content presentation differs from theirs and whether you need to make revisions.

✔ **Learn about content that is buried.** You will see content that is not featured and should be brought up to a higher level on the site.

✔ **Determine whether there is content you should immediately create or repurpose.** Seeing what's featured will show you where your gaps are and how they can be remedied.

✔ **Use the map to determine whether a redesign is needed.** Mapping website content almost always ignites a conversation about whether you are focusing on current business goals. You may choose not to do a redesign immediately, but you may want to budget for one in the future.

✔ **Use the map to get changes made to content navigation.** When you look at navigation, you may find that your priorities have changed and a revision would be useful.

As you can see, mapping your website and other important sites will facilitate a lot of discussion and insights. In Figure 10-6, you can see an example of a map template that you can use as a model.

(You can also download this map — and see it in color — at www.dummies.com/extras/contentmarketingstrategies.)

Figure 10-6:
Model of a
website
map.

Creating Your Plan

It's time to create your content plan. In Table 10-1, you see the components that go into developing it. Note that the table includes the chapters that refer to specific worksheets and related content.

You can download all the worksheets for this book at www.dummies.com/extras/contentmarketingstrategies.

Table 10-1	Components of Content Strategy	
Component	*Why It's Needed*	*How to Prepare*
Stakeholders	To ensure that you have information from all those who can make or break the project	Conduct one-on-one interviews. Hold group meetings.
Content audit	To determine existing content	Do a content audit using the content audit worksheet.
Personas	To know who is the target of your content	Use the information you develop from the Persona worksheet referred to in Chapter 7.

(continued)

Table 10-1 *(continued)*

Component	*Why It's Needed*	*How to Prepare*
Customer journey	To know what the customer needs to see on his journey to buy	Use the information you develop from the customer journey worksheet refered to in Chapter 8.
Story	To create a context for your prospect's choice and establish your "why"	Use the information you develop from the section "Crafting the story" in Chapter 12.
Governance, systems, and editorial calendar	To determine how content is judged, assigned, and moved through to completion	See Chapters 13 and 14 for more on these topics.
Metrics	To be able to determine metrics that tie back to your KPIs	Choose metrics (see the bullet about key success metrics in the list that follows).

The following list describes how each of the components in Table 10-1 helps you determine what goes in your content plan:

- ✔ **The business case for content:** If you created your content marketing strategy (Chapter 1), you have made a business case for your content. Use the business case you created (or will create) for your content to inform your plan.

- ✔ **Stakeholder interviews:** Your stakeholders will provide you with a wealth of knowledge and insights about what has been done and why. Using this knowledge will ensure that your content plan with be better defined and executed.

- ✔ **A completed content audit:** After you have completed your content audit you will know what content you currently have and what you need to create going forward. Obviously, this is crucial to your plan's success.

- ✔ **Defined personas for your market niche:** Your personas will tell you who you are targeting with your content. If you don't have personas you won't be able to create content that resonates with your customers. It will be generic content that will not engage anyone to pay attention to you.

- ✔ **A map of your customer journey:** By determining your touchpoints along the customer journey you can now see the content you need for each stage and persona.

✔ **Your business story:** Obviously, your business story will determine the themes you choose to write about. Storytelling is a key way to engage your prospects.

✔ **Key success metrics:** Choosing your success metrics is a very important part of your content plan. They will tie back to the key performance indicators (KPIs) that you determined were important when you developed your content marketing strategy. (See Chapter 1 for suggested metrics.)

With this information, you can begin to outline your content using the content plan worksheet. Note that you should complete a separate sheet for each persona.

You can download the content plan worksheet at www.dummies.com/extras/contentmarketingstrategies.

After you have completed the content plan worksheet, you are ready to fill in the editorial calendar that you choose in Chapter 13.

Focusing on Specialized Content

Before you leave the topic of content planning, you should know about several kinds of content that should be on your radar screen. These include pillar content, evergreen content, visual content, and viral content. Read on to see why you should keep them in mind when developing your content plan.

Creating pillar content

Do you know what pillar content is? I'm sure you're using it even if you don't know the term. Pillar content is quality foundational content that you create to represent your brand. This content can be as e-books, tutorials, or other substantial content pieces that provide value.

From this content, you create a variety of other pieces of content that function as a pillar "supporting" a topic. This means that you can take the tutorial you created and turn it into a

✔ Video

✔ Podcast

✔ Mind map

✔ Google Hangout

✔ Guest post

✔ Webinar

You really have no limit to the amount of pillar content you can create (see the "Content pillar success" sidebar for an example of pillar content).

Content pillar success

Here's how one cloud content center software company found success using pillar content. Liz O'Neill Dennison details this case study in her 2014 Kapost blog article, "How a Content Pillar Increased New Business by 3X" shown in the following figure (http://marketeer.kapost.com/content-pillar-five9-case-study/#axzz3lAETBT7b). Kapost's client Five9 (http://www.five9.com), was just getting started with its content marketing.

After a previously unsuccessful content campaign, Pat Oldenburg, Director, Marketing Operations, Content and Web for Five9, decided to use pillar content to launch the company's next initiative, an e-book called "Practical-Tactical: A Comprehensive Guide to Maximizing Agent Efficiency."

Using Kapost software, Oldenburg's team created 63 different assets from the e-book — 63! According to Oldenburg, "The e-book drove 4 times as many leads, and 3 times as many closed deals as the company's previous campaign." These results made pillar content a staple of Five9's content marketing efforts. Shouldn't you consider trying this tactic?

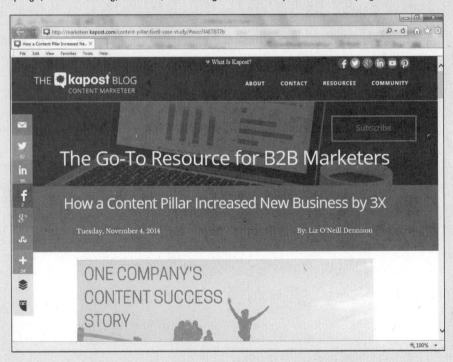

Utilizing "evergreen" content

Evergreen is an important concept that you should consider when you are creating content. Evergreen content is content that can be enjoyed without regard to when it was created. For example, a blog post about "how to be a productive entrepreneur" can be read any time of the year in any recent year. It's timeless and can keep readers interested whenever they come upon it.

Some examples of evergreen content include:

✔ Tutorials

✔ Support content and FAQs

✔ e-books

✔ Online tools lists

✔ Favorite resources

✔ Company stories

So what should you keep in mind when creating this type of content? You should

✔ **Make it easy to consume:** Visitors appreciate content that doesn't take a long time to read and isn't overly complex.

✔ **Create only high-quality assets:** If the content is going to be around for a while and represent your brand, you want to ensure that it can delight and engage customers.

✔ **Include visuals:** As discussed earlier, visuals are key to creating great content. Make sure that all evergreen content has graphics, photos, and so on.

✔ **Create a series:** It's helpful to create evergreen content that is in series form. Readers look for the other articles in a series after they find one of them.

An interesting article by Julia McCoy, CEO of Express Writers called "Why You Need to Start Creating Long, Evergreen Content Today" was published in the Search Engine Journal, shown in Figure 10-7 (`http://www.searchenginejournal.com/need-start-creating-long-evergreen-content-today/132598/`).

In the article, she discusses why small business owners specifically benefit from long evergreen content. She lists several reasons that could also apply to any size business:

- Google rewards more in-depth content, and placing you higher in search results.
- Your visitors appreciate content that is not overly complex but is instructive and useful.
- You can get leads over a sustained period of time with less effort.
- Evergreen content keeps you relevant and provides quality content whenever visitors find it.

Using graphics and other visuals

Throughout this book, you see how visuals enhance your content marketing efforts. Here, I want to briefly emphasize this point again. Here are just a few stats that show how using visuals powers up your content:

- When you include an image with a tweet, you get 18 percent more clicks than those without images, and you get 150 percent more retweets (Buffer).

✔ Eighty-six percent of buyers want interactive/visual content on demand (Demand Gen Report).

✔ By 2019, 80 percent of all consumer Internet traffic will be video traffic (Cisco).

Your customers respond to visuals, and taking advantage of this responsiveness is imperative. A wide variety of choices are available to you, such as infographics, memes, comics, doodles, sketches, photos, wireframes, custom graphics, and more.

Going viral

What about viral content? Everybody wants to create it, but do we really know how? Some research done by Jonah Berger and Katherine L. Milkman suggests that we at least know some of the components that make up viral content.

Berger and Milkman published an article in the Journal of Marketing Research called, "What Makes Online Content Viral?" (To download the PDF, use this link: `https://marketing.wharton.upenn.edu/files/?whdmsaction=public:main.file&fileID=3461`). They analyzed *New York Times* articles and determined that emotion played a large part in creating sharing behavior.

Specifically, they found that:

✔ Positive content is more likely to go viral than negative content.

✔ High psychological arousal fuels viral content. Content that evoked such strong emotions as awe, anger, anxiety, and sadness was more likely to go viral than weaker emotions. (For more on why people share content, see Chapter 15.)

This research can help you when you're creating content with an eye toward going viral, but it can't ensure your success. One sure-fire way to get some power from viral content is not to write it, but to curate it.

After you know that a piece of content has gone viral you can ride its coattails by creating an article that uses the viral content in it. You may not get a huge reaction, but at least you know that people will be interested in viewing and sharing it.

Check out the next page for a mind map of this chapter's content, and download a color version at `www.dummies.com/contentmarketingstrategies`.

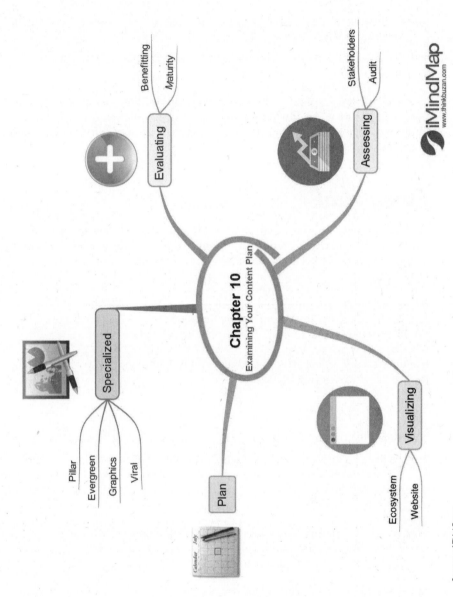

Courtesy of ThinkBuzan.

Chapter 11

Exploring Content Types

· ·

· ·

At the heart of your content marketing strategy is, of course, your content. If you have a strong collection of content, it is a company asset. Building this asset takes time and effort. But with the right strategy, you can create valuable content from several different content types.

In this chapter, you find out how working with a variety of content types helps you effectively reach your customers and win the sale. You have numerous categories to choose from, and when you combine them, you get even greater results.

Dipping into Content Categories

Eight different content categories are available to you. Rather than write everything from scratch, you can create unique content by taking one of the eight content categories shown in Table 11-1 and turning it into a custom piece that has value to you and your customer. By paying attention to your audience personas, you can develop exactly what your personas need for each stage of the buyer's journey (see Chapter 8 for details about the buyer's journey).

Table 11-1	Content Categories	
Technique	*Description*	*Examples*
Original content	Content written for your owned media, such as a website or blog	Blog post; e-book for lead generation
Curated content	Other people's content with your opinions and recommendations; articles must be credited to the original writer	Round-up article; guest post (A round-up article is one in which the author interviews subjects, collects information, and puts it into an article that contains the latest information on the topic.)
User-generated content (UGC)	Content your customers create about your company	Pictures on Instagram of customers using your product; video sent in by users
Repurposed content	Content that is refreshed to republish	Webinar repurposed for SlideShare; podcast audio repurposed as an article
Aggregated visual content	Graphics and images published on sites like Pinterest and Instagram	Pin boards on Pinterest; photos on Instagram
Streaming video content	Live streaming to an audience using an app for iOS or Android	Periscope, Meerkat, Blab.im
Press releases and business news	Original content developed by your company specifically for the purpose of promoting your business	A press release about a new product launch submitted on a PR site and articles written to put on your website about charitable endeavors
Online courses	Content that is either new or repurposed to create a training course	Udemy, Skillshare

Here's a look at each type mentioned in Table 11-1:

✔ **Original content:** Content that you write to inform, attract, and sell to your customers. This is always your most valuable content because no one else can use it without crediting you. Unfortunately, it is too costly to create all original content.

✔ **Curated content:** Other people's content to which you add value. You add your own opinions and recommendations to personalize the content for your audience. The key is to make sure to add enough new ideas and opinions to make it more than just a rehash of other people's work.

✔ **User-generated content (UGC):** Content that your customers and others create. This is valuable to you and your customers because it's unique and cannot be duplicated by your competitors. In addition, it gets your audience members engaged and interacting with one another.

✔ **Repurposed content:** Content that you have already published is reworked to become a new asset. Repurposing your content helps you make it more cost effective. You take something that has already been seen by your audience and update it. You can also change the format so that in your audience's mind, it's new. For example, if you take a popular blog post and turn it into a video, you have a new asset. Just make sure to refresh the text so that it fits with your current audience's needs.

✔ **Aggregated visual content:** This is a category that has recently been added. It refers to content you aggregate on visual sites like Pinterest and Instagram. Examples include a Pinboard with your company's products displayed and an Instagram collection with user content. These tactics can have great value now that Pinterest and Instagram have added "buy" mechanisms (see Chapter 8 for more about the buying buttons for Pinterest and Instagram). As you know, visual content is a key component of your content strategy.

✔ **Streaming video content:** This type of content is relatively new. It allows you to live-stream directly to your audience. As of August 2015, Periscope (owned by Twitter) had ten million registered accounts. Because the app only launched in March of 2015, its quick growth is an indication that this type of app has captured the imagination of both marketers and consumers.

✔ **Press release and business news:** This is original content developed by your company specifically for the purpose of promoting your business.

✔ **Online courses:** This type of content can be collected from all your training materials to create a cohesive online course for customers that you can sell or give away.

Read on to see how you can benefit from including each of these categories.

Working with Original Short- and Long-Form Content

Creating original content isn't easy, but it can deliver the greatest punch. However, the companies who have gained the most traction have figured out how to distinguish their content from that of their competitors, regardless of length. For this reason, you should consider using both short- and long-form content.

According to the Social Media Examiner's marketing industry report, 58 percent of marketers said that "original written content is the most important type of content, above visuals and videos" (`http://www.socialmediaexaminer. com/social-media-marketing-industry-report-2014/`).

See whether these comments sound familiar to you: "You should create only short-form content because people don't have the time to spend reading long articles" or "Your audience wants long, thoughtful pieces and expects you to spend the time and money to create them." Directly contradictory, right? Well, which statement is right?

The content community continues to debate whether long- or short-form content is preferable. Although some claim to know the answer, I think it really depends on what your specific audience prefers. For example, it may like long-form how-to blog posts but prefer short list posts. You can find the answer by looking at your own data. In addition, some content is determined by its platform. Tweets are short, content on Pinterest is visual, and posts on the blogging platform Medium (`https://medium.com`) tend to be longer. You need original content in all these spaces.

People generally agree that long-form content comes in at about 2,000 words and short-form content is approximately 800 words or fewer. You won't have trouble recognizing which is which. The following lists highlight the benefits of each type.

Using long-form content can be a benefit because

- ✔ Google has declared that it values this type of content, and its algorithm supports it.
- ✔ Your audience will reward you highly for this content. It not only informs them but also demonstrates that you're a credible expert who cares about the audience.
- ✔ It provides greater online visibility from backlinks and shares.
- ✔ It causes readers to stay on your site longer and perhaps look at more of your content.
- ✔ You can turn some of the longest content into lead-generation pieces to help you determine what your audience values.
- ✔ You can take older content and combine it into long-form content to get more value from pieces that have already been created.

Short-form content is valuable because

- ✔ It's quick and can be published on a regular basis
- ✔ It's less expensive to write

✔ It attracts readers who want to have a quick read and move on

✔ It lends itself to multipart posts that get readers coming back for the rest of the series

You can see that each type of content has value regardless of the current fads. Experiment with both types to ensure that all parts of your audience are satisfied and that you have data to analyze.

Using Curation

Content curation can seem complicated, but it is really very straightforward. What can actually be complicated is the delivery of a curated article that adds value. Although you can take an article you like and share it on social media, that's sharing, not curating. Curating takes more effort than mere sharing, as I explain shortly.

According to a 2014 survey by Trapit (`http://trap.it`), shown in Figure 11-1, 74 percent of marketers say that curation is important to their content marketing strategy.

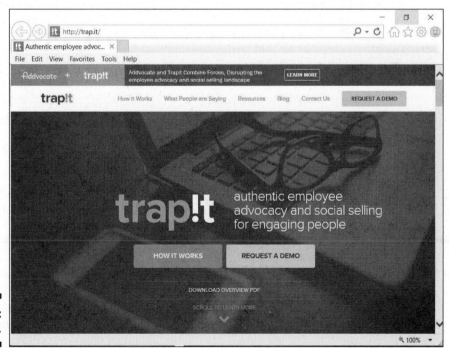

Figure 11-1:
Trapit.

You and your audience benefit when you curate content because it allows you to

- ✔ Demonstrate your ability to analyze and add value to content topics
- ✔ Organize the information to make it easier to understand
- ✔ Provide a new viewpoint on an old idea to make it usable
- ✔ Inspire trust in you as a thought leader
- ✔ Put the information in a different format — such as an infographic — to make it more digestible
- ✔ Create content that can supplement your original content, thus providing quantity and quality

So what exactly is curated content? Here are some examples. You can

- ✔ Round up information and package it together with your comments. This helps your readers find information they might miss.
- ✔ Collect media from a variety of articles in formats like slides, videos, and podcasts and create a slide show on a topic.
- ✔ Develop a visual timeline that shows the development of a topic based on historical content.
- ✔ Uncover a new trend and create a report about it using the content of others.

Examining five curation models

Rohit Bhargava laid out a framework for content curation in his prescient 2011 article, "The 5 Models of Content Curation" http://www.rohitbhargava.com/2011/03/the-5-models-of-content-curation.html. You can use these models as prompts when you are considering what kind of article you want to create. The prompts are as follows:

- ✔ **Aggregation:** When you aggregate content to curate, you're gathering what you consider to be excellent material about a topic. You then add your own opinion and give the reader a new way to think about the content you've presented.
- ✔ **Distillation:** The word *distill* means to reduce something to its essential components. When you use distillation to curate, you boil down all the material and keep only the most important points.
- ✔ **Elevation:** When you use elevation to curate, you look for the bigger picture or expose a trend. This is a very valuable form of curation because it offers the reader a fuller understanding of a topic.
- ✔ **Mashups:** *Mashup* is a term that is often used by software vendors to describe a new functioning app that's derived from two already existing

programs. In relation to curating, a mashup takes different types of material and brings them together with a new way to provide a new way to think about the topic.

✔ **Chronology:** When you use chronology to curate content, you're using a timeline of events to explain a topic.

Understanding how to curate

Curation is not a new concept. For example, curators have been employed by museums to look at their holdings and pick out the most representative pieces to tell a larger story. You do the same with web content. You use other people's content as the foundation of a new story you want to tell.

You can use the following list as a checklist of the 11 actions you need to take to ensure a quality curated post:

✔ **Give credit to the writers of the content you choose.** You must give attribution to the writers of the content you curate. There should be no mistaking which content is theirs and which is yours.

Check out Curator's Code (`http://curatorscode.org`), shown in Figure 11-2, to ensure that you are correctly attributing the content.

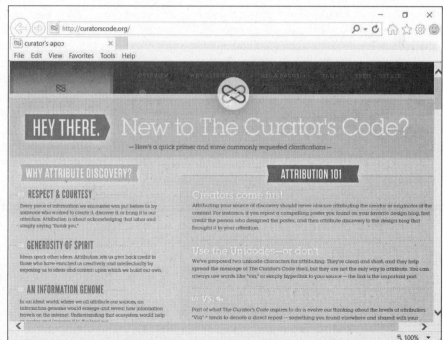

Figure 11-2: Curator's Code.

✔ **Use quality content as the basis for your new content.** Choosing poor-quality content as the basis for your new content doesn't make sense. You have so many quality sources to choose from that you never have a good reason to use badly written material.

✔ **Develop a new headline.** You are creating a new piece of content. This means that you need a new title that reflects your point of view.

✔ **Use a new image.** Just as you should use a new title, you also need a new image that sets your content apart from the content you're curating.

✔ **Reduce the articles you are curating to their essence.** This item is especially important. Don't think that you need to include a lot of content from each article you have chosen. You will have links to the full article right in the piece. What you want to include are the few sentences that represent the most important part of the content.

✔ **Remember to do your keyword research.** Using the right keywords for your audience is just as important for curated articles as it is for original content. Remember that keywords are used to find your content, so they need to be present whenever you publish.

✔ **Don't choose only the low-hanging fruit.** You and everyone else in your field can find the most popular content. That's great when you want to know what topics would make good original posts. But if you stop at the most popular content for your curated articles, you are not adding much value. Make an effort to find some good content that hasn't already been read by your audience.

✔ **Include your branding to ensure brand recognition and awareness.** Any content your company creates or curates should have your branding visible. Both types of content are of value and should let people know they're from you.

✔ **Include a call to action (CTA).** As you know, whenever you publish content, you want to tell your audience what to do next. A CTA lets your audience know what that next action should be. For example, you may want people to go to a landing page or subscribe to your blog.

✔ **Decide which channel you will be publishing on ahead of time.** Pick the channels you plan to publish on before you write. Be sure to determine that it will satisfy that specific audience.

✔ **Be clear about how the content will be measured before it's published.** The only way you can judge whether your content is successful is to choose some metrics to evaluate it. Those metrics can also help you determine whether you should create more content just like it.

Even though curating content seems to take a lot of effort, remember that it's still faster than creating an original article of similar length.

Making Use of User-Generated Content

Next in our list of content types is user-generated content (UGC). For better or worse, this is not content created by you but rather your audience. UGC is any content that is published to an online site by an end user to be seen by other users. If you've ever asked your customers to submit pictures of themselves using your product or to send photos using a specific hashtag, you've dealt with UCG.

UGC can be positive or negative, depending on the mindset of the user. By its very nature, it's uncontrollable. You will get UGC whether you want it or not. It's the voice of the customer weighting in on you and your brand. It includes such content as user reviews, videos, photos, and ratings. UGC can be your greatest sales driver or your worst nightmare. If you launch a specific campaign and you tap into some major customer dissatisfaction, it can be a recipe for disaster.

A great example of positive UGC would be a tutorial on YouTube from a user who loves your product. I've been delighted to find great step-by-step videos on products I've just started using. In many cases, users are excited by the product and feel that they have something to contribute. This lends credibility to the product and engages your customers.

Understanding the positives

Some online influencers believe that UGC can be a great tool for brands. An op-ed by Aliza Freud on DIGIDAY recommends that 'brands should use more UGC in 2015" (`http://digiday.com/brands/nielsenes-op-ed-brands-use-ugc-2015/`). Freud cites the following three reasons. UGC is

- ✔ **Plentiful:** Social media followers of brands are a ready-and-waiting audience who are eager to share their thoughts and opinions.
- ✔ **Compelling:** Users value the opinions of other users over that of a brand. Reviews of products are sought after and read by people who are interested in learning about a product.
- ✔ **Scalable:** Friends will tell friends. You can get your message shared by people in groups on social networks in ways that you never could get on your own.

You can see that major benefits can accrue to any brand that generates positive UGC. Brands establish strong relationships with their customers by constantly monitoring what is being said on their sites and on social media. In this way, they know where the bumps may be.

You should make sure that you have customer service reps reporting problems on a daily basis. Things can go south in the blink of an eye on social media.

One example of a UGC campaign that succeeded was reported on by EngageSciences (`http://www.engagesciences.com/marketing-campaigns-36/`). A contest was created by North Face and Peets Coffee. As of this writing, the latest contest in the series was in July of 2015. Users were asked to send in photos of their adventures based on the hashtag #PeetsBoldyGoes. The ten winners get prizes that include a North Face back-pack and some great coffee. Users were excited to share their photo adventures, and the contest has been a great success.

Dealing with the negatives

The pain of failed UGC campaigns has been well-documented. Sometimes companies launch a new UGC campaign and get a barrage of nasty comments and images. Could the companies have avoided them? Maybe. It depends on how connected the brand is with its customer.

What should you do before you launch a UGC campaign? Here are some things to consider:

- ✔ **Take your time:** You can't walk back a failed campaign. Think carefully about your goals for the project. Make sure that everyone is clear about it and that you have buy-in from management.

- ✔ **Look at other UGC campaigns:** See what has already succeeded and failed. Have competitors tried something similar? Were they successful?

- ✔ **Experiment:** Try something small that can give you a feel for your user's sentiment.

- ✔ **Listen to your users on a daily basis:** I am assuming that you are con-stantly listening and engaging with your audience. If there are sore spots, you should already know about them. If you think you aren't sufficiently plugged in to your audience, don't go forward with a UGC campaign.

- ✔ **Go in with your eyes wide open:** No matter how well you plan, you can still encounter a problem. Keep a close watch on your launch and respond immediately if things get out of hand. Be transparent and open. If you act in a heavy-handed manner, it will make things worse.

Repurposing Content to Add Value

Your collection of content is a company asset. When you consider other company assets, such as hardware, do you ignore them and let them fall into disrepair? Not likely. So why do you treat your valuable content this way?

When you repurpose content, you can change the format, update the material, or both. Doing both is wise so that your content always feels up-to-date.

Benefitting from repurposing

Repurposing your content makes sense for many reasons. It helps you:

- **Spread ideas:** It extends the reach of your ideas by giving new audiences the chance to see it.

- **Extend content life**: It demonstrates a breadth of knowledge over the lifetime of the content.

- **Provide a variety of formats:** It enhances the value of content by changing the format to reach people who prefer that format.

- **Make content more cost effective:** Obviously, when you use content several times, you get back the cost of creating it.

To do a first-rate job with your repurposing efforts, you need to go about it systematically. First consider which content will be repurposed and then deal with how it gets done and who does it.

Planning goals and picking content

The first step in repurposing your content is to decide what your goals are. Next, choose the content you want to work with. You should have the following information when you start:

- **A list of the content available to repurpose organized into topic categories:** You should have this list from your content audit. (See Chapter 10 for how to perform this audit.)The list shows you the topic, format, keywords, and other pertinent facts. If you have not done a content audit, your choices are limited. You can sort the content you have at hand, but you will surely overlook some of your best material buried in your database.

✔ **Your editorial calendar and a list of upcoming campaigns:** Make topic choices based on what you need immediately. Look at your editorial calendar and upcoming campaigns that require content.

✔ **Pick the content that suits the business goal you have for this content:** You use your repurposed content most effectively when you tie it to actual goals you have. Sometimes you may repurpose something because it lends itself to a format change. But the best way to do it is to match the current asset to a real need.

✔ **Determine the resources you need and the implementation cost to determine the best fit:** After you get rolling, you see all kinds of things you want to do to repurpose the content. Make sure your choices reflect your resources and current budget.

I recommend that the person making editorial decisions about content repurposing use a reference chart. If you start with a ready-made list, you can develop your own "best format" chart for your audience.

If you want to use one of the ultimate content guides, check out Robin Good's "The Ultimate Guide to Editorial Content Types and Formats" (http://www.masternewmedia.org/guide-editorial-content-types-formats), shown in Figure 11-3. What I like about this guide is its inclusion of almost every format available. It's also good to use when you are creating original content.

Figure 11-3:
Robin
Good's
"Ultimate
Guide."

Viewing Aggregated Visual Content

How did we satisfy our need to share and stare at visual content before Pinterest, Instagram, Tumblr, and others? Frankly, I can't remember, and I bet you can't, either. But surprisingly, only six years have passed since the first of these visual aggregation sites was launched (Pinterest in 2010).

As you know, organizing photos and images on a board is not a new idea. People kept their tools organized on peg boards and displayed photos of their collections on their home bulletin boards. Obviously, when this activity became available in digital form for all the world to see, the concept exploded. Now everyone can see your collection!

In the earlier section about user-generated content, I talk about the value of encouraging users to share their visual content. But what about creating your own branded visual content for these sites? Will it engage your users?

According to Forrester's Nate Elliott, a study was done to analyze customer engagement on seven social networks. The study found that Instagram was the clear winner: ". . . Instagram delivered these brands 58 times more engagement per follower than Facebook, and 120 times more engagement per follower than Twitter" (`http://blogs.forrester.com/nate_elliott/14-04-29-instagram_is_the_king_of_social_engagement`).

I see your future

In 2015, Millward Brown Digital and Pinterest collaborated on a study to see whether they could determine the process people use when they plan for upcoming events. They made an interesting finding: Forty-seven percent of people began pinning items for a major life event in the previous six months before the event. During that time, those people were on the site actively researching new ideas and brands on a regular basis.

This should encourage you as a content marketer to build branded collections of images specifically labeled for major life events. You can include events such as having a baby, buying a house, or taking a trip. You will have active pinners at all times of the year. The good news is that many products can come under this major-life-event umbrella if you think expansively about what might be needed `https://www.millwardbrowndigital.com/pinterest-and-the-power-of-future-intent/`.

Dealing with Live Video Content

Now, live from anywhere — you can reach your audience using one of several new live-streaming apps like Periscope (http://periscope.com), shown in Figure 11-4, or Meerkat, for both iOS and Android. These are new and exciting marketing tools that certainly add a real-time dimension to anything you promote or share. But, as with any new tactic, you need to think about how to integrate it into your larger content strategy.

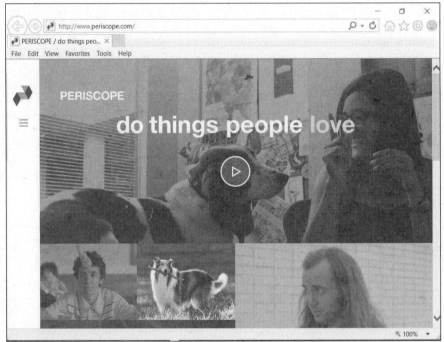

Figure 11-4:
Periscope.

Consider the emotional value of live video. As you know, when you can tap into customer emotions, you can accelerate your ability to win new customers. With live video, you can evoke the

✔ **Element of surprise:** Live video definitely has the element of surprise. Your audience doesn't know what will happen.

✔ **Ability to create excitement:** You can generate enthusiasm for a new product or feature you are launching, akin to hosting a physical event.

✔ **Opportunity to demonstrate that you care:** Customers can ask you questions, and you can help solve their problems.

✔ **Belief that you have skills:** You can provide information, training, or demos to show your credibility as a thought leader.

✔ **Feeling of camaraderie:** Viewers can comment and respond to one another and you.

Although you broadcast live, the broadcasts can be replayed on tools like Periscope. Replaying gives you the opportunity to create some great word-of-mouth exposure and possibly even wind up with a viral video.

So what kind of things can you try with this new real-time tool? Here are some suggestions:

✔ **Document a live event:** When you launch your latest new product or feature, get your prospect's attention by creating a live video event and give discounts or gifts to the audience.

✔ **Develop user-generated content:** Others might use a replay of your video and promote you. This is the best kind of sharing because you are being recommended by someone else, but you get to deliver the actual message via your original video.

✔ **Take a look behind the scenes:** Several TV shows have used these tools to take viewers behind the scenes with their favorite actors. This gets a viewer's attention and enhances the value of the show.

✔ **Interview someone at a conference:** Interviews can be a really fun way to generate excitement for your prospects. You can show viewers what is happening at the conference and interview top speakers.

✔ **Provide training or demos:** Your prospects are hungry for valuable training opportunities. Provide a live demo or special training to develop trust with your audience.

Extending Business News

Content that is created specifically to promote your business is not like other original content. Of course, all the content you create will have some value to your company. But there is specific content that you write for press releases, stockholders, potential investors, and others with goals that are different from all your other content.

I mention this type of content here because it can have additional uses and is often overlooked. After you've created this content, you can feed it back to your editorial group to repurpose it. For example, you might want to take the written content on the charitable causes you support and add it into a video you're creating for your blog. The key is to document everything you create so that you can consider other places to use it.

If you think that PR content is not suitable to be repurposed, you are not creating the right type of content. No audience wants to read stodgy paragraphs of corporate speak to find out what your company does. If you're relying on that old-school content, you're wasting your money. Press releases now have multimedia components that you can use in a variety of ways. Don't forget to include this content in your repurposing efforts.

Offering Online Courses

When Lynda.com (`http://lynda.com`; see Figure 11-5), a company that offers online training, was sold in 2015 to LinkedIn for $1.5 billion, every online marketer took notice.

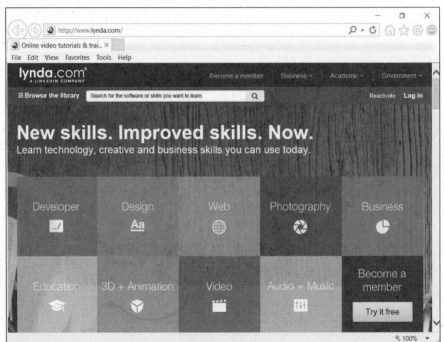

Figure 11-5:
Lynda.com.

Online training is big business. People are willing to pay to enhance their skills because the market is competitive and employees look for ways to set themselves apart.

Several major learning platforms have sprung up in recent years, including Udemy, shown in Figure 11-6. Udemy has courses for all sorts of business and personal skills. One of the interesting aspects of the company is that both individuals and companies use the platform to provide customer training.

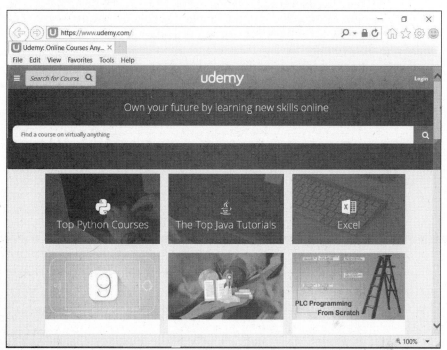

Figure 11-6:
Udemy.

One great thing about online courses is that they can be created by repurposing content along with some original content. After you examine your content for its ability to teach and inform, you're likely to be amazed at what you can repurpose.

So how can you as a content marketer benefit from creating online training? You can use it for a variety of marketing efforts, including the following:

- **Revenue generation:** You can sell the training as well as have affiliates sell for you to widen your audience.

- **Development of customer relationships:** You can distribute the training to special customers as a perk.

- **Lead generation:** You can use the training as gated content to grow your list. That is content that requires an email address in exchange for viewing it.

- **Customer retention and loyalty:** You can give some of your training away to show customers that you care about them.

Managing Content Formats

Whereas the previous sections explore content categories. this section points out popular formats that you should deploy. I show seven of those formats in Table 11-2 along with distribution channels that you can use to promote them.

Table 11-2	Content Formats
Format	*Distribution Channels*
Video	YouTube, Vimeo
Slide shows	SlideShare, Slideboom
Infographics	Cool Infographics, Visually
Webinars	GoToWebinar, Eventbrite
Audio/podcasts	iTunes, Blog Talk Radio
Mind Maps	Biggerplate
Presentations	Prezi

Here's a look at the formats discussed in the table in more detail:

- ✔ **Video:** As you know, video is wildly popular with customers, only second to articles. With the addition of the new, live video tools, it will remain so. Some helpful tools to create videos include Camtasia (http://camtasia.com), shown in Figure 11-7, and Brainshark (http://brainshark.com).

- ✔ **Slide shows:** This format has become much more popular with the advent of sites like SlideShare (http://slideshare.com), shown in Figure 11-8, and Scridb (http://scribd.com), which allow you to post a presentation for wider distribution.

- ✔ **Infographics:** This is another very popular category for content. Audiences find infographics easy to understand and fun to share. If done right, the visuals can be repurposed and used in a variety of ways. Some helpful tools you can use to create them include Canva (http://canva.com), shown in Figure 11-9, and Piktochart (http://piktochart.com).

- ✔ **Webinars:** Webinars have been popular for some time because they allow companies to interact with their customers and provide valuable training. Major tools to deliver webinars include GoToWebinar (http://gotowebinar.com), shown in Figure 11-10, and Eventbrite (http://eventbrite.com).

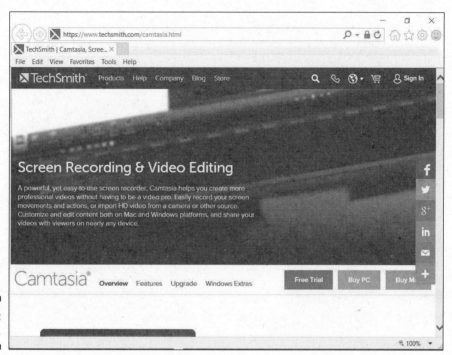

Figure 11-7:
Camtasia.

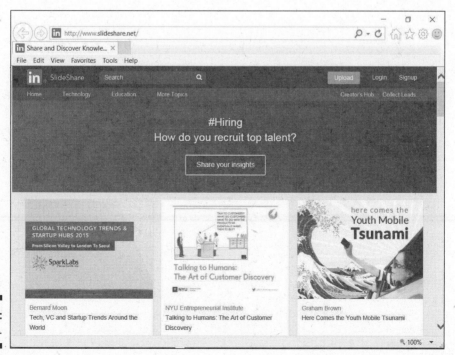

Figure 11-8:
SlideShare.

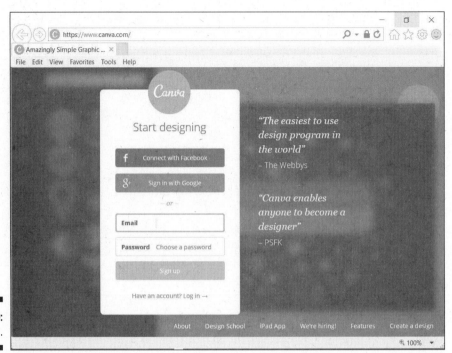

Figure 11-9:
Canva.

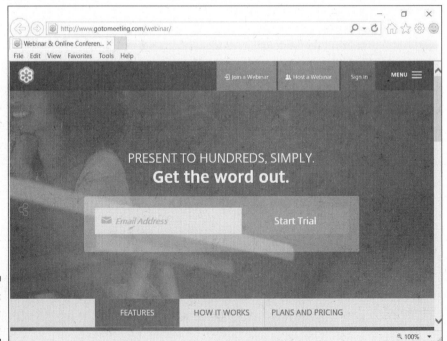

Figure 11-10:
GoTo-
Webinar.

✔ **Audio:** Podcasts have been regaining popularity again in 2016 after an earlier downturn in interest. One reason for the renewed popularity is that the technology is easier to use and the distribution is very wide on places like iTunes (`https://itunes.apple.com/us/genre/podcasts/id26?mt=2`), shown in Figure 11-11, and Blog Talk Radio (`http://blogtalkradio.com`).

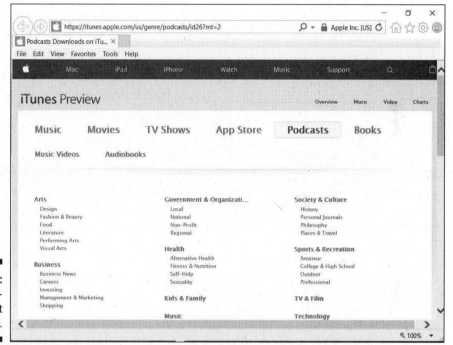

Figure 11-11: iTunes podcast directory.

✔ **Mind maps:** Mind maps have been around a long time and have been gaining in favor in recent years to help marketers explain their ideas to prospects. Some helpful tools to create them include iMindMap (`http://imindmap.com`), shown in Figure 11-12, and bubble.us `https://bubbl.us`. (Full disclosure, I am a Buzan Certified Mind Mapping Instructor.)

As a mind mapping enthusiast, I have included mind maps at the end of every chapter that give you a visual look at the content covered. The mind maps can help you organize your thoughts and add your own notes about the content being presented.

To distribute your mindmaps, you can upload them to an innovative company called Biggerplate (`http://biggerplate.com`) run by Liam Hughes, shown in Figure 11-13. It has a large community of mind mappers who share their own maps and promote the use of mind maps around the world. If you're interested in finding out about mind maps, this is one great place to go.

Figure 11-12:
iMindMap.

Figure 11-13:
Biggerplate.

✔ **Presentations:** Presentation tools such as PowerPoint have been around for a long time. Newer tools bring a new dimension to the average presentation. These are tools such as Prezi (`http://prezi.com`; see Figure 11-14), which offers zooming and movement, and Zoho Show, a cloud-based tool (`https://www.zoho.com/docs/presentation/features.html`) that lets you present from anywhere on any device.

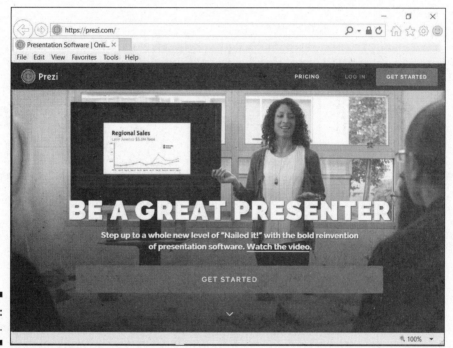

Figure 11-14: Prezi.

Check out the next page for a mind map of this chapter's content, and download a color version at `www.dummies.com/contentmarketingstrategies`.

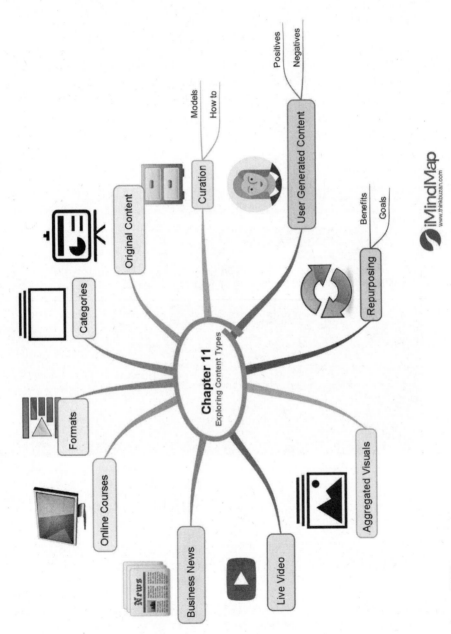

Models
How to
Curation
Positives
Negatives
User Generated Content
Original Content
Benefits
Goals
Repurposing
Categories
Chapter 11
Exploring Content Types
Formats
Online Courses
Aggregated Visuals
Business News
Live Video

iMindMap
www.thinkbuzan.com

Courtesy of ThinkBuzan.

Chapter 12

Storytelling for Content Marketers

In This Chapter

▶ Understanding the science of storytelling

▶ Constructing product stories

▶ Writing great headlines

Most great content marketers know that storytelling is their secret weapon. They know that stories engage us; they have for centuries. Stories can be motivating and give us heroes to emulate. They can teach us how to act and how to cope. They also perform a critical function for the content marketer — persuasion.

In this chapter, you consider the value of storytelling, how to develop a compelling product story, and how to write headlines that capture attention.

Storytelling to Engage Your Audience

Now that the web helps everyone share stories, you need to create brand stories that others can tell for you. A great story can capture your customer's attention as no other feature or benefits package can.

Seeking the science behind stories

We are hard-wired to love stories, but why is this so? A brief look at neuroscience holds the answer. More has been learned about the brain in the last ten years than the one hundred years before that. We are able to analyze what happens to the chemicals in our brains as they respond to different stimuli.

We've learned that the brain has three main "parts": (1) the neocortex, where thinking, imagination, and problem-solving happen; (2) the limbic brain, where we retain memories, experience emotions, and form value judgments (consciously and unconsciously), among other things; and (3) the reptilian or "lizard" brain, which controls automatic physical functions and signals our "fight or flight" response in an attempt to keep us safe. Why am I taking this quick foray into neuroscience? Because it relates to how the stories we tell influence our customers.

Consider this: The lizard brain responds when your customer perceives a threat. Even though the threat is not a stampeding animal herd, as it may have been in our ancestors' day, customers may still perceive a kind of danger. In this case, it could be a high price or an assault on their time. They need to decide whether to stay or retreat. As a content marketer, your job is to mitigate that fear long enough to get your customer interested in your brand. So how do stories do that?

In his article in the Harvard Business Review, "Why Your Brain Loves Good Storytelling" (`https://hbr.org/2014/10/why-your-brain-loves-good-storytelling/`; see Figure 12-1), neuroscientist Paul J. Zak talks about the effect of the brain chemical oxytocin. He calls it the "it's safe to approach others" brain signal that engenders empathy and cooperation. In the lab, Zak found that character-driven stories produce this effect.

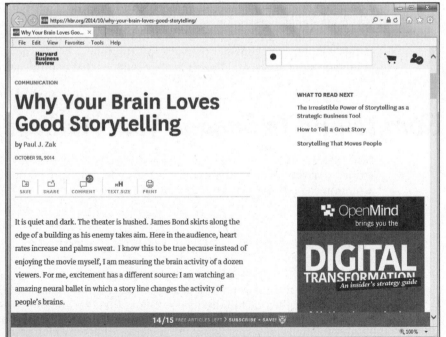

Figure 12-1:
Harvard
Business
Review.

Another study by Zak is reported in Jeremy Dean's PsyBlog, shown in Figure 12-2. The blog quotes Zak as saying that "results show why puppies and babies are in toilet paper commercials. This research suggests that advertisers use images that cause our brains to release oxytocin to build trust in a product or brand, and hence increase sales" (`http://www.spring.org.uk/2014/01/the-psychology-of-storytelling-and-empathy-animated.php`).

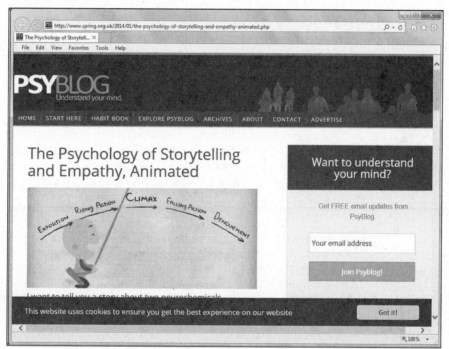

Figure 12-2: PsyBlog.

The lizard brain is quieted by stories that help build trust. Such stories actually cause a chemical reaction. Every content marketer knows that trust is the key to building a lasting customer relationship. The screenwriter and teacher Robert McKee says that for business communication, you need to "unite an idea with an emotion." So when you see long, boring articles about a product, you know they are missing the mark.

So what are some keys to help you recognize good business stories? They include the following characteristics. They should:

- **Be simple and straightforward:** Have you ever stopped reading a novel because the action was hopelessly confusing? You probably decided that you didn't want to waste your time trying to follow the plot. People have even less patience for a business story — they need a simple plot. That doesn't mean that the story can't be complex, but if you confuse your prospect, you've lost him.

- **Evoke emotions:** Attention is affected by our brain chemistry. If you don't provide some suspense, mystery, or conflict, you have no story.

✔ **Use visuals:** Web stories should have visuals to support them. An abundance of free, online sources of visual materials are available. Many social media studies show that content with visuals are understood and shared at a much higher rate than content without visuals. Imagery powerfully affects our limbic brains. Also, although some people are much more visually inclined than others, we think not just in words but by imagery as well, so you need to show *and* tell.

✔ **Connect directly to the customer:** Customers are seeking advice when they learn about your products. They want to know whether your products are a good fit for them. Telling stories about how great the company is doesn't create the emotional connection. The connection comes when you tell customers how great *they* can be using your product.

The point is really very simple. Customers are moved to spend money on your product when they believe that it will make them feel better, look better, or be better in the eyes of those around them. Think about that fact when you write your content.

✔ **Have a beginning, middle, and end:** As with any good story, you need to have the three story components. Leave something out and you've got some details, but not a cohesive story.

✔ **Be authentic:** Okay, I know you've heard this time and time again, but authenticity is critical to business storytelling. Telling a phony story is anathema to everything you know about engaging customers and building relationships. You can't win. In addition, millennials are particularly captivated by stories about company values and giving. If you lie, you are lost.

Finding your product stories

This section begins with a basic rule. The product stories you tell should have the customer as the hero of the story. You can make your product the hero, but then you lose the interest of the customer. The customer's focus is on himself, not you.

Your company has many stories to tell. Key among them are the messages that are derived from your mission and goals. (See Chapter 1 for help with defining those goals.) These messages tell your customers how you will serve them. In this section, I focus on the stories you post every day on blogs, in articles, and on guest sites. You know the ones I mean: the ones that keep your audience loyal and engaged. These stories are the bread and butter of content marketers.

Major bloggers focus their blogs on you. How you can be better, how you can serve your audience, and how you can make a difference. When people read Seth Godin's blog (http://sethgodin.typepad.com/), for example, they often come away feeling inspired. This is how you want your readers to feel about you and your brand.

"Puppy Love"

Several marketers are using the valuable information about brain chemistry to enhance their ability to capture your attention and your emotions. An article by Alyssa Hertig called "Is Neuroscience the Future of Content Marketing Measurement?" reports that Budweiser used knowledge of brain chemistry to enhance its hit Super Bowl commercial "Puppy Love" (`http://contently.com/strategist/2014/10/08/is-neuroscience-the-future-of-content-marketing-measurement/?goal=0_855cf0c201-2da44d4e63-315209537`). Budweiser marketers determined when people were likely to want to cut away from the commercial and enhanced it to prevent that outcome. Surprised? I'm sure you aren't. You know that advertisers will use any tools available to them to give themselves a competitive edge.

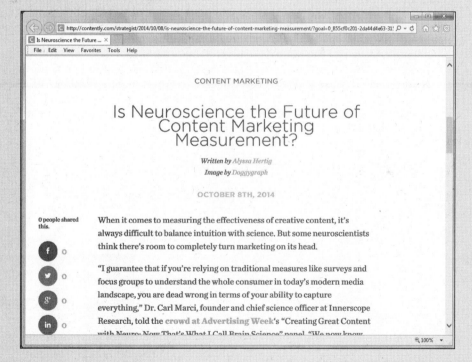

So where can you find material for these company stories? You can get them from

> ✔ **Loyal customers:** Make sure that you and your team regularly interact with your best customers. They will always give you feedback about what you're doing right. The stories about how they are succeeding with your product are crucial to capture. They can also let you know what you can do better.

- ✔ **Customer support staff:** These people are on the front lines with your customers. They solve problems and know where the fault lines are. Make sure that they know you want to hear their stories.

- ✔ **Other employees around the company:** Don't assume that only support people have stories to share. People throughout the company gain knowledge about customers that will help you create your messages.

- ✔ **Vendors and colleagues**: Your company is being talked about by customers and everyone who does business with you. Capture the good stories and try to fix the bad ones.

In short, stories are lurking everywhere. You just need to listen for them. These stories are the raw material that you use to make your content come to life. Another way to find stories is to look at what your data says. You can gather lots of great insights from your analytics that can be told as a story. When you marry data with a story, it's easier to remember.

Jennifer Aaker of the Future of Storytelling organization (`http://www.futureofstorytelling.org`) talks about this concept in her YouTube video, "Persuasion and the Power of Story: (Future of StoryTelling 2013)" (`https://youtu.be/AL-PAzrpqUQ`; see Figure 12-3). Aaker says that because we are overloaded with information, stories cut through the noise and help us to decide "what to believe in."

Figure 12-3: Jennifer Aaker.

Storytelling posts

Here's an example of an article that successfully blends storytelling with facts. The article, "11 Examples of Killer B2B Content Marketing Campaigns Including ROI," was written by popular blogger Lee Odden on his TopRank Blog (`http://www.toprankblog.com/2013/05/11-examples-killer-b2b-content-marketing/`).

I encourage you to check it out; it's well written, and I think you'll find it instructional. Odden begins with a statistic that sets the tone: "According to a CMI and MarketingProfs study, 91% of B2B Marketers are using content marketing and that means a few things." He then goes on to tell about his presentation at a DemandGen conference.

Next, he discusses the awards made at the conference and shares brief stories about the winners. At the time of this writing, his article had been shared 1,700 times. It demonstrates the power of blending storytelling with facts to make the post memorable.

According to Aaker, three major characteristics of stories are what can make them so powerful. Stories can be (1) memorable, (2) impactful, and (3) personal. We think that we convince people by using statistics. But statistics alone don't have an emotional impact. If we conjoin statistics with a story, the listener connects with the storyteller as well as the story, and persuasion becomes possible.

Keep these characteristics in mind when you are putting together your next product presentation. Straight statistics and facts will not be as persuasive as a good story to go with them.

If you're looking for an interesting way to share a curated collection of stories, you might want to check out Roojoom (`http://roojoom.com`), shown in Figure 12-4. Roojoom provides an easy-to-use platform that lets you select and display a collection of posts around a topic to tell a story.

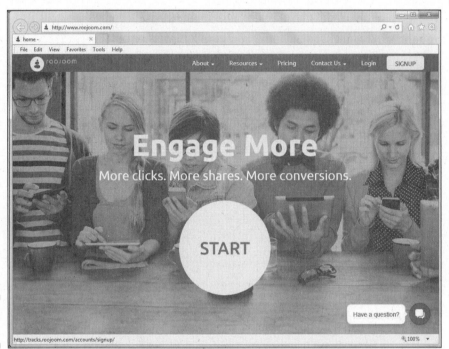

Figure 12-4:
Roojoom.

Structuring Your Content Using Stories

So, how can you develop your own stories? If you've tried in the past but were less than successful, you likely didn't use a tried-and-true storytelling structure. There's no need to reinvent the wheel. Storytelling has been codified since Aristotle's time (the fourth century).

Crafting the story

A great many story templates are available to you, and they can help you construct your brand story. They are all a variation on the hero's journey, articulated by Joseph Campbell in his book *The Hero with a Thousand Faces*.

If you aren't familiar with the hero's journey framework, you can download a PDF from the Mythology Teacher website that gives you a good overview: `http://mythologyteacher.com/documents/TheHeroJourney.pdf`.

In brief, the framework involves a hero who will be taking a journey and will come out the other side a changed person. Here are the components and how they relate to a product story:

- **Start with a look at the current reality:** You start the story by telling the audience about the marketplace or give them some information to set the stage.

- **The hero has a problem:** You introduce the hero, which in this case would be one of your customer personas. You want your prospects to make the connection to the hero as themselves and relate to his struggle. You talk about the problems and the feelings the hero is experiencing. These are the problems and feelings your customer has. For example, the hero could be short on time, overwhelmed by work, or be focused on some other problem.

    You are telling this story to evoke emotions as well as recognition of the problem.

- **A mentor is introduced:** The hero meets a guide who understands his fears and can help him with his struggle. The guide is your product or brand that has the answer to his problem.

- **At first, the hero doesn't want to accept the journey:** This element adds drama to the story and reflects your customer's indecision.

- **Eventually, he takes action:** The hero accepts the challenge to solve his problem using the guide's advice, or he fails to take his advice and proceeds on his own. This is your call to action and the struggle itself.

- **He succeeds or fails:** As a result of his actions, the hero succeeds or fails. This result is determined by his execution of the guide's advice. He can fail miserably if he doesn't take his advice, or succeed if he does.

You can tell an unlimited amount of brand stories using this framework. As you work with it, you will recognize how common it is.

Incorporating copywriting

Okay, it's time for some more definitions. In Chapter 10, I discuss the difference between content marketing strategy and content strategy. Copywriting and content marketing have the same kind of difference. They are not one and the same; instead, they complement each other. Here's a comparison of the two:

- **Content marketing:** You're marketing your content to achieve business goals. The content you write is determined by what you want to accomplish from a macro perspective.

- **Copywriting:** You look at copywriting from a micro perspective. When you focus on copywriting, you consider the words and other devices, such as visuals, that you choose to compel your reader to do something specific. You are enticing her to give you her email address, buy your product, or sign up for your newsletter. To this end, you use copywriting tactics such as great headlines or metaphors (and stories) to persuade her.

Because I think that the use of great headlines is one of the most important copywriting techniques for content writers to employ — and do it well — I go into some detail here on headlines.

Why do headlines matter? Some people never get past them. I read somewhere that only two in ten people will go past the headline to read the article. You need all the help you can get to create compelling headlines so that you entice people to read further.

When you create headlines, you want to:

- **Evoke emotion:** As you've seen, emotions trigger attention and persuasion. If your headline is bland, the reader will pass it by on the way to something juicier.

- **Attract the right reader:** You headline should make it clear who the article is targeted at — CEOs, small business owners, or others.

- **Assist with search engine optimization (SEO):** All this means is that if you use a keyword in your headline, you will help your customers find you.

- **Make a meaningful promise:** Readers always want to know what they will get from reading your article. Make that clear.

- **Do the work of the entire article:** As you know, some readers will never get past the headline, so create a headline that has impact.

When you are crafting your headlines, you don't need to reinvent the wheel. Several good, free tools are available to assist you:

✔ **CoSchedule's Headline Analyzer (**`http://coschedule.com/headline-analyzer`**):** This tool gives you an overall score and breaks down your headline into several measures to help you improve it.

✔ **Headlinr (**`http://headlinr.com/`**):** This tool is unique because it provides you with proven headlines that match your keyword or topic. You can invoke it right from your browser, so it's always there.

✔ **Hemingway App (**`http://www.hemingwayapp.com`**):** You can use this tool to test both your headline or your entire post. It makes suggestions about improving your content to make it clear.

✔ **The Readability Test Tool (**`http://read-able.com/`**):** This tool helps you determine whether your writing is appropriate for the targeted audience. It will help you simplify and make your content more readable.

See Chapter 23 to find out about the Emotional Marketing Value Headline Analyzer (`http://www.aminstitute.com/headline/`).

Check out the next page for a mind map of this chapter's content, and download a color version at `www.dummies.com/contentmarketing strategies`.

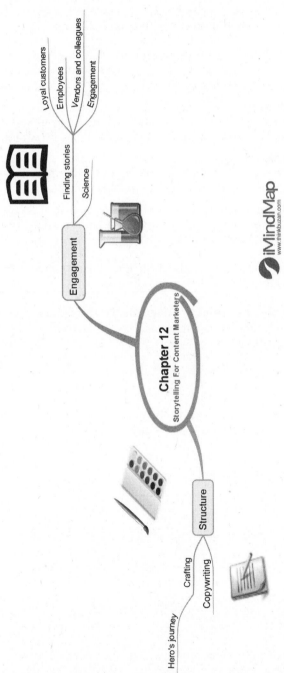

Courtesy of ThinkBuzan.

Chapter 13

Creating Processes and Systems for Your Content

A chapter about systems and processes? You may be thinking that this content is reserved for people who love to talk about workflow. Well, it is. But it's also important for everyone else who has to participate in getting his or her content to market. So that must include you, too.

In this chapter, you get into the nuts and bolts of your content framework. After your marketing strategy is in place and you know what kind of content you need, you'll want to create a system that you can rely on to get the job done. This chapter also delves into how content systems and documented procedures make everything easier.

Organizing the Content Process

Why should you care about developing a system for your content efforts? The best answer is that everyone benefits, even those who are not directly involved in the process. You would probably not consider mounting any other kind of project in your organization without detailing how things will work. The same should be said for your content system.

Of course, if you're a solopreneur who doesn't use freelancers, you can probably get away without documenting anything. But the moment you bring on another person, you need to let her know how things are done so that she doesn't reinvent the wheel.

Benefiting from a defined framework

When you implement a documented content marketing process, you provide everyone in the organization with clear expectations about

- Who is in charge (and responsible) for each part of the process
- How long your different campaigns and tasks take to complete
- How to avoid bottlenecks and mistakes
- What the budget will provide for and what resources are needed
- Whether you are meeting your content and business goals
- Whether you are meeting your legal requirements
- How security is implemented and preserved

On the opposite side of the coin, here's a brief look at what can happen if you don't have your content systems in place. You could have the following:

- **Violations of copyright laws:** Copyrighted images or content is published without permission.

- **Dissemination of inaccurate information:** Angry customers see inaccurate information that was not vetted by a content manager or editor.

- **Sloppy design:** No approvals were obtained for design consistency, making your brand look amateurish.

- **Poorly written articles:** Without editorial guidance, your posts could have misspellings and typos that will turn your audience off.

Obviously, people make mistakes. Even with a content system in place, you will still incur errors. A content framework simply helps you eliminate as many nasty errors as possible.

Enumerating these issues is often a good way to get managers on your side. Talking about corporate exposure always gets people's attention.

Examining the systems needed

You can begin by focusing on what's involved in putting your content system together. No magic is involved. As with any project you create, you need to know what the tasks are, how to get them done, and what your budget constraints are. It's important to make sure that everyone on the team understands how you deliver quality content using the highest standards.

You should have a documented process that everyone can follow. According to the Content Marketing Institute, research shows that those companies that have a documented framework believe that it helps them be more successful content marketers.

It's also critical to give all team members the opportunity to make suggestions and improve procedures. In fact, even those who are not actual team members can benefit from understanding the content process. You should welcome anyone who is interested in learning how he can assist or support your efforts.

You should also watch out for office politics related to your project. Big projects usually engender big emotions. Make sure that everyone is heard. Also be aware that not everyone will want your project to succeed, for reasons known only to them. (See more about resistance to change in Chapter 4.)

So, now you are tasked with getting the system in gear. You have buy-in and you need to get to work. What needs to happen next? The next paragraphs consider just a few of the tasks ahead of you.

If your company has a formal Content Management System (CMS), that system should have specific guidelines about the ways in which you have to input and manage your content. Here, I'm dealing with the general tasks needed to put procedures in place.

You need to

- **Assign roles and responsibilities:** Everyone must know what he or she is responsible for and in what time frame.

- **Establish governance rules to be followed:** Governance rules need to be created so that people know how to make decisions.

- **Put editorial guidelines in place:** Editors need rules, too. Don't forget to create these for everyone to follow so that your content will have quality and consistency.

- **Develop a writer's resource system:** You need to identify where to get writers (if they are not in-house), how to assign them to specific tasks, and what and how to pay them. (Same goes for designers and other technology workers if they are contractors.)

- **Select and use an editorial calendar:** Everyone needs to see what is being created. A calendar is also used to assign other project tasks that complete the content process. (See "Using an editorial calendar," later in this chapter.)

- **Create content guidelines for authors:** Writers need to know what is expected of them in terms of style and content.

✔ **Ensure that you have visual guidelines for designers:** Your content much be visually appealing and conform to all guidelines that have been documented in your brand guidelines.

✔ **Make sure that your taxonomy is in good order:** This is just a fancy way of saying that your keywords and other data classifiers should be kept up-to-date so that they can be tagged correctly and people can easily find you.

✔ **Develop the workflow to revise and approve content:** After content is written and has gone through the editorial process, you need to make sure that people know who is responsible for approving the content.

✔ **Publish content to multiple channels:** Have channel guidelines in place for each social platform to which you publish. You don't want to go through all that effort to create content and then fail to publish it correctly.

✔ **Ensure that training is in place:** If new people join the process, you want to be sure that they can get up and running quickly.

You also need to evaluate and measure the results of your efforts, as I cover that in Part V of this book.

How's that for a list of tasks? Now that you understand the magnitude of the project, you can work on getting your systems in place.

When you think about content writing and publishing, you probably don't think about governance. In reality, though, governance is crucial to your content strategy. Governance refers to the rules of the road that guide your decision-making throughout the content lifecycle. After you determine the scope of your project, you have to create the rules that guide you.

For example, if you, as the editor, intend to publish a controversial article on the company blog, how will you go about reviewing it and getting approval? When everything goes smoothly, the topic of governance seems unnecessary or heavy-handed. When you run into a conflict, however, either internal or external, you're glad you have them.

So what goes into preparing for governance? You need to

✔ Develop roles and responsibilities

✔ Establish workflow

✔ Create documentation

You also need to ensure that there is adequate training for all involved. The following sections look at each of these governance roles in turn.

Determining Roles and Responsibilities

When it comes to the average workplace, sometimes it's hard to know who is in charge. People often assume the mantle of authority even when they have no real power. But before you determine who is in charge, it's important to know how decisions about the project will get made. Governance models are typically one of three types:

- ✔ **Centralized model:** In this model, all decisions are made by a central committee that has the authority to consult anyone in the hierarchy to make decisions. This committee could include the legal department, advertising, and other departments. This model works best in small companies with a localized editorial team.

- ✔ **Hub-and-spoke model:** This model allows different teams to take responsibility for their own decisions. These teams may be spread across the globe, thereby making a central model impractical. Obviously, the model makes having a high standard of consistency less likely unless guidelines are strictly enforced.

- ✔ **Hybrid model:** As you might guess, this model is the most popular. It is more informal and allows teams to use the best of both models. It does require that some matters, such as legal aspects, be controlled centrally.

After your organization has decided on the method of making decisions, several roles must be assigned in a content management system, as described in Table 13-1.

Table 13-1	Roles Needed for a Content System
Role	*Description*
Project Leader	Corporate leader who approves the overall budget and goals and is ultimately responsible for the overall success or failure of the project
Project Manager	Manages budget, staffing, guidelines, and so on
Content Managers	Determine what topics are written about and what formats are used
Editors	Assign and schedule writers; evaluate writing; supervise revisions; approve for publication
Contributors	Write articles, e-books, and other content
Designers	Create images and design page layouts
Content System Administrators	Evaluate content to ensure that it will render correctly; create pages; check links
Web Administrators	Ensure that content is formatted for publication and meets all web standards

Managing the Workflow

Developing an efficient workflow is a vital part of the content system. When you document your systems, you help yourself and others learn the process. You also make it easy for others to spot mistakes.

Here are several tasks to consider in your workflow process:

✔ How contributors are found and assigned

✔ How contributions are scheduled

✔ How the content gets reviewed and approved

✔ How the content is published

The following sections explain each of these tasks.

Workflow documents should include visual elements. If you can capture screen shots, that's great. Flow charts are also helpful. Keeping the use of visual elements in mind will be valuable when you are trying to streamline the process.

Finding and assigning writers

Your content is only as good as the people who create it. If, like IBM (`http://IBM.com`), you have subject matter experts (SME) in almost all technical and business fields, your problem is solved. You can have your in-house writers interview an SME and create great content.

But what if you have only a few people who can write, or worse yet, no one who can produce content? You need to look outside of your organization to engage writers and editors to do the job. Doing so requires a budget and an understanding about what constitutes great content specifically for you.

To assemble a team of content creators, you have several options that vary in the amount of time and money you have to spend. Here are some options that you can try:

✔ **Harness your own in-house talent and create a content writing team.** If you choose this path, you will have to take on a great deal of the management yourself. You will have to determine how much time and effort you need and figure out how to use your resources. One major disadvantage is that you are stuck with the writing talent you have. If your writers are very good, you're lucky. If not, you may have weak content and nowhere to go to improve it.

✔ **Hire individual contractors and create an external writing team that you manage.** This path gives you the potential to find good writers. You'll still have to manage their time, but only in the sense that you assign work and expect to get work returned in a timely manner. The major disadvantage here is that you may have to test and audition several writers before you find the ones who suit you. Also, as freelancers, they can move on and you'll have to replace them. Some sources for freelance writers are

- *Contently (*`http://contently.com`*)*

- *WriterAccess (*`http://www.writeraccess.com/`*)*; see Figure 13-1

- *Zerys (*`http://www.zerys.com/`*)*

Figure 13-1:
Writer-
Access.

✔ **Hire a writing service.** When you hire a writing service, you're getting someone else to manage your writers. The service fulfills your requests by finding a suitable writer among its stable of contributors and getting the content written. Using such a service can save you time and effort, and you'll typically pay a premium for that fact. However, if you are looking to save time, perhaps you should consider this. Here are several writing services to get you started:

- *Internet Marketing Ninjas (*`http://www.internetmarketing ninjas.com`*)*

- *Express Writers* (`https://expresswriters.com`)
- *Brafton* (`http://www.brafton.com/`); see Figure 13-2.

✔ **Contact influencers who will create guest posts for you.** To supplement your content, you may want to have guest posts done by your industry's influencers. I discuss working with influencers in depth in Chapter 18. These people may want a byline credit, and they will be happy to have the exposure.

✔ **Pay a premium for special writers.** You may know of professional writers who would provide exactly what you need. If so, you can offer to pay them a premium rate.

Figure 13-2: Brafton.

Of course, you can mix up all these options and build a system that's perfect for you. As you experiment, you'll find the best combination of services for your needs.

Using an editorial calendar

Would you schedule a trip without looking at a calendar? Probably not. So why not use an editorial calendar when scheduling your content? If you wonder whether a calendar is necessary, you're not alone. Some content marketers don't want to be bothered with establishing one and keeping it current.

If you're a solo business operator or have a very small team, you might think that a calendar is overkill. Think again. Would you prefer to keep the schedule in your head and have everyone ask you about it? And could you even keep everything straight in your mind? Why take the chance of missing deadlines?

If you work in a large corporation, you probably already see the need for a robust organizational tool and may be looking for a good editorial calendar. You have several good options to choose from, and I describe them shortly. But first, take a look at the tasks that a calendar helps you perform. When you have a calendar, you can

- ✔ **See the big picture of how your content is distributed throughout the months.** A calendar gives you an at-a-glance view of the content that is in the pipeline and that has already been published, helping you avoid redundancies.

- ✔ **Ensure that you will have the people and resources that you need when you need them.** To avoid long gaps in the schedule, you want to get writers lined up in advance. If someone drops out or you want to add something special, you can prepare ahead of time. Also, Google loves consistency, and you don't want to disappoint Google!

- ✔ **Develop content for specific promotions and campaigns.** Product managers, marketers, and sales managers want to get their campaigns put at the head of the line. A calendar can help to control the potential chaos of conflicting demands.

- ✔ **Assign people to specific content tasks and then follow up with them**. A documented schedule allows you to follow up with the people to which you assign tasks. You can see whether a deadline is fast approaching with no word from your contributor.

- ✔ **Prevent the problem of not knowing what to write about with a deadline looming.** A calendar will allow you to schedule topics in advance so that you're never wondering what your people should be writing about.

It is critical that you keep a steady stream of content ideas so that you can plug them in and get them written. Keep a growing list of ideas for content in online tools like Evernote (`http://evernote.com`), a content organizing tool.

Or you might use Trello (`http://Trello.com`) a collaboration tool. If your group already has a collaboration tool, use that. The key is to make sure that you capture ideas as you think of them so that you're never at a loss for a juicy topic to write about.

✔ **Make sure to vary your content formats so that you delight everyone in your audience.** Scheduling ahead of time allows you to look at content formats. You will want to have a variety — lists, videos, and audio — to entertain your audience.

✔ **Help your team be more productive because they know what to work on when they're ready to work.** People are more productive when they manage their own time. Not waiting for the last minute ensures that project members turn in their assignments on time. Or at least they will know that they are going to miss a deadline and inform you!

Using a calendar makes it easy to show your manager what you're doing when it's performance review time. It also allows you to review your strategy at given intervals. When you're ready to revise and optimize, you'll have all the information you need in your calendar, along with supporting documents.

So what calendar tool should you choose? That depends on what's available to you. Here are some options to consider:

✔ If you use a formal content management software platform (CMS), you may already have a calendar tool built right in. An example of a CMS with a built-in calendar is the Kudani Cloud (`http://Kudani.com`) content platform. It has all the built-in features you need for finding content and publishing it to your blog or website — all without leaving the application.

✔ If you want to use a stand-alone calendar, you might try the one from CoSchedule (`http://coschedule.com`).

✔ If you have a simple blog and are looking for a WordPress plug-in, you can use the one shown in Figure 13-3 (`https://wordpress.org/plugins/editorial-calendar/`).

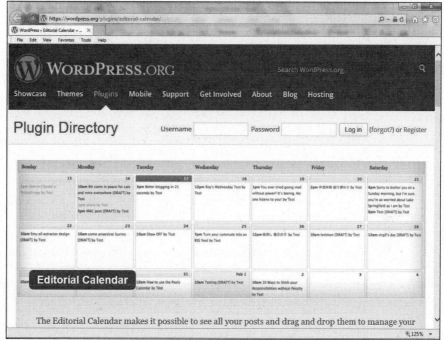

Editorial Calendar

The Editorial Calendar makes it possible to see all your posts and drag and drop them to manage your

Figure 13-3:
WordPress
Calendar.

Can your editorial calendar increase your number of followers?

You know that using an editorial calendar can help you with your scheduling, but can it actually get you more attention and Facebook followers? According to the co-founders Dechay Watts and Debbie Williams of SPROUT Content, a content and inbound marketing services firm, it can. On their blog (http://www.sproutcontent.com/blog-editorial-calendar-case-study-copy), they detail how they were able to help a regional restaurant group in Florida with several locations get into social media and create excitement for its brand. One of the first things

Watts and Williams did for this client was to create a three-month blog editorial calendar for each restaurant.

Within a two-year time frame, the company accrued more than 23,000 Facebook fans, a metric it could never have obtained if it didn't use its editorial calendar to apply long-term thinking to their content creation.

Perhaps you thought that using an editorial calendar wasn't valuable. Now you see that it can be.

Documenting Your Policies and Procedures

Documentation isn't considered a very exciting topic, but it's certainly a very necessary one. As I explain in Chapter 5, documenting your content strategy can mean the difference between the success and failure of your project. This is also true of documentation for your systems and procedures. You need to ask several key questions about your documentation on an ongoing basis. These questions include:

✔ **Does everyone know where to find documentation?** It's great to have documentation, but if no one knows where it is, it's useless. A central repository should exist on the company server to house all your documentation regarding content processes.

✔ **Is there a method to let everyone know about changes made to documentation?** Having a way to keep everyone in the loop concerning changes is key, because tracking changes can be a bit complex. You want to figure out the best way to let people know who care about the changes and not annoy those who aren't. Some companies issue alerts to specific teams when guidelines have changed. Make sure that you know who is on each team, for example, editorial versus technical, so that the right alerts go to the right people.

✔ **Are you guarding against "walking documentation"?** The term *walking documentation* refers to the information that is known only to specific employees, who walk out the door each night. You need to ensure that everything that should be known by the group is written down and kept in an accessible place, rather than existing just in the mind of a few employees.

Table 13-2 lists the kind of documentation you need for each of the content system areas. In the upcoming sections, I explain each of these areas.

Table 13-2	Documentation Needed for a Content System
Who Uses It	*Documentation*
Content managers	Taxonomy
Editors	Editorial guidelines
Writers	Style guides
Designers	Visual and branding guides
Content system administrators	Social platform requirements, CMS
Web administrators	Systems and security

Content managers

Content managers are somewhat new to the party. In larger organizations they are different from the editor, who ensures that the content meets its goals and doesn't violate any company policies. A content manager has a more strategic role. She is responsible for knowing about the customer personas and the data collected about customers. With that knowledge she maintains the taxonomy (as described above) and determines what topics and formats of content should be created.

Editors

Editorial guidelines are critical for any publisher. They explain to everyone concerned what your goals are for publishing. The guidelines tell your contributors who your audience is and what you want them to get from reading your content. It also explains the approval process so that writers know how their work will be evaluated.

Writers

Obviously, documenting what authors need to know about writing content for you should be available in a style guide for authors. The type of style guide you provide for your in-house writers will be extensive and will also include specific information about your CMS, if you have one.

HubSpot provides a free style template (see Figure 13-4) that can be helpful if you need to create guidelines from scratch. Go to `http://blog.hubspot.com/blog/tabid/6307/bid/31247/The-Simple-Template-for-a-Thorough-Content-Style-Guide.aspx`.

Blogs that use outside contributors normally have a document available on the blog's website that informs contributors about what is acceptable and desirable in a post they submit for publication.

One great example is available on the Boost Blog Traffic blog written by Jon Morrow and guest posters. They have a page dedicated to information about how to write for them. `http://boostblogtraffic.com/write-for-us/` shown in Figure 13-5. This is a great page from which to model your own page.

Figure 13-4:
HubSpot content style template.

Figure 13-5:
The Boost Blog Traffic page with editorial guidelines.

Designers

Designers rely on the visual guidelines that have been created for the website properties. They will also refer to brand guidelines if issues arise.

Content system administrator

The content system administrator makes sure that the CMS is functioning and will refer to the CMS documentation when necessary. He also keeps social platform guidelines with the details about formatting content for other channels.

Web administrator

The web administrator is the keeper of the important security guidelines for the company's web properties. She's also responsible for system maintenance documentation.

Of course you know that getting all the systems in place is only half the job. People must be trained to effectively use the systems. Some of the training occurs by using the systems and getting comfortable with how they work.

 The technology you put together for your system may include software tools for writing, designing, and editing. This means that you expect your team members to be well-versed in the software skills needed for their work.

Your content could be intelligent

Recently, content marketers have been hearing about "intelligent content." This term doesn't refer to content that is written for power users. Rather, it's content that is structured to make it more useful. Scott Abel, the Content Wrangler (http://contentwrangler.com), calls it "content that can be read by people and machines." The value of making your content intelligent is that by providing a structure, the content can be found and used throughout the organization. Robert Rose of the Content Marketing Institute is quoted in Scott Abel's SlideShare presentation as saying, "Intelligent content is an approach. A way of thinking about how we structure and manage content" (http://www.slideshare.net/abelsp/intelligent-content-in-the-experience-age-49565442). Intelligent content is content that is broken out into its components (such as Meta data) so that it can be structured into the output that's needed.

Is intelligent content something that you need to consider for your company? It depends. If you are a small company with a limited amount of content, the answer is, not right now. If you have a big organization and lots of different forms of content, developing intelligent content will help you deliver the best content to all your customers. You want to be able to get the right content to the right customers at the right time.

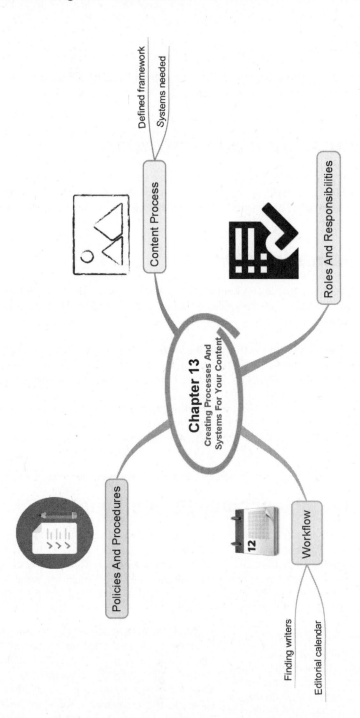

Defined framework
Systems needed

Content Process

Roles And Responsibilities

Chapter 13
Creating Processes And
Systems For Your Content

Policies And Procedures

Workflow

Finding writers

Editorial calendar

iMindMap
www.thinkbuzan.com

Courtesy of ThinkBuzan.

Part IV
Developing Channel Promotions

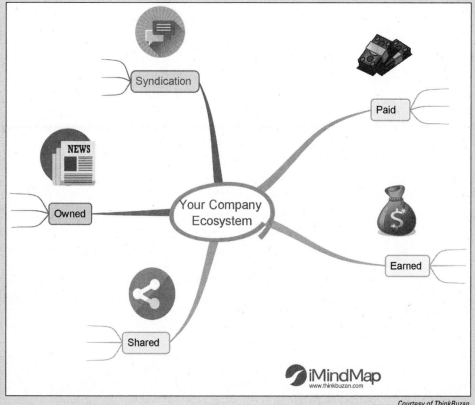

Courtesy of ThinkBuzan.

The quality of your content won't matter if no one sees it. Discover five ways to encourage content sharing at www.dummies.com/extras/contentmarketingstrategies.

In this part . . .

- ✔ To coordinate your promotions, you need to create a channel plan for each of your channels. See how to easily put plans in place.

- ✔ Creating shareable content will help your bottom line. You look at the "Five *W*s and one *H*" of sharing.

- ✔ I recommend using the PESO model (paid, earned, shared, and owned media) and show you how to implement it.

- ✔ Syndication and guest posting are two important tactics. See how they can fit into your content marketing strategy.

- ✔ Finding the right influencers is crucial to your success. I provide you with a downloadable worksheet that will help you develop partnerships with the right influencers for you.

Chapter 14

Examining Channel Plans

*H*ow often do you ask yourself whether you'll ever distribute your content to all the places you'd like to send it? If you have a team dedicated to filling and managing those channels, you are probably less concerned. If you are a solopreneur or a small business owner, it's a major headache. There are more channels than you could ever hope to address.

In this chapter, you look at how the hard work you have done to set things up in other areas culminates in successful channel plans. The chapter shows you how to create a plan for each channel, a plan that meets your objectives and delights your audience. The key to creating great channel plans is to focus on what your prospects are thinking and doing when they are on that channel. You must focus on giving your customers exactly what they want to see from you on a particular channel.

Your customers are on a journey to accomplish something. They are thinking about how they will accomplish their mission. That's what you should be thinking about when you create your channel plans.

Getting Started with Your Channel Plan

Creating channel plans can be complex if you haven't done the work of analyzing the components that go into devising a plan. I'm sure you've been tempted, as most of us have, to publish the same content to every channel. If you've already created your personas (see Chapter 7 for details on developing personas), you know that your audience is not a monolith. Having the wrong content on a channel is just as bad as having no content at all. For this reason, you need to carefully pick your channels and put the right type of content there. For example, you shouldn't be posting the same content to your Facebook and LinkedIn accounts.

You know that when you're on Facebook, your audience is most likely communicating with friends and family. On LinkedIn, you're communicating with colleagues in a business setting. Clearly, the content should not be the same for both. So what are some of the benefits you derive from creating a channel plan?

Benefitting from planning your channel content

Understandably, you'd like to skip creating individual channel plans. You have enough to do creating systems, procedures, calendars, and content. All that effort could be wasted, however, if you aren't strategic about where your content will be seen. A channel plan helps ensure that you can

- ✔ Choose the right content for users on that platform
- ✔ Guide your content writers to formulate articles that meet your objectives for that channel
- ✔ Effectively measure your results on each channel by using channel-specific analytics
- ✔ Obtain the knowledge you need to determine when and how often to post
- ✔ Determine whether your prospects could be viewing their content on a mobile device
- ✔ Get buy-in from team members who are not directly involved in the process, such as sales reps
- ✔ Gain a competitive edge against competitors who haven't created their own channel plans
- ✔ Prevent yourself from creating the wrong assets and duplicating efforts

Something that you should keep in mind when developing your channel plans is how a channel can be used. This may sound strange to you, but sometimes people get stuck thinking about a particular channel in only one way. You can use your channel in the way that makes sense for your audience. Depending on what you determine your persona needs, you can use a channel to

✔ **Sell:** You can always provide a link to buy the product from almost any channel. The key is to use the appropriate style for that channel.

✔ **Highlight your brand:** Provide content that will demonstrate credibility and brand awareness.

✔ **Facilitate sharing of content:** Content will get shared from everywhere by readers. Don't feel that you can't encourage sharing from any platform.

✔ **Encourage recommendations:** You know that your viewers are your best salesforce, so help them to recommend your product from any channel.

✔ **Offer discounts and other savings:** People love to get deals, so don't hesitate to offer them from wherever you distribute your content.

✔ **Allow free trials and samples:** This is another category that should be used for any channel on which you are distributing content.

✔ **Announce new products:** People want to know what's new, so share news on all your channels.

Knowing what you need to create a channel plan

In other chapters of the book, you develop a variety of strategies, audience tools, and your brand story, for a total of six methods. You can use all six of these methods to formulate the channel plan. They are your

✔ **Content marketing strategy.** This strategy tells you how your content supports the overall goals of your business. It dictates where you will publish your content, which is key to the channel plan.

✔ **Customer data.** A knowledge of the customer data you're collecting lets you know whether you will have what you need to analyze your results and what measures you need to use to determine whether your channel plans are successful.

✔ **Customer personas.** After you know your personas, you will know a host of other pieces of information as well, including which channels are most valuable to your personas. If you know that your persona isn't likely to frequent a particular channel, you can make that channel a very low priority.

✔ **Buyer's journey.** Understanding the stages that your customer goes through informs you which channels to target for each stage.

✔ **Content strategy.** Your content strategy guides the creation, management, and governance of your content. Without knowing this strategy, you can't populate your channels with content.

✔ **Brand story.** This is the foundation from which you build the content you need for your personas on their buying journey.

Preparing for a Channel Audit

Beginning a channel plan requires that you do a channel audit. This means that you need to know what you are currently doing on your content distribution channels before you make any changes or additions. You want to make sure that you keep the best and toss the rest.

Although no easy way exists to complete this task, you can break it into three phases that will help make it less daunting. I hope that doing this will encourage you and your staff to get started, rather than put it off. It's not unusual for teams to avoid doing this job because it requires lots of time and effort. But the effort pays off.

The three phases of a channel audit are as follows:

✔ **Phase One: Current Channel Audit.** You create a list of the current channels you're using and include information from the recommendations I list in the sections that follow. You want to make sure that you understand which channels are successful and why.

✔ **Phase Two: Channel Content Review.** You document the content that is on each channel. You can do that here if you haven't done that in your content audit described in Chapter 10. If you do a thorough job, you will identify lots of content to repurpose.

✔ **Phase Three: New Channel Plans.** When you know which distribution channels you're using and the content you have used to support it, you can develop a new one-page document for each channel's plan.

I cover each of these phases in turn.

Phase One: Current Channel Audit

Your goal in Phase One is to identify the channels on which you currently distribute content. Although you think you're on just a few, you may be surprised to discover the number when you investigate. Occasionally, someone might add a channel at the spur of the moment without alerting others.

Obviously, if the addition is just a one-off and is temporary, it won't matter. But if it becomes an ongoing channel, you want to have a plan to make the most of it.

Begin by making a list of all your channels other than your paid and syndicated ones. Those will be handled separately but will become part of the bigger picture.

To look at content distribution via paid channels, see Chapter 16; Chapter 17 covers distribution via syndication.

To create your list, here are some examples of channels you may be on:

- ✔ Blogs
- ✔ Social media platforms (Facebook, Twitter, Pinterest, Instagram, LinkedIn, and so on)
- ✔ YouTube and other video channels
- ✔ SlideShare and other presentation sites
- ✔ Email and newsletters
- ✔ Landing pages
- ✔ Owned communities and forums
- ✔ Answer forums, such as Quora
- ✔ Social bookmarking sites, such as Reddit

For each one of your current channels, you want to list the following:

- ✔ Name of the channel
- ✔ URL and the name of the property
- ✔ Your current goals for that channel
- ✔ Current status

You may need to look at data to determine how successful you are on the smaller channels, but I'm sure you know which major ones are succeeding or failing.

In addition to the items in the preceding list, you may want to document the following as applicable:

- ✔ **The number of followers you have on the social media platforms:** The number of followers you have is not really a measure that will tell you how many people will buy your products. It does show you a measure of brand awareness.

✔ **The size of your email list or subscribers to your newsletter list:** Again, the size of your lists is not an indication of how well they perform, but you'll want to see changes over time.

✔ **General success metrics on your most important channels:** You will want to look at the analytics for the channels that are most important to you to get current metrics.

Note that you should use gross measures in this phase. The idea is to get a sense of whether you are currently succeeding on these channels. You will develop more specific measures going forward. An example of the basic audit of your current channels is shown in Table 14-1.

Table 14-1		Basic Channel Audit	
Channel	*Name/URL*	*Current Goals*	*Current Status*
Website	Corporate name http://*companydomain*.com	Sales; drive traffic; lead generation	Needs redesign; traffic inadequate; email list 20K
Blog	Blog name http://*companyblog*.com	Brand awareness, drive traffic to website; credibility	Good driver of customer engagement; subscriber list 45K
Facebook	http://facebook. com/*company*	Brand recognition; engagement	Lack of customer engagement; followers 20K
Twitter	@*company*support	Customer retention; brand loyalty	Working well; followers 40K

Even though you know that you may be eliminating channels or changing goals, make sure to document them here. It's always helpful to have a historical document to compare with your new one so that you know what you were thinking.

As you do your audit, here are some questions to ask yourself:

✔ **Based on data and your personas, do you know that your customers are on this channel?** Ensure that you have data telling you that your prospect is on this channel. You don't want to spend time and money on something that won't further your goals.

✔ **Have I been successful on this channel?** To plan a new strategy for the channel, you need to know how you are currently doing. Is this channel failing to meet the goals you set for it? Why or why not?

✔ **Based on what I find now, should this channel be a priority going forward? Should I eliminate it?** You may be on a channel that does not provide your customer with any value. On the other hand, you may find that the channel should be elevated on your priority list.

✔ **Is this channel currently integrated with our present goals?** Determine whether the channel is currently part of your working content marketing plans and how it performs with other channels.

When you complete Phase One, you will know a great deal more about what you should do next than you did before this exercise. For this reason, you should make sure to document all your takeaways.

Phase Two: Channel Content Review

If you have already done a content review (see Chapter 10 for how to conduct this review), this phase will be easy. You simply need to identify a representative sample of what you're doing on each channel. If you haven't done a full content review yet, you'll need to collect some information here and then go back and do a full review of your content when you're ready.

Of course, some channels, such as SlideShare (http://slideshare.net), are easier to audit than channels like Twitter. You probably won't have thousands of slide presentations. You may choose to do some channels at this time rather than wait for your full content audit.

Here's what you want to do in Phase Two:

✔ **Document the type of content you have placed on a channel:** For example, if you have succeeded with long- or short-form content on a particular channel, you want to note that.

✔ **Be aware of the tone:** You want to determine the tone you're using for the content on that channel. Remember that now that you're targeting specific personas, you have to match the tone to the persona.

✔ **Document the structure:** Gather information about the different structures you are distributing on that channel. Note whether it's long- or short-form content and whether that content is a list, a how-to, or something else.

You want to collect any information in this phase that will help you determine how to modify your plan for each channel going forward.

Phase Three: New Channel Plans

Finally, the moment you've been waiting for. You've done the hard work of collecting everything you need. Now you can develop channel plans with the best information available. It's not going to be a quick process, but you already guessed that.

To start, consider the customer mindset. To create a great plan for each channel, you want to think about what your specific customers will be doing on the channel and how they are thinking about it. Read on for an example.

If you are beginning your channel plan for Tumblr, you want to start by looking at two things: (1) the general user profile for that channel; and (2) your user personas and how they use the channel. The demographics are easy to find and the personas are already created so that you get a full picture of the channel and the users.

So, for example, you find that according to Quantcast (`http://unwrapping.tumblr.com/post/43854304176/tumblr-demographics`), the profile of a Tumblr user is the following:

- **Majority gender:** 56 percent female.
- **Largest age group:** Age 18–34.
- **Income:** 68 percent lower than 50K.
- **Education:** 46 percent are college educated.
- **How the persona you are targeting is using it:** This requires that you look at the personas you are targeting that use Tumblr to see what they might be thinking, feeling, and doing.

It's important to look at these items for each channel (see examples in the upcoming section) because you want to be sure that you're keeping your customers at the center of the plan. You can easily forget that you're trying to reach "the right customer at the right time with the right content." Making a plan to distribute content to Tumblr or any channel without a specific goal is a waste of effort.

What questions should you be asking yourself for each channel? Consider these:

- What are my new goals for this channel?
- What will my success measures be?
- Which persona am I targeting based on real data?
- What are the dominant content types that would be appropriate for this channel?

Dipping into Some Major Channel Examples

When creating your channel plans, you have a lot of data to draw from. The following sections cover examples of using the four top social media channels in 2015 to show how the market is segmented. I drew each channel's statistics from the Pew Research Center Social Media Update for 2014 (`http://www.pewinternet.org/2015/01/09/demographics-of-key-social-networking-platforms-2/`), shown in Figure 14-1.

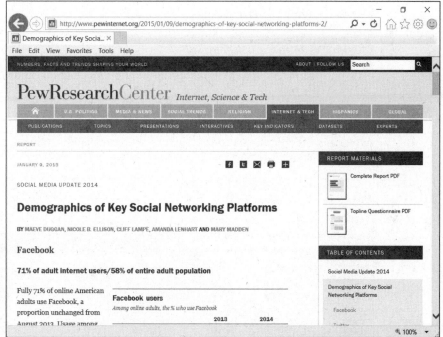

Figure 14-1:
Pew Social
Media
Update
2014.

The statistics are based on U.S. adult Internet users in 2014 versus the entire adult population. (They don't add up to 100 percent.)

In addition, the examples show how brands are effectively using a given channel. You can use these examples to derive some ideas about what you can do.

Using Facebook for customer support: Avon

Who is on Facebook? Seventy-one percent of adult Internet users versus 58 percent of the entire adult population.

Demographics for Facebook

- ✔ **Gender:** 66 percent male; 77 percent female
- ✔ **Largest age group:** 18–29
- ✔ **Income:** 72 percent less than 75K
- ✔ **Education:** 74 percent college educated

Channel example: customer support

How is Avon effectively using Facebook? To provide customer support and engagement.

According to an article by Jim Belosic, CEO of ShortStack (`http://www.socialmediaexaminer.com/10-facebook-tactics-by-top-brands/`), Avon uses Facebook, as shown in Figure 14-2, to provide amazing customer

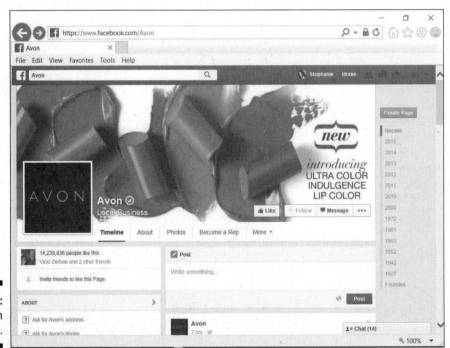

Figure 14-2: Avon on Facebook.

service. This is something you should, of course, consider as you create your channel plans. Having an alternative channel for customer support in addition to your website is a smart way to use a channel.

Tweeting for customer engagement: Warby Parker

Who is on Twitter? Twenty-three percent of adult Internet users versus 19 percent of the entire adult population.

Demographics for Twitter

- ✔ **Gender:** 24 percent male; 21 percent female
- ✔ **Largest age group:** 18–29
- ✔ **Income:** 27 percent under 75K
- ✔ **Education:** 30 percent college graduate

Channel example: User-generated content and engagement

How is Warby Parker effectively using Twitter? By encouraging engagement and user-generated content.

Michael Thrasher, writer for Business Insider (`http://www.business insider.com/best-brands-to-follow-on-twitter-2013-9?op=1`), reports that Warby Parker is using Twitter to entice customers to send in photos on Instagram with the promise of showing the best ones in their catalog, among other enticements. This demonstrates the use of two channels to feed into one another. (See Figure 14-3.) You definitely want to explore integrating your channels to engage your customers.

Influencing through LinkedIn: Microsoft

Who is on LinkedIn? Twenty-eight percent of adult Internet users versus 23 percent of the entire adult population.

Demographics for LinkedIn

- ✔ **Majority gender:** 28 percent male; 27 percent female
- ✔ **Largest age group:** 30–49
- ✔ **Income:** 44 percent less than 75K
- ✔ **Education:** 50 percent college graduate

Figure 14-3:
Warby
Parker on
Twitter.

Channel example: Influence and product education

What is Microsoft doing effectively on LinkedIn? An article by Amanda Walgrove, lead writer at Contently, reports that Microsoft uses LinkedIn to showcase Microsoft's founder Bill Gates as an influencer (`http://contently.com/strategist/2015/02/24/5-b2b-brands-that-rock-linkedin/`; see Figure 14-4). Gates has garnered more than 5.5 million followers on his personal LinkedIn page and Microsoft provides educational content about its products. You don't have to be Microsoft to use LinkedIn to educate your customers about your products.

Using Pinterest to gauge user interest: The Container Store

Who is on Pinterest? Twenty-eight percent of adult Internet users versus 22 percent of the entire adult population.

Figure 14-4:
Microsoft
on LinkedIn.

Demographics for Pinterest

✔ **Gender:** 13 percent male; 42 percent female

✔ **Largest age group:** 18–29

✔ **Income:** 34 percent less than 75K

✔ **Education:** 32 percent college graduate

Channel example: New content ideas

How is The Container Store effectively using Pinterest? Adam Weinroth, CMO of OneSpot, reports that The Container Store uses Pinterest to see what content is resonating with customers (https://www.onespot.com/blog/the-best-brands-on-pinterest-and-what-theyre-doing-right/; see Figure 14-5). The company's Pinterest board becomes the best focus group it could ever have. The Pinterest board tells the company what its customers care about most.

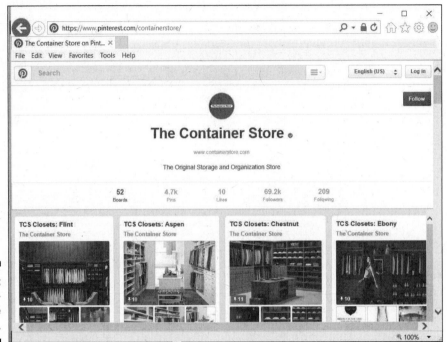

Figure 14-5:
The Container Store on Pinterest.

Documenting each channel's plan

This short section suggests a template for documenting each of your channels. For each one, you want to list the following:

- ✔ Channel name
- ✔ Targeted personas
- ✔ Frequency
- ✔ Goals
- ✔ Success measures

Items like keywords and content due dates don't get listed here. This is not your content planning sheet. (Chapter 10 tells you where to find that.) An example of a very simple channel plan for Facebook is shown in the following mini table. Yours will be much more detailed to capture everything you learned in Phase One.

Channel Name	Targeted Personas	Frequency	Goals	Success Measures
Facebook	Persona1 Persona2	Two posts daily	Brand awareness; Drive traffic to website; Credibility	Shares; likes; referrals to website shown in Google Analytics; followers

Check out the next page for a mind map of this chapter's content, and download a color version at www.dummies.com/contentmarketingstrategies.

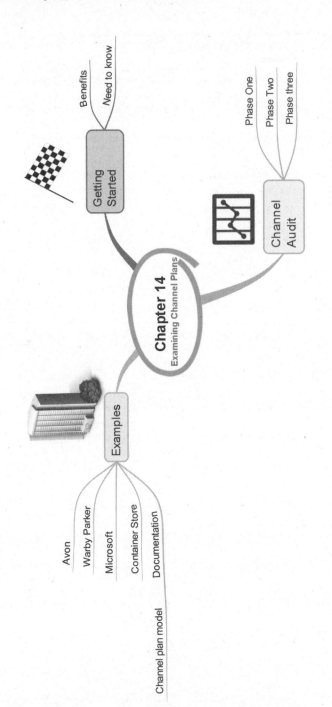

Getting
Started

Benefits

Need to know

Phase One

Phase Two

Phase three

iMindMap
www.thinkbuzan.com

Channel
Audit

Chapter 14
Examining Channel Plans

Examples

Avon

Warby Parker

Microsoft

Container Store

Documentation

Channel plan model

Courtesy of ThinkBuzan.

Chapter 15

Sharing Your Content

. . . .

. . . .

*W*hen the web was still a novelty, getting people to read your online posts was easy. When I started working at AOL in 1994, people would rejoice at the sound of "You've got mail!" Well, those days are clearly over.

The likelihood that someone will read something you wrote gets more remote all the time. Who knew that getting people to read and share what you create would be one of the biggest problems faced by content marketers in 2015?

In this chapter, you examine how strategically sharing your content can make the difference between a wildly popular brand and one that is ignored. You also look at why people share content, as well as where and how they share it.

Embracing Shareability As a Strategy

One battle cry that can be heard throughout marketing departments today is the notion that sharing content should be everyone's job. It used to be that only customer-facing employees were encouraged to share. Now everyone across all departments is expected to help the company gain a wider audience.

Understanding sharing patterns

There are two immediate ways for you to make content sharing a company-wide endeavor:

- ✔ **Focus some attention on your "employee channel."** A new term has cropped up — the *employee channel* — which refers to the pipeline of company content that you supply to your employees so that they can champion the company. Your job is to help your employees share content and promote the company regardless of which department they're in.

  By encouraging what the Altimeter Group, a leading research and consulting company, calls the Culture of Content (CoC), you can develop a cycle of production and promotion that boosts the profile of all your content and makes your company smarter.

  The Altimeter report "The Culture of Content Best Practices," by Rebecca Lieb and Jessica Groopman with Susan Etlinger (http://www.altimetergroup.com/pdf/reports/Culture-of-Content-Altimeter-Group.pdf) includes the following recommendations:

  - Let an obsession with the customer guide content creation.

  - Align content with your brand.

  - Constantly evangelize your content among employees to maintain the CoC.

  In Chapter 9, which deals with sales enablement, I tell you about the need to give all employees who deal with customers the most up-to-date information. Having an employee channel takes that idea even further, requiring that you help all your employees participate in sharing content regardless of department.

- ✔ **Be channel agnostic after developing content to share.** The idea of being "channel agnostic" may seem counterintuitive. When you develop content, you want to pay attention to the audience demographics on that specific channel. Doing so is important, especially when you're creating ads on that channel, such as through Facebook. What being channel agnostic means is that you shouldn't be so channel focused after content is shared. For example, Copyblogger eliminated its Facebook account in 2014, yet still gets a lot of its content shared on that channel. Copyblogger understood that its audience would be sharing its content across all the social media platforms and didn't want to expend energy directly on Facebook for what it found to be a minimal return.

  I am not necessarily recommending that you do the same — you know your audience best. But you should understand how content spreads before you create a sharing strategy. An article on Contently, a company that helps companies and freelancers deliver content (`http://contently.com/strategist/2015/04/29/buzzfeed-just-cracked-the-code-on-how-social-content-spreads-and-its-a-big-deal/`), detailed how BuzzFeed (`http://buzzfeed.com`), used a proprietary software technology called Pound to determine how content spreads on the web. Contently found that content spreads in clusters. Someone may share a post on Twitter, which in turn gets shared on Facebook, which then kicks off a flurry of activity on Google+. The most important takeaway from this is that you do everything you can to make your content shareable.

Sharing as a bottom-line issue

Ratings, reviews, recommendations — doesn't it seem that nothing can be sold without someone's having first voiced an opinion? Actually, that is the case. If you see a product that doesn't have reviews or ratings, you may be reluctant to be the first person to buy. Items such as books and movies have always been rated and discussed, but now every grocery product and children's toy needs to have a host of opinions before it's considered by a buyer.

So you need to have your products and services reviewed, but should you care about getting that content shared? Does it really make that much of a difference to the bottom line?

Two online companies — ShareThis and Canva — think so.

A study done by ShareThis (`http://sharethis.com`; see Figure 15-1), a company that makes sharing tools, set out to determine the answer to the question, "Does sharing matter to the bottom line?"

The study, called "The Return on a Share," found that, indeed, a distinct business case can be made for sharing. Findings include:

- An excellent recommendation boosts the average value of a share by 9.5 percent over a neutral one
- Positive shares created a 9.6 percent increase in purchases
- Bad recommendations instigated lower purchases by 11 percent
- Recommendations exceed price and brand when considering purchases

If you need to convince your manager that sharing is key to your content marketing strategy, show her these statistics as part of your argument. (For more on obtaining buy-in from management and other colleagues, see Chapter 4.)

Figure 15-1:
ShareThis.

Another interesting finding from the Return on Share study: "Mobile is considered two times as social as desktop." Don't forget your mobile audience!

Another company that presents compelling evidence for the value of sharing content is Canva, a design company. Andrianes Pinantoan, Head of Growth Marketing for Canva, details on the Convince & Convert blog (http://www.convinceandconvert.com/content-marketing/how-to-increase-shareability/) how Canva increased the traffic to its design school blog (https://designschool.canva.com/; see Figure 15-2) by over 220 percent.

Canva decided to focus on shareability by testing everything it posted to its blog, and then it developed its content strategy by doing the following:

✔ Looking at the content that was being successfully shared by its competitors

✔ Focusing on writing in-depth posts

✔ Using storytelling to make its content more interesting

✔ Developing great headlines

✔ Adding more visuals

Figure 15-2:
Canva
Design
School.

In 60 days, Canva increased its traffic by 226 percent. Not bad for two months of effort! Can you apply some of these tactics? They are best practices that should help you make significant progress.

To encourage more sharing, you can create an inline tweet that is irresistible to share by using Click to tweet (`http://coschedule.com/click-to-tweet`). It's a WordPress plug-in by CoSchedule. All the user has to do is click the ready-made box within the post, and off the tweet goes. Now that's easy!

Uncovering the Five Ws and One H of Online Sharing

All journalism students are taught to cover the Five *W*s and one *H* in their reporting — who, what, when, where, why, and how. This is a framework for asking questions that will uncover the most important information. Using this structure to understand online sharing works quite well.

Knowing who shares content, and why

It's important to know what motivates people to share content so that you can effectively appeal to your constituency. The Consumer Insight Group at the *New York Times* recently did a study called "The Psychology of Sharing: Why Do People Share Online?" (`http://nytmarketing.whsites.net/mediakit/pos/`), shown in Figure 15-3. The study's methodology included in-person interviews, a quantitative survey, and a one-week sharing panel.

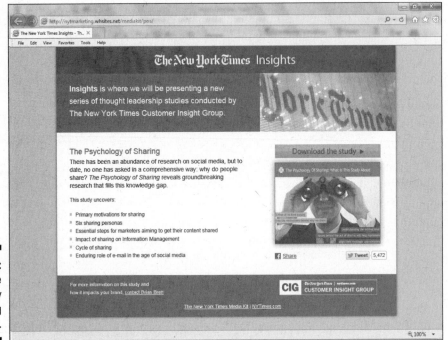

Figure 15-3: The Psychology of Sharing study.

Among the very interesting findings was the fact that they found six personas of online sharers. Table 15-1 lists these personas and how, what, and why they share.

Table 15-1	Key Insights from the "Psychology of Sharing" Study		
Persona	*What/Why They Share*	*Keywords Commonly Used*	*Preferred Way to Share*
Altruists	Content that serves the needs of friends and family, such as health and finance articles	*Helpful, reliable*	Email

Persona	What/Why They Share	Keywords Commonly Used	Preferred Way to Share
Careerists	Content on business-related ideas to improve their company	*Valuable, network*	LinkedIn
Hipsters	Content that defines who they are	*Cutting edge, young*	Less likely to email; prefer to share on social networks
Boomerangs	Content that gets them noticed and provokes a reaction	*Validation, empowered*	Twitter and Facebook
Connectors	Deals and introductions to make everything better for friends and family	*Creative, thoughtful*	Facebook
Selectives	Careful about what they choose to share with individuals; they want to hit the mark	*Resourceful, informative*	Email

This knowledge of personas and why and how they share content is very valuable when you're putting your own personas together. (See Chapter 7 for more about your own personas.) Here, I examine personas through the sharing lens to help you determine the motivations of your specific audience.

For example, if you are a health-related company, you know that you will have one group of sharers who want to educate people (altruists). A great illustration of this motivation, reported by the Sales Lion blog (http://www. thesaleslion.com/content-marketing-companies-b2b/), is Health Catalyst. The Health Catalyst is a data warehousing and analytics company that was able to get its doctors and nurses to share information in the form of e-books and blog posts and put them in a Knowledge Center, shown in Figure 15-4. The Health Catalyst reports that this education effort was, in part, responsible for getting the company $50 million in investor funding. Even though its direct customers were hospitals, the company's willingness to share its knowledge resulted in a high profile for a small-sized company.

Want a really simple yet effective way to determine the shareability of your blog posts? Have your users take Guy Kawasaki's "reshare test," described in an interview on the Social Media Examiner blog at http://www.social mediaexaminer.com/content-sharing-with-guy-kawasaki/. The test involves asking users "Are you sharing something that other people will share with their friends and followers?" Their answers give you information about how your readers view the value of your content.

Figure 15-4:
Health
Catalyst
Knowledge
Center.

Considering what they share

A valuable study was undertaken by BuzzStream (`http://buzzstream.com`), a company that provides link building and PR tools, and Fractl (`http://frac.tl`), a content-marketing agency, to find out what types of content was shared over a six-month period. These companies analyzed 220,000 pieces of content using BuzzSumo (`http://buzzsumo.com`), a content-analysis software company.

MarketingSherpa created a chart showing the types of shared content across eleven industries, as shown in Figure 15-5 (`http://www.marketingsherpa.com/article/chart/most-and-least-shared-social-content`).

Most helpful to the question about what gets shared, Andrea Lehr, Brand Relationship Strategist at Fractl (see Figure 15-6), identified the content types:

- **How-to:** The standard problem — solution post
- **Lists:** A numbered or bulleted list about a specific topic
- **What-if posts:** Typically, comparisons of one thing to another
- **Why posts:** The author picks a topic and provides points that support the argument
- **Video:** An article with accompanying video that explains the topic

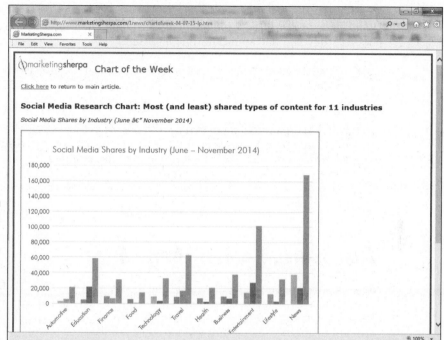

Figure 15-5:
A Marketing-Sherpa chart of the most and least shared social content.

Figure 15-6:
Fractl.

Curious about what type of content made the "most shared" lists? Steve Rayson, co-owner of BuzzSumo, looked at the data collected in the aforementioned study and had some additional findings:

✔ List posts were the most shared content format; how-to articles were the second most shared.

✔ Long-form content performed best (articles over 3,000 words).

✔ Individual picture-list posts have the potential to go viral. These are posts that have pictures as their list items instead of text. Although text list posts did better overall, BuzzSumo found that picture lists were more likely to go viral if they were shared. (`http://buzzsumo.com/blog/buzzfeeds-most-shared-content-format-is-not-what-you-think/`)

Discovering when they share

Several studies concerning the best time to share on social media have been done in recent years. Anyone interested in succeeding at content marketing pays some attention to timing. It makes sense that you'd want to at least attempt to share your content when people are likely to see it.

I found a variety of data presenting conflicting times and recommendations. I share the following findings because this study looks specifically at resharing. Many of the other studies focused on clicks only.

In 2014, Kissmetrics (`http://kissmetrics.com`), an analytics company, reported on the findings collected by Dan Zararella. He looked at when to tweet and post to get the most reshares on Twitter and Facebook (`https://detart.files.wordpress.com/2014/08/science-of-social-timing-part-1.png`). Zararella found that:

✔ **On Twitter:** Six percent of all retweets occurred at 5 p.m. EST, and the best days to tweet were in midweek and on weekends.

✔ **On Facebook:** The best time to get reshares is around noon and a little after 7 p.m. EST, and the best day is Saturday.

It's great to be mindful of general times to get reshares, but you still want to test and experiment. Use these findings as guidelines when you are testing your own social media campaigns. Audience preference can change overnight.

Observing where they share

If you were asked in October of 2015 to list the five most popular social net-working sites, you probably came up with the same list that ebizMBA (http://www.ebizmba.com/articles/social-networking-websites) did:

1. Facebook

2. Twitter

3. LinkedIn

4. Pinterest

5. Google+

These are the go-to sites for sharing that most companies (and users) turn to first. When it comes to your specific audience, some sites may place higher up or down, but these would be the likely choices.

When looking at where your communities congregate, you also want to study niche sites that your audience frequents. For example, if you are a design company you might want to visit Stack Overflow, (http://stackoverflow.com), a Q&A site for developers, or SourceForge (http://sourceforge.net). If you sell electronics and gadgets, you should check out a site like Gizmodo (http://gizmodo.com).

Looking at how people share content

The biggest surprise about sharing is *how* data is shared. Josh Schwartz is a data scientist at Chartbeat (https://chartbeat.com/), a company that measures real-time traffic (see Figure 15-7). Schwartz was asked by Farhad Manjoo at Slate to look at the scrolling and sharing behavior of Slate's audience (www.slate.com/articles/technology/technology/2013/06/how_people_read_online_why_you_won_t_finish_this_article.html), and his findings were very disconcerting. He found that people frequently tweet links to articles they've only partially read. In Slate's case, people scroll only 50 percent of the way before tweeting them. BuzzFeed and other online sites have found similar results.

Think about the implications of this behavior. When you read about how people respond to long-form content, it may mean that they like to share long-form content, but not necessarily read it through to the end. As Manjoo stated, "We're in the age of the skim."

Unfortunately, you can't simply shorten your content if your audience responds to the longer format. You need to give your readers what they want and share. However, you might want to put the most important points and your call to action up higher in the content.

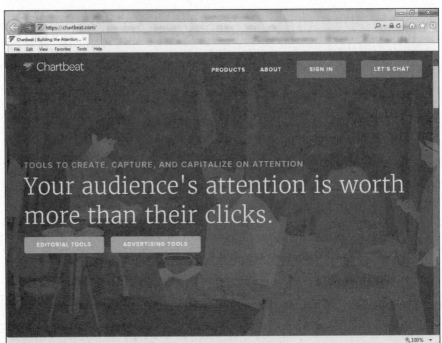

Figure 15-7:
Chartbeat.

In an attempt to more effectively evaluate audience interest, companies like Upworthy, a breaking news site, are looking at "attention minutes." (`http://blog.upworthy.com/post/75795679502/what-uniques-and-pageviews-leave-out-and-why`). This means that companies consider the total amount of time spent on their sites and the total attention given to a specific piece of content. In this way, they can assess audience interest instead of just scrolling behavior.

Adding Social Bookmarking

When you're looking at places where content is shared, don't overlook book-marking sites. Users on these sites share articles they find interesting, and others read them and vote on the ones they like. If your content shows up on one of these sites, it can

✔ Drive traffic to your site

✔ Help you rise in Google search results

✔ Give your content more visibility and brand recognition

✔ Increase your domain authority

Being tagged on one of these sites does not guarantee that the traffic that is generated will stick with you. Don't be disappointed if the increase is a one-off. At least you got some recognition.

The top three bookmarking sites you may want to consider are

- ✔ **StumbleUpon** (`http://Stumbleupon.com`): Now owned by eBay, StumbleUpon is the oldest of the bookmarking sites (2002). This site has a team of searchers who work to find quality content to share.

- ✔ **Digg** (`http://digg.com`): Unlike some of the other sites, Digg has a curated front page. Its content is separated into articles and videos. Users vote by clicking a digg link to signal their approval. You can sort content by time or "most shared."

- ✔ **Reddit** (`http://reddit.com`): On this site, you can create a community of your own called a subreddit. Each community has its own moderators and is separate from the others.

Are you wondering whether you can do anything to make your content even more shareable? Former Wall Street Internet analyst Mary Meeker says that a post gets half of all its shares within 6.5 hours on Twitter and 9 hours on Facebook. So you need to take some actions to keep your content from disappearing. One approach is to keep your tweets under 125 characters, which allows people to add text of their own.

Making SEO a Priority

When it comes to content marketing, the concept of Search Engine Optimization (SEO) is often misunderstood. When SEO was fairly new, content writers were tasked with stuffing as many keywords as possible into a blog post to attract the search engines. This tactic is long gone along with the people who wanted to help you game the system. Google is aware of all the "black hat" techniques that people try to deploy and frequently changes Google's algorithm.

At this point (2016), Google's clear directive is to have you produce quality content that employs keywords that help people find you. Your SEO strategy needs to be well thought out to ensure that your customers can find the content you so carefully planned to share.

Rather than create a complex list of things you need to do, focus instead on a few SEO tasks that will have the biggest impact. You can:

- ✔ **Use long-tail keywords.** You still need to use keywords to be found by the search engines. *Long-tail* keywords, which means keywords that are really phrases, work best. For example, in place of the broad phrase "red shoes," narrow the phrase with "red sandals wedge discount womens."

In other words, make sure to be very descriptive so that when someone is searching for your specific shoe, she can find it.

✔ **Pay attention to mobile.** According to predictions, your mobile audience will soon make up approximately 50 percent of your total audience. Look at your site on all possible devices to ensure that it's mobile ready. The Google Developers site has a "Mobile-Friendly Test" tool that you can use to test your site, as shown in Figure 15-8.

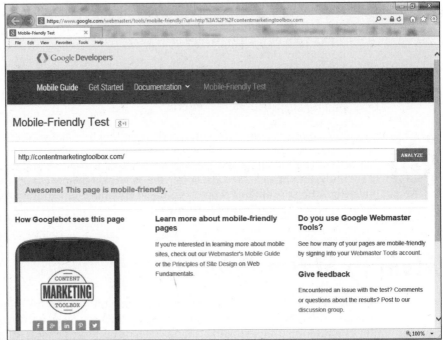

Figure 15-8:
Google site test for my Content-Marketing-Toolbox.com site.

✔ **Make sure that your keywords are in the right places, such as in titles.** Because you're not going to "stuff" your site full of keywords anymore, put them in the places where they can do the most good, such as in your title tag. Google uses a limited number of characters (55) to display what your site is about. Make sure to use them wisely.

✔ **Evaluate results often.** You should use analytics to measure what your users are clicking on. Don't guess.

✔ **Improve site load times.** This is a boring task, but one that you should not overlook. People don't have the patience to wait for your site to load. Ask your webmaster to check loading times and fix if necessary.

✔ **Make sure to optimize for video.** This one is similar to the preceding item about loading times. Even though users love video, they won't wait for yours.

✔ **Play the long game.** The most important Google SEO rules don't really change that much. You need quality content to drive your traffic. Optimization doesn't happen overnight. Prepare to do the right thing year after year and you will be rewarded.

You can always dig deeper into SEO when you have more time or want to engage a professional to work with you.

Looking for some free SEO Tools to get started? Try these:

✔ **Moz (**`https://moz.com/`**):** This company, shown in Figure 15-9, offers great free tools and a paid subscription. The free tools include Open Site Explorer, Followerwonk, MozBar, Moz Local, and MozCast. I mention Followerwonk in Chapter 18 as a great Twitter tool. The rest are equally good. Using these tools, you can do keyword searches, analyze anchor text, and a lot more.

✔ **Ubersuggest (**`http://ubersuggest.org`**):** This free tool, shown in Figure 15-10, is so easy to use that it's perfect for beginners (and experienced users.)

✔ **SEMrush (**`http://www.semrush.com`**):** This is a multifaceted set of tools, shown in Figure 15-11, that helps you develop your SEO, advertising, and link-building strategies. SEMrush also offers paid tools.

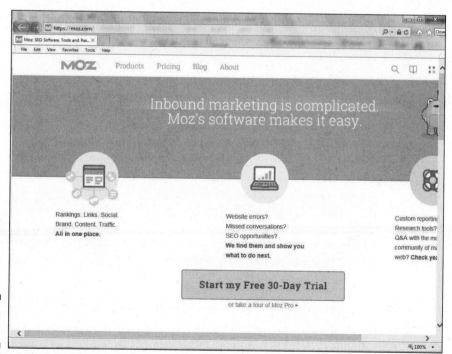

Figure 15-9:
Moz.

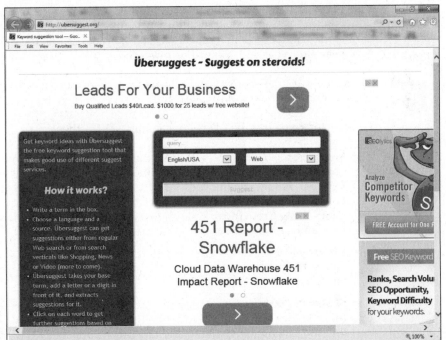

Figure 15-10:
Uber-
suggest.

Figure 15-11:
SEMrush.

Deploying Hashtags to Encourage Sharing

Many people use hashtags on social platforms as an afterthought (or not at all). Don't be one of them. Hashtags really do give your content more visibility and increase the likelihood that you'll be reshared on places like Twitter, Pinterest, and Instagram. People set content alerts for brand names, products, and specific keywords. By using hashtags, you immediately get on people's radar screen and encourage them to check you out.

Understanding hashtags

Although they may seem unfamiliar, hashtags are simply a way to categorize keywords. By adding the # symbol in front of the keyword, you are telling the search engine to pull out and display content designated that way every time someone uses that term. So, if someone on Twitter or other social platform types in the # before a term, that person will be able to see all the tweets that contain it. People can get right to the content that interests them most.

Twitter recommends no more than two hashtags per tweet. The concept of "less is more" applies here.

It's helpful to look at the usefulness of hashtags from two angles. The first is that a hashtag helps you find something; second, it helps you to be found. Sound simple? It really is. For example, if you want people from a specific area — for example, New York City — to find your content, you can add a hashtag like #nyc that makes it easy to spread your message locally. How about borrowing a hashtag that has a devoted group of followers? If you're a writer, you can use #amwriting or #writing to speak to that community.

Using hashtag tools

To search out and use hashtags, you should consider using some of the hashtag tools created to make using them easier. Here are a few to consider.

Do you want to:

- **Participate in a high profile chat?** If you are hosting an online chat, it can get confusing when you try to follow responses in the stream. Using a tool like TweetChat (http://www.tweetchat.com), shown in Figure 15-12, you can isolate your specific tweets posted in real time during the chat.

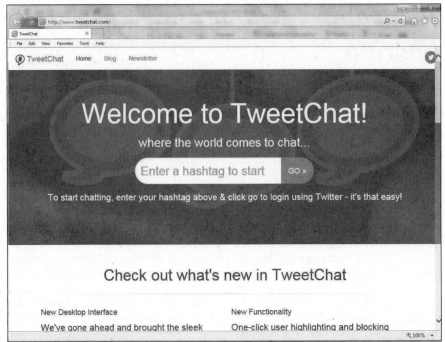

Figure 15-12:
TweetChat.

✔ **Determine which hashtag to use in real time?** When you are creating a tweet, you want to know what tag will most likely garner the highest visibility. A tool such as RiteTag (https://ritetag.com/), shown in Figure 15-13, can help you make the best choice.

✔ **Understand how the tag is being used and who is using it?** Hashtagify (http://hashtagify.me), can show you everything you ever wanted to know about a hashtag you may want to use as your own.

✔ **Register or brand a hashtag?** Using a tool such as http://twubs.com, shown in Figure 15-14, you can register a hashtag as your own.

Still want more sharing tools for your blogs, landing pages, and websites? You can use such free tools as SumoMe (http://sumome.com/) or the WordPress Social Sharing Optimization (WPSSO SSB) tool (https://wordpress.org/plugins/wpsso-ssb/). Both offer free versions.

Check out the last page of this chapter for a mind map of this chapter's content, and download a color version at www.dummies.com/contentmarketingstrategies.

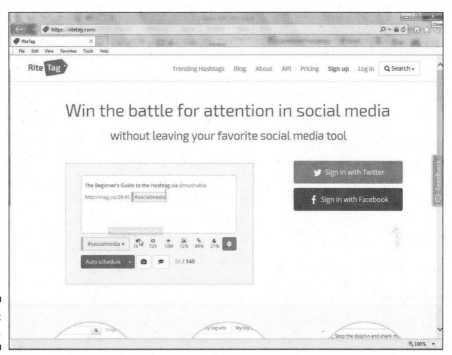

Figure 15-13:
RiteTag.

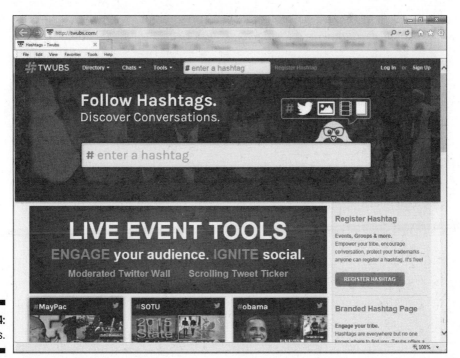

Figure 15-14:
Twubs.

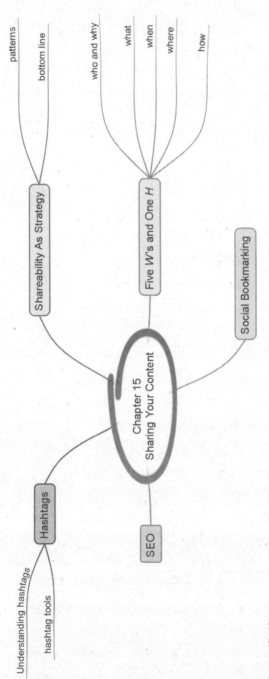

patterns

bottom line

who and why

what

when

where

how

Shareability As Strategy

Five *W*'s and One *H*

Social Bookmarking

Chapter 15
Sharing Your Content

Hashtags

SEO

Understanding hashtags

hashtag tools

Courtesy of ThinkBuzan.

Chapter 16

Looking at Paid, Earned, Shared, and Owned Media

In This Chapter

▶ Considering when to use paid media

▶ Discovering the value of retargeting

▶ Understanding why owned media is important

Have you struggled with the concepts of Paid, Earned, Shared, and Owned media? It's no wonder. Within each of these categories is a rotating variety of options that could confuse even the most seasoned online marketer. Also, because the allocations for each type vary widely, the stakes can be high. Getting it wrong is not an option.

Content marketing has added another layer to the promotion puzzle. Now marketers have to decide the budget mix as well as what to market. Should they pay for product, service, or content promotions, or a mix of all three? In this chapter, you look at each type of media to understand the pros and cons of each. You also see how to put together a strategy that fits your specific needs.

Understanding Types of Media

The notion of Paid, Owned, and Earned media has been the accepted model for several years. In 2014, Mashable reported on a new version of the model in the article, "Why PR is embracing the PESO Model" (`http://mashable.com/2014/12/05/public-relations-industry/`) as shown in Figure 16-1.

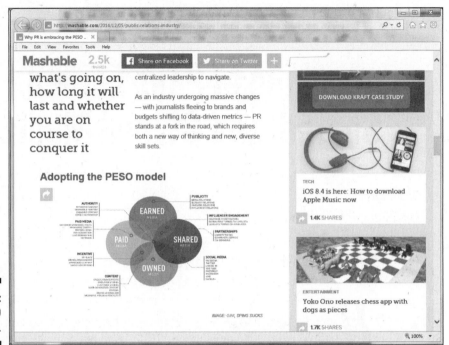

Figure 16-1:
The PESO
model.

The article discusses the PESO model (Paid, Earned, Shared, Owned) suggested by Gini Dietrich, founder of the nontraditional PR firm Arment Dietrich (`http://spinsucks.com`). The PESO model blog post (`http://spinsucks.com/communication/pr-pros-must-embrace-the-peso-model/`), adds Shared media to the traditional mix of Earned, Owned, and Paid. Previously, the media model did not specifically segment out Shared media but instead included it as part of Earned media. It's now segmented as a separate media type because of its importance to the mix.

When you break out Shared media from Earned media, you can evaluate how you will specifically deal with your Shared media strategy. Shared media is not under your control, whereas Earned media can be influenced by your relationships with traditional PR sources such as influencers and publishers.

Reviewing each media type

To help you understand the PESO model, I begin by defining each of the four media types:

✔ **Paid media:** This type of media refers to the advertising promotions that you pay for. When choosing these options, you need a budget and a conviction that you will get a return on the money you spend.

Examples: Facebook ads, promoted tweets, traditional and native advertising, print ads, paid search, mobile ads, app ads, and Amazon ads

✔ **Earned media:** This is the media that you get when other sources recognize and promote your content for you. Your brand or your content is deemed valuable and is showcased in some way or reshared.

Examples: Influencer reviews, traditional PR, and media relations

✔ **Shared media:** This refers to the shares you get from others on the various social media platforms.

Examples: Shares on Facebook, Twitter, Google+, Tumblr, and others

✔ **Owned media:** This type of media is controlled by you and is becoming more and more important as time goes on. I explain why later in this chapter.

Examples: Website, blogs, emails, micro sites, apps, collateral, user-generated content

With shared media, you are part of the conversation without having to specifically buy your way in. That's a great place to be.

Control is a big factor when choosing the media you want to use. When you have a major campaign coming up, you want to know to what extent you can impact the outcome. Table 16-1 shows the amount of control you have over each type of media and the audience target. When making decisions, be aware of these factors.

Table 16-1   Attributes of Paid, Earned, Shared, and Owned Media

Type	*Control of Distribution by Brand*	*Audience Targeted*
Paid	Medium to high	Potential customers
Earned	Low	Potential and current customers (fans)
Shared	Low	Potential and current customers
Owned	High	Current customers

Determining your needs

So how do you determine how much of each media type you should use? You have to strike a careful balance, and this is a question you should frequently revisit. You don't want to spend on ads when your content is effectively being shared organically. Revisions to the mix depend on

✔ **How well your current mix is doing.** Are you satisfied with the recognition and traffic you are getting? If not, you need to take action. But even if you are satisfied, you should plan to check back monthly (or weekly, if you see significant changes) to see whether you're still satisfied with your results.

✔ **How often you launch promotions.** If you frequently launch new campaigns for your products or services, you'll want to prepare special targeted campaigns to get the word out. These could include emails or mini sites. After you've launched a timed campaign, don't let it sit online past its prime.

Make sure you've assigned someone the job of monitoring the promotion site. When the promotion is over, revise the site to send visitors to something new. You never know when someone will find the link and go there. Disappointing a new visitor is lazy marketing and bad for your brand.

We've all gone to dead campaign links that make us feel annoyed or forgotten. Don't be guilty of ignoring old links. You're wasting the effort and money you put into getting someone to notice your brand.

✔ **How and where you want your customers to encounter you in their daily online travels.** If you are targeting customers on a particular platform, you need to buy the ads that will reach that specific audience. It can be money well spent. It will also feed your organic traffic. If you are unsure whether your audience is on that platform, you'll want to test first. Don't guess.

Utilizing Paid Media

Of all the categories in the PESO model, Paid media is the easiest to understand. It includes traditional advertising like paid search as well as the newer forms of advertising such as retargeting and native advertising, discussed next.

Discovering retargeting

Over the last few years, banner advertising has had a bumpy ride. Because of the constant barrage of these ads, online customers developed what is known as *banner blindness*, the ability of users to ignore (subconsciously or otherwise) banner ads on websites.

According to the Content Marketing Institute, "consumers reject banner ads at rates greater than 99%" (http://contentmarketinginstitute.com/wp-content/uploads/2013/10/B2B_Research_2014_CMI.pdf).

For this reason, companies had to figure out how to make their ads visible again. Enter retargeting. You've probably heard the term retargeting but may not be sure what it's about. Retargeting refers to the ad tactic that allows a brand to anonymously place a bit of code (called a pixel) on a user's site when she clicks on items on her website but doesn't buy. Then when the user is browsing around the web and hits one of the ad servers purchased by the marketer, the product is displayed again. This gives the marketer "a second bite at the apple." The marketer is paying to offer the customer another chance to buy its product.

This tactic has proven to be very effective. One obvious reason is that you are showing people things they expressed an interest in. Suddenly you are not an anonymous advertiser but rather someone showing them an item that got their attention.

Retargeting also works well to retrieve abandoned carts on your websites. According to JeremySaid.com (http://www.jeremysaid.com/turn-shopping-cart-abandonment-secret-weapon-creating-sales/) up to 72 percent of visitors may return to purchase something within 12–24 hours. By sending an email that is triggered by an abandoned cart, you can significantly increase your sales. In Figure 16-2, you see an example of a retargeted ad in my Facebook feed.

According to AdRoll's 2015 "State of the Industry" report, more than 90 percent of marketers say that retargeting converts better than search, email, and display advertising.

Dealing with native advertising

As we discussed, banner blindness caused advertisers to seek new ways to capture attention. One method they have increasingly begun to use is called native advertising (NA). NA refers to advertising that is made to match the editorial content on its respective platform.

Business Insider, a business, celebrity, and technology news website that has done extensive research on Native Advertising (http://www.business insider.com/spending-on-native-ads-will-soar-as-publishers-and-advertisers-take-notice-2014-11), predicts that by 2018, spending on native advertising will double to more than twenty billion dollars. Clearly, advertisers see it as a valuable form of advertising.

Figure 16-2:
Retargeted
ad.

Retargeted ad on Facebook

One humorous example of native advertising was produced by Gawker Media and Newcastle Ale using the native format to showcase its product. `http://studioatgawker.kinja.com/weve-disguised-this-newcastle-ad-as-an-article-to-get-1508339241`. The ad is titled "We've Disguised This Newcastle Ad as an Article to Get You to Click It" and is shown in Figure 16-3.

This form of advertising has raised the hackles of journalists who feel that this practice can be deceptive. Readers, on the other hand, haven't voiced a major concern and these ads are performing well.

Both sides of the controversy have their defenders. Some journalists feel that readers won't recognize the content as an ad. Publishers say that as long as the ad says "sponsored" or "advertisement," no confusion should ensue. You'll have to decide for yourself whether this type of media should be included in your ad buy.

Figure 16-3:
Native ad
from
Gawker and
Newcastle
Ale.

Considering programmatic buying

The ability to make ad decisions in real time is another innovation for advertisers. It's called programmatic buying and allows brands to send ads to their potential customers via such things as emails or mobile phone numbers based on their current website behavior.

The use of programmatic buying requires that brands put automated functions in place on their owned channels. The customer data that's collected triggers the buying of specific ads that are directly responsive to users' behaviors. This is different from real-time bidding (RTB), which is associated with inexpensive inventory. Proponents of programmatic buying emphasize that their ads are linked to quality interactions from buyers.

This type of paid advertising has several benefits, which include the following:

✔ Ads can be seen across the consumer's devices — mobile devices as well as laptops. They don't have to be in one place.

✔ Advertisers have greater control over what their customers see, and when. They don't have to wait until the customer triggers the ad online.

- ✔ Real-time customer interactions can be measured to provide valuable insights and help advertisers make predictive decisions.

- ✔ This type of advertising replaces the tediousness of making individual buying decisions manually.

Programmatic buying is still evolving, so do your homework.

Finding out what you need to know from advertisers

Knowing your budget is not the only thing you need to concern yourself with when you are spending money to advertise. Because of all the decisions you have to make, you want to make sure that you have all the facts about the platform on which your ad will be placed. Here are some items you'll want to consider when making choices:

- ✔ **Demographics:** Who is the audience that receives these native ads? How do the platform owners slice and dice their measures?

- ✔ **Geographics:** What kind of geographical information does the native advertising platform collect and how granular can it get?

- ✔ **Reporting functions:** What and when are analytics available to you? Can you get custom reports?

- ✔ **Creative materials necessary:** What do you need to supply your advertising platform, and in what time frame?

- ✔ **Special sauce:** What does this platform offer that you can't get elsewhere?

Championing Earned Media

Earned media is prized because it gives you the boost that you hoped for when you planned your content. You and your team dreamed of hitting the front pages of digital magazines and the local news with the content you carefully crafted. Unfortunately, in today's crowded market, garnering headlines takes a lot more effort.

Want to capture the media's attention for your content? According to the Statistic Brain Research Institute website, the average human's attention span in 2015 is 8.25 seconds, down from 12 seconds in 2000 (http://www.statisticbrain.com/attention-span-statistics/). The average goldfish's attention span is nine seconds. That's why your job is so hard.

In Chapter 18, you delve into the role of influencers who are crucial to making your earned media campaign a success. In this section, you look at the role that journalists play in spreading your message. Several groups have suggested that hiring a journalist to work on your content marketing efforts is a good idea. Journalists know the lay of the land and are familiar with what will get you the right kind of attention.

So how do you reach out directly if you want to make contact with journalists who cover your subject? Several tools can make this outreach easier:

- Help a Reporter Out (HARO) (`http://www.helpareporter.com`), shown in Figure 16-4. This service was started as a small business by Peter Shankman and purchased by Vocus in 2010. It helps reporters find sources for their stories and helps marketers find journalists who want to write about them.

- Media Kitty (`http://www.mediakitty.com/`), shown in Figure 16-5. This service lets journalists and marketers contact each other via the online platform. You can access the journalist database or connect with reporters who have a specific story they are researching.

- Muck Rack (`http://muckrack.com/`), shown in Figure 16-6. This service keeps you in touch with the stories that reporters are interested in, and much more. You can sign up as a marketer and get in touch with journalists who are interested in your specific topic.

Figure 16-4:
Help a
Reporter
Out.

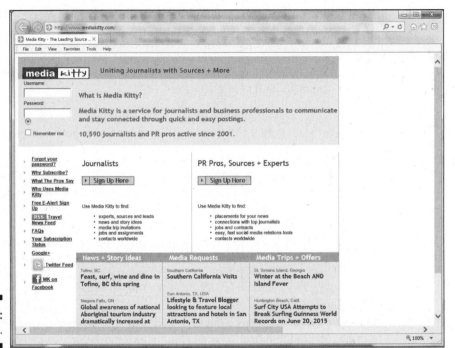

Figure 16-5:
Media Kitty.

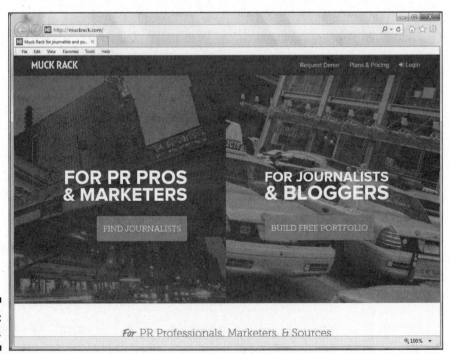

Figure 16-6:
Muck Rack.

How much does your CEO make?

One the best examples of earned media is Gravity Payments (`http://gravitypayments.com/`), a credit card payment company. Dan Price, 30, CEO of Gravity Payments, announced in April of 2015 that he was going to take a pay cut and raise the lowest salary in his company to $70,000 over a three-year period. He decided to sacrifice his own million-dollar salary to improve the lives of people in his company. He read that people who had a baseline salary of $70,000 would be able to lead fulfilling lives without having to worry about paying their bills.

After this announcement, Dan was featured on multiple news shows, and articles about him appeared in all the major media outlets, including the *New York Times* and *Money*

magazine. Social media was ablaze with information. He was thrust into the spotlight and hailed as a hero. His company got more publicity in one day than it did in all ten years of its existence.

His plan was to do something worthwhile for his employees rather than get free publicity. However, he got both, because overnight Gravity Payments became a company that cared about its employees and, by extension, their customers.

Even if your company cannot make such a generous contribution, it is worth the effort to look at how you can contribute to the improvement of your community.

Enhancing Shared Media

You'd be hard pressed to find an online business today that doesn't try to make the most of its social media efforts. Whether it succeeds is another question. Businesses know that shared media is low cost and packs a powerful punch. You've heard that friends and other customers make up the most powerful and credible sales force for any product. But are you maximizing the effects of shared media? Doing so can be difficult when you realize that the social referral half-life of the average tweet is 6.5 hours, according to Mary Meeker's 2014 Internet Trends Report. The PDF can be found here: `http://kpcbweb2.s3.amazonaws.com/files/85/Internet_Trends_2014_vFINAL_-_05_28_14-_PDF.pdf?1401286773`.

Some marketers focus the majority of their attention on shared media. You could be making a big mistake if you do that, however. Why? Isn't social media sharing the best way to reach new customers? Yes, but not having a balanced mix puts your media plan in jeopardy.

The problem with focusing all your attention on social media is that the platform your content is on is "rented," so to speak. That is, you don't own the land on which your content is sitting. The community you have built is not really your own. If one of those social platforms decided to limit the amount of content you can share about a specific topic, you'd be hard pressed to get that platform to reverse its decision. It cares about its business model, not yours.

In addition, the attention given to content on social platforms is unpredictable. If you want to participate in a topic that's trending, social platforms are the best place. If you want to develop in-depth content, be sure to balance your mix.

Amplifying Owned Media

As the creator and distributor of your content, you are free to publish as much and as often as you like. You don't have to worry that Facebook or Twitter will change their policies and wipe out your best content. Owned media is becoming ever more important because of the control it provides the marketer. According to Melissa Hoffmann of Adweek, July 20, 2014, 27 percent of marketers surveyed believe that in five years, earned media will be more important than paid and owned (including shared) media.

Owned media is not free media. You have to budget for the creation and development of it. So when you are planning your media mix, bear in mind that it may cost as much to create it as it does to use paid media with something you can repurpose.

Looking at the role of press releases

I'm sure when you see the term press release you think that they are past their prime. But think again. Press releases have a place in your current media strategy. Just don't consider them strictly owned media. Press releases have evolved along with all the other practices that marketers utilize. In addition, Google has changed its algorithm with regard to the value of press releases for SEO, so the game has changed. Throwing a bunch of keywords into the release will not gain you any additional page rank.

The dissemination of press releases is under your control, so that is partly why earned media is in the mix. But you also need to look at how press releases are received by customers. In today's marketplace, a press release should be considered more of a paid advertorial, according to Cheryl Conner in Forbes (http://www.forbes.com/sites/cherylsnappconner/2013/08/28/do-press-releases-still-matter-yes-but-not-like-you-think/). This means that people will consider the content of your release to be sponsored material.

Here are three ways you can improve the value of your press release:

- ✔ If your press release is picked up by a major outlet like Forbes, link that on your website to drive traffic.

- ✔ In the press release, insert a call to action (CTA) to a landing page that has clear value to your customers (such as a free trial).

- ✔ In the press release, link to a piece of content on your site that has already garnered great publicity so that even more people can find it.

The downside to press releases is that it's difficult to determine the return on investment (ROI).

In case you're wondering what would be an effective topic for a press release today, these topics still carry enough weight to make it worth your while:

- ✔ Significant financial news about your company

- ✔ A major shift in business model

- ✔ Corporate giving to charities

- ✔ A new product announcement

- ✔ Additions in staff and promotions

Spreading the message

One of the truly inspired examples of owned media was detailed by Contently in a blog post written by Aaron Taube (http://contently.com/strate gist/2015/05/06/how-the-big-marketing-activity-coloring-book-fueled-marketos-insanely-lucrative-lead-gen-machine/). It recounts how Marketo (http://marketo.com), a marketing software company, created a piece of content that generated more than $500,000. What was this marketing masterpiece? It's a 30-page coloring book called "The Big Marketing Activity Coloring Book" (http://www.marketo.com/ebooks/the-big-marketing-activity-coloring-book), shown in Figure 16-7. You probably agree that at first blush the idea sounds a bit crazy. Do professional marketers want to spend time coloring and filling in puzzles? Perhaps. What is clear is they wanted to download and see the inventive marketing piece.

The e-book was entertaining and educational. It was a creative break from the norm and garnered a great deal of attention. Most important is that when they go to the link, potential customers can see a demo, get a free trial, or contact the company. That's a big win!

Figure 16-7:
Marketo's
Big
Marketing
Activity
Coloring
Book.

The coloring book idea is inventive and fun. Couldn't your company come up with a content piece that is fun and inviting? The landing page isn't costly or difficult to construct. It just requires you to think about luring your visitors to a page that entertains and sells.

Creating a Framework for Achieving the Right Mix

Unfortunately, you have no sure-fire way to guarantee that your content will be seen and shared, so it becomes even more necessary to leverage Paid, Earned, Shared, and Owned tactics. The strategy of bringing the four types of media together is called *converged media*, a term coined by the research company Altimeter Group (http://altimetergroup.com).

Are you curious to know how other companies are dividing up their spending? According to the Econsultancy Marketing Budgets Report 2015, created in association with Oracle Marketing Cloud (https://blogs.oracle.com/marketingcloud/new-2015-marketing-budget-benchmarks), their survey found that the marketers were dividing up their budgets as follows:

✔ **Paid media:** 39 percent

✔ **Owned media:** 35 percent

✔ **Earned media (includes shared):** 26 percent

Are you surprised to see that Paid media is leading the list? Don't be. With all the new tools I've discussed, such as native advertising and retargeting, marketers are spending more on new technology to solve advertising problems. Also note that Owned media is next. Both types give more control to the marketer.

The framework shown in Figure 16-8 and described in the following sections illustrates one way to think about putting a converged strategy together. You can use this framework as the catalyst for your own custom plan. Be aware that because of the cyclical nature of media, you won't be able to assess each type in a vacuum. The ability to use the data you collect at each stage will improve the ongoing decisions you make. What I've depicted here is a way to think about how this media can work together.

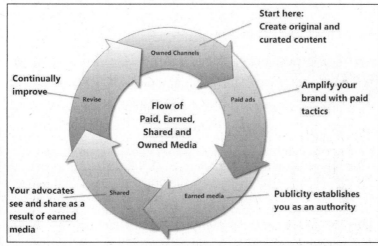

Figure 16-8:
Diagram of a framework for finding the right balance.

Section 1: Owned Channels

Begin your plan in the upper-right section of the cycle called Owned Channels (refer to Figure 16-8). Remember that this includes both your original and curated content on the channels you own. Starting here to develop your strategy makes the most sense because it is controlled by you. These are your company's assets, and improving the way you develop and distribute them can only make them more valuable.

Some questions to ask:

- Do you know what topics your audience wants to learn about?
- Have you done an evaluation of the content you have so that you know what you can repurpose?
- Do you have the people and technology in place to get your content out quickly?

Owned content is the foundation of your strategy. Give careful consideration to how much of your budget to dedicate to this part of your strategy, because owned content is what gives your brand visibility. Don't skimp on this. It is the raw material you will use to get results.

Section 2: Shared Media

In Section 2 (refer to Figure 16-8), you need to look at the traction you've gained from the content you published.

Some questions to ask:

- How much content was shared on all your social platforms?
- Did some topics resonate better than others?
- Did some formats get people's attention?

Shared media gives you an indication of what resonates with your current audience. Is your fan base sharing your content in large numbers? Use the information about how your content is being shared as a barometer to determine how your relationship with customers is faring. In this section, you see the traction you got from news outlets, influencers, and other high-value attention for your content. You evaluate the content you created and curated and determine what has garnered the most attention. The caveat here is that depending on how large your audience is, you may not have received the attention you expected.

Section 3: Paid Ads

Based on the response you received to your new content, you need to decide what to promote, and which advertising methods to use. These methods can include such things as Facebook ads or Promoted Tweets. Using this method at this stage helps you to leverage advertising to gain visibility for your content.

Some questions to ask:

- ✔ Do you know how much you can spend on several pilot experiments to test what works best?
- ✔ Should you consider native advertising?

Section 4: Earned Media

After you've paid to get your brand story out there into the world, you can push the story even further by connecting with influencers and others who might be interested in your content.

Some questions to ask:

- ✔ Have you identified several influencers to whom you can reach out when you have content you want to promote?
- ✔ Do you have media relationships that you have developed over time?

Section 5: Evaluate and Revise

In Section 5, you evaluate the results of your PESO strategy and make plans to revise your mix.

Ask whether you have selected the metrics you will use to determine whether your efforts are successful.

You should alter your strategy to incorporate what you've learned in the first complete cycle. This is the time to consider whether you're clear about your goals and perhaps revise them to incorporate what you've learned.

As suggested in the preceding plan, many marketers are starting to see better results when they focus more directly on getting the content out into the world rather than just creating more and more content. If no one sees it, your efforts are wasted. You might mistakenly believe that your content doesn't have value, when in reality, it just wasn't seen by enough people to have an impact.

Check out the next page for a mind map of this chapter's content, and download a color version at www.dummies.com/contentmarketingstrategies.

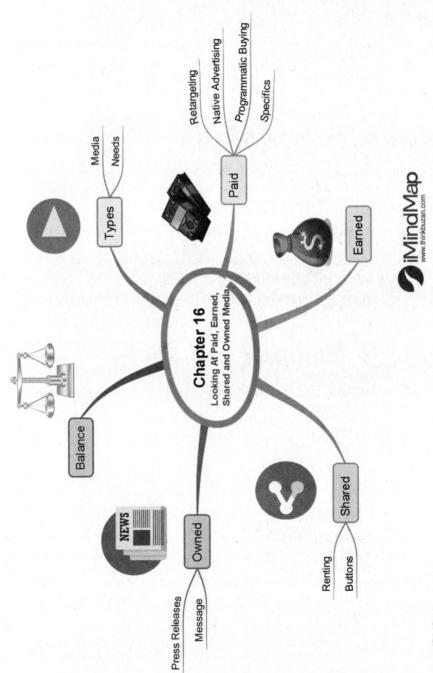

Chapter 17

Delving into Syndication and Guest Posting

*I*t's great when your content is discovered by a new audience. Your ticket to recognition is to distribute your content to as many eyeballs as you can. But how do you make that happen? You can't count on getting all your traffic from your owned media, such as a blog or website. To get the word out, you need to use other venues, such as social media and other people's blogs.

Two great strategies you can use to find new audiences are syndication and guest posting. Some people get confused and think they are the same thing because they involve posting content on someone else's site. But the two actually have very different characteristics and benefits, which I discuss in this chapter. The main difference between syndicated content and guest posting is that with syndicated content, you are sharing content that was already posted on your site. When you guest post, you are creating original content that is first seen on an influencer blog with a link back to your site.

In this chapter, we look at the ins and outs of syndication and guest posting and the need to distribute your content to as wide an audience as possible.

Understanding Syndication

Syndication is the distribution of your content on other blogs and websites so that it can be found by people who might not frequent your blog. The Internet Content Syndication Council (`http://www.internetcontent syndication.org/`), shown in Figure 17-1, defines syndication as follows: "Internet content syndication is the controlled placement of the same content on multiple partnering Internet destinations." The council defines *controlled placement* as content that is placed on destination sites, "by the content owner or its syndication agent," with the goal being to "maximize the content's exposure to desired audiences."

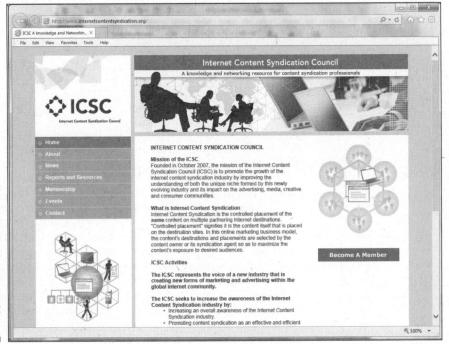

Figure 17-1: The Internet Content Syndication Council promotes the growth of content syndication.

A key part of that definition is the notion that the content owner is in charge of deciding what content to use and how it will be placed. We break each of those out for you below.

But first, you're probably curious to know how much of your content is wise to syndicate. Should you consider syndicating everything? The recommendation of major content marketing platforms like Curata (`http://curata.com`) is to strive for the balance shown in Table 17-1.

Table 17-1	Suggested Content Mix	
Type of Content	*Description of Content*	*Amount of Content Recommended*
Original	New content written by you and posted on your blog	65%
Curated	Content written by others which you comment about on your blog	25%
Syndicated	New content written by you shared on other people's blogs	10%

As you can see, syndicating a lot of your content is not recommended. You want to provide enough content to get people's attention, but not so much that you weaken your own site's authority.

 According to the Content Marketing Institute's survey "B2B Content Marketing: 2013 Benchmarks, Budgets and Trends-North America," 26 percent of B2B content marketers used licensed or syndicated content. (B2B stands for companies that market as a business to another business.)

Looking at content specifics

When you consider syndicating your content, you have some choices to make. None of your choices are irrevocable. You can choose to try something and see how it works. With that in mind, here are some decisions to make:

✔ **Type of content:** There is no real limit to the kind of content that can be syndicated. As long as it's digital, a place to syndicate it on the web probably exists. Types can include:

- Blogs
- Articles
- Video
- Audio
- Landing pages
- Micro sites
- e-books
- Slide shows

✔ **Amount of content:** When you syndicate your content, you don't necessarily have to show the entire post. You can choose to show snippets, thumbnails, or just the links to video and audio. What you show very much depends on what's right for you and what the syndicator requires.

In case you're confused about how you might slice and dice your content, here are some thoughts about what to display for specific purposes:

- ✔ **To get traffic, try snippets and backlinks.** That way, the reader has to come back to your site to see the original post.

- ✔ **To build awareness and thought leadership, use the full article.** You want the reader to see your full post on the authority site.

- ✔ **To expose your products, use headlines, paragraphs, and images of the product.** You want to pique potential customers' interest.

One central issue that arose about syndication deals is how Google rates syndicated content. Google penalizes duplicate content, so some bloggers were afraid that their syndicated article would be considered duplicate content. But there is a simple solution to this problem that your webmaster can quickly put in place. A syndicated article can be tagged (`rel=canonical`) so that it will not be seen as duplicate content. There are also other methods to deal with this issue, and your webmaster should be familiar with those methods.

Uncovering syndication types

Not all syndication is created equal. There are three primary ways of syndicating your content that you should be aware of. You can use a mix of these to suit your needs, as described in the following sections.

Free content

You can freely syndicate your content using a method called Really Simple Syndication (RSS). This tactic is sometimes referred to as self-syndication because you don't need anyone's approval to set it up. To get started, you create a free feed of the content you're interested in sharing (usually a blog, but you're not limited to that).

The most popular tool used to set up a feed is FeedBurner, owned by Google. Sign into your free Google account from this link: `https://accounts.google.com/signup` and then follow the steps to create the feed. FeedBurner also provides a way for people to receive your updates via email.

After your feed is created, anyone interested in reading your updates with be able to subscribe and view it in a blog reader. Current blog reader favorites include Feedly (`http://feedly.com/i/welcome`), a free service shown in Figure 17-2.

Digg Reader (`http://digg.com/reader/#sign-in`), shown in Figure 17-3, is another free service and is easy to use.

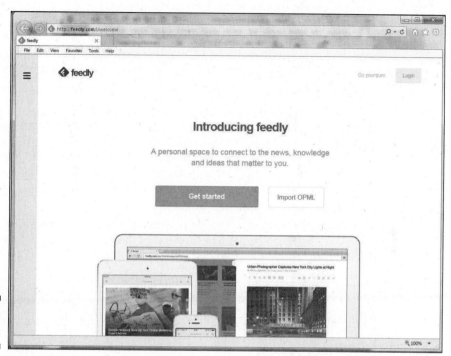

Figure 17-2:
Feedly.

Figure 17-3:
Digg
Reader.

Licensed content

When you license your content, you make an agreement to allow either a syndicate or an individual publisher (such as Social Media Today (`http://socialmediatoday.com`; see Figure 17-4) to distribute your content after it is published on your site.

As you would expect, major syndicators who distribute to popular blogs like FastCompany.com or Forbes.com have strict quality standards. If they determine that you meet these qualifications, you can sign up to have your content distributed. It is usually charged as a pay per click (PPC) fee. You set a budget using their tool and you can get clicks until that budget is reached.

Supported content that you advertise

These syndicators have agreements with advertisers to display ads along with your content. You get a percentage of the revenue that is generated from the ads that are clicked.

Figure 17-4:
Social
Media
Today.

Looking at Online Syndicators

To give you an idea of what you will find when you begin to investigate syndication, here are some specific examples of two of the larger syndicators:

✔ **Outbrain** (`http://www.outbrain.com/`): Major syndicators like Outbrain, shown in Figure 17-5, produce results that can be measured based on their pay per click technique. They work with a variety of high-quality publishers.

Figure 17-5:
Outbrain.

One example of how content was used to great effect appears in the work Outbrain did for The Line (`https://www.theline.com`), a new luxury fashion brand. The Line has an online store and an interesting story to tell about its retail space. That space is an apartment (actually called "The Apartment") on Greene Street in Manhattan, New York. You have to make an appointment to see the merchandise.

The Line's online content is composed of stories and photos that relate to art and fashion icons (go to `https://www.theline.com/stories`), as shown in Figure 17-6. Outbrain was able to use The Line's unique content to get one hundred million impressions in three months. The Line also saw a 72 percent increase in transactions.

✔ **Taboola** (`http://www.Taboola.com/`): Shown in Figure 17-7, Taboola operates in a similar fashion to Outbrain and has a proprietary search engine that determines where your content should be placed. It also does native advertising.

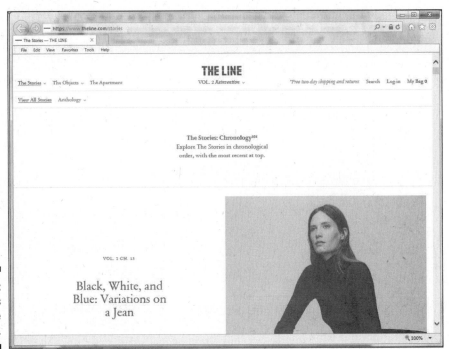

Figure 17-6:
The Line's
online
content.

Figure 17-7:
Taboola.

Establishing Your Syndication Plan

When you are new to syndication, you should educate yourself about the companies and their pros and cons. Here are some things you can do before you choose a syndicator:

- ✔ **Determine your syndication goals.** It's important that you understand your goals for syndication. Goals may include getting more traffic to your site, exposing your products to a new audience, or establishing your own thought leadership.

- ✔ **Evaluate your content.** Obviously, your goals determine the type of content that you pick to syndicate. For example, if you want to become a thought leader, you want to use content that shows off your particular expertise. If you want traffic, you might choose a how-to or a list article about a particular topic.

One idea to consider when writing content with an eye toward syndication is to provide inline links. An *inline link* is a link to another piece of content from within your post. When you write a quality post, you likely reference other people's articles with a link. Adding a link or two to relevant articles on your site is also permissible and can encourage readers to click back to your site. But use these links with care. You don't want to seem to be engaging in blatant self-promotion.

- ✔ **Choose the type of syndication that will work for you.** As mentioned previously, three types of syndication are available to you. Determine the types that will fit your audience and your goals. Be willing to experiment.

- ✔ **Investigate options.** Each syndicator will have different requirements. Look at each one to understand its business model.

- ✔ **Look at what you will be required to supply.** Many of the large syndicators will help you get your content set up and distributed. Find out how much support you can expect and what resources, if any, you need to supply. Also find out what content formats are required. For example, some syndicators may require a thumbnail or an image.

- ✔ **Find out how often new content is distributed.** Learn about the schedule the syndicator uses to refresh your content. How often will new content be seen?

- ✔ **Length of the deal and renewal options.** Find out how long a term you need to sign up for and what the cancellation policy is.

After you have collected all this information, you will be ready to select a syndicator and look at the contract it's proposing.

Discovering Guest Posting

Guest posting has become very popular with bloggers and brand representatives because it helps them cut through the noise to reach a new audience. A guest post is a post that has been written and accepted for publication to a popular blog. It exposes that writer to people who might not be aware of the writer's (or company's) brand.

Benefitting from guest posting

Many great benefits can be derived from guest posting. It can help you in several areas:

- **Company brand awareness:** It can help new audiences find your brand.

- **Personal thought leader status:** It can demonstrate your knowledge and expertise. It will also serve as a sample of your writing skills.

- **Product and service exposure:** It may potentially drive the sales of a product or service that is discovered when readers go to your site after reading your post.

- **Link building:** You are building links to other popular sites.

- **Social proof:** It will demonstrate that a major blogger deems your content worthy of a posting on his or her site.

- **Traffic:** New readers may visit your site and spend time on it.

- **Shareability:** It offers great potential for your content being shared on social platforms.

Guest posting: According to Matt Cutts

In 2014, controversy developed over the tactic of guest posting. Matt Cutts, head of the Google Webspam team wrote a post on his personal blog at https://www.mattcutts.com/blog/guest-blogging/ that included the following: "Okay, I'm calling it: if you're using guest blogging as a way to gain links in 2014, you should probably stop. Why? Because over time, it's become a more and more spammy practice, and if you're doing a lot of guest blogging, then you're hanging out with really bad company."

The web exploded the way it often does when any web tactic is pronounced dead, especially by a distinguished blogger. Much back and forth ensued. People wrote to say that he was wrong and misguided. Finally, Cutts clarified that what he meant to say was don't use guest blogging for search engine optimization purposes. Crisis averted. Using guest posting is okay if you create valuable posts and share them on well-regarded sites — which is what you were planning to do anyway, right?

Guest posting is not necessarily a quick way to promote your work. It takes some solid investigation and effort. But as you can see, the benefits can be significant.

Pitching your guest posting to a blogger

If you are going to pitch a guest post to a blogger with a large audience, you'd better do exhaustive research and know exactly what the person's blog is about. The following sections cover seven actions you need to take before you ever write a single word. Each section also provides cautions against what *not* to do.

Be clear about your goals for guest posting

Earlier, I list several benefits that you can derive from guest posting. Figure out which benefits you need so that you can write a post that will target those specific goals. Well-known blogger Danny Iny from Firepole Marketing (`http://FirepoleMarketing.com`), shown in Figure 17-8, credits 80 guest posts he wrote with increasing his blog traffic by 1,000 percent in one year.

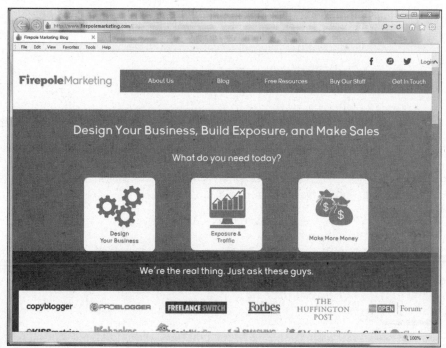

Figure 17-8: Firepole Marketing.

Possible fatal mistake: Writing a guest post that doesn't help you with your own business goals. If you just want to be noticed, then being accepted for publication is good. But you might have additional goals that require you to think more carefully about what you put into your author bio or call to action.

Find the right blogs in your niche that accept guest posts

As you study the blogs in your niche, make sure that your post speaks directly to those blogs' audiences. To gain this knowledge, you have to actually read and evaluate the blog as a whole. No cutting corners.

One of the quick ways to find blogs that accept guest posts is to search Google for "guest posting blogs list." This search returns lots of lists of blogs in various niches that you can investigate.

Possible fatal mistake: Sending a pitch to a blog that is in your niche but isn't right for that blog regardless. It will be immediately apparent to the blogger that you don't understand her blog.

Learn about the blog's readers

It's one thing to *think* you know what a blog audience is interested in. It's another to *really* know. Make an effort to learn about the audience you will be writing for. Read the comments; also, create Google alerts (`https://www.google.com/alerts`; see Figure 17-9) for specific product names or people related to the blog.

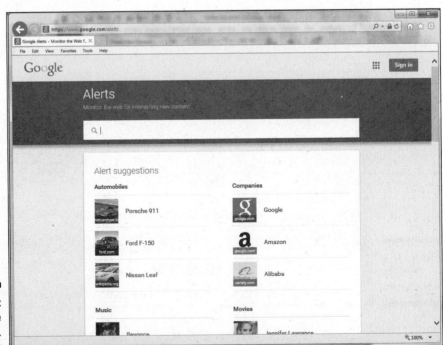

Figure 17-9:
Google
Alerts.

Possible fatal mistake: Writing for the wrong audience.

Evaluate the tone, language, and style of the post

This step is a crucial one that many writers skip. You want to understand the specific way in which the blog addresses its readers. You also want to look at the headlines and see the blog's style. Because headlines are the key to getting any post read, it's important to make sure you match the blog's headline style. I cover headlines in depth in Chapter 12.

Possible fatal mistake: Writing too informally or not matching the tone. If a blog's headlines eschew hype, don't send one that has exclamation points.

Discover the topics that resonate with the audience and pick two or three to pitch.

Here's where the rubber meets the road. You need to get into the blog and see what specific topics the audience cares about. Look on the home page to see the list of top articles. If the blog has a word cloud, check it out to see what the major topics are. Posts also will most likely have article keywords listed below them. Check those out as well.

Another quick way to see what posts are the most popular is to go get a free account at Ahrefs (`http://ahrefs.com`) and choose Site Explorer, as shown in Figure 17-10. Type in the domain name of the blog. You can

Figure 17-10: Ahrefs search for a blog domain.

see all sorts of helpful information, including top content, global rank, and domain rank.

Possible fatal mistake: Picking topics that don't serve the blogger's community. Don't decide to talk about something that isn't of interest to the blog even if it's a pet topic of yours. Focus on serving that blog's audience.

Pitch according to the instructions on the blog

If the blog's owner or staff accepts guest posts and has taken the time to write instructions for submission of guest posts, don't ignore them. Follow those instructions to the letter and show the blog's creators that you are respectful of their time and objectives.

Possible fatal mistake: Not checking first to see whether they even accept guest posts, or just winging it on how you write the post. You'll probably get back an answer that says, "Please resubmit your request and follow our submission guidelines."

Send your pitch and wait to hear back

Write your pitch and send it off. Of course, check for misspellings, bad grammar, and typos before you send anything. You can follow up with the blog if you don't hear back, but wait a couple of weeks. Popular bloggers get many pitches a week. Don't sound impatient — just ask about the pitch.

Possible fatal mistake: Sending a pitch that doesn't recognize the human connection. In a recent blog post called "How To Land a Guest Post Every Time: 21 Secret Tips," Mary Jaksch, Editor-in-Chief at Write to Done (see Figure 17-11), had some pointed tips about relationships when sending a pitch. Here's a sampling:

- ✔ "Remember that you are an equal human being."
- ✔ "Check your tone — do you sound confident and respectful, or arrogant?"
- ✔ "Compliment the blogger — but don't compromise your integrity" (http://writetodone.com/how-to-land-a-guest-post-every-time-21-secret-tips/).

In a nutshell, you should be respectful but not submissive. You want to demonstrate clear leadership in your own right. The authority blogger wants to know that she is introducing her audience to a qualified leader.

Preparing to guest post

Your pitch has been accepted! Here's what to do next.

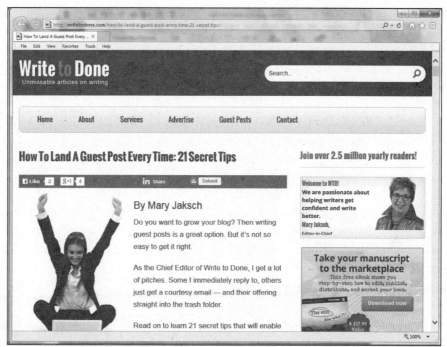

Figure 17-11:
The Write to
Done blog.

Take the time to create a masterpiece

Now is not the time to be lazy. You worked hard to get this gig, so make it worth your while. Make sure to check the requirements so you know what length the post should be.

If you have leeway, recent studies show that 1,500–2,000 words is the most popular length for a blog post.

Possible fatal mistake: Not taking the care and effort required. Ramit Sethi, the owner of the popular blog "I Will Teach You To Be Rich" (http://www.iwillteachyoutoberich.com/; see Figure 17-12), said that it takes him roughly 12 hours to complete a guest post. Sethi is a bestselling *New York Times* author and yet he devotes a substantial amount of time to each of his guest posts. If you hope to get your guest post on a major blog, you'll have to match his dedication.

Including graphics and other images guarantees that more people will read and share your guest post. In fact, according to Twitter, photos average a 35 percent boost in retweets.

Spend time on the author bio and prepare your links carefully

The author bio serves as your publicity billboard. It's your only chance to get readers to pay attention to either your call to action or a link back to your

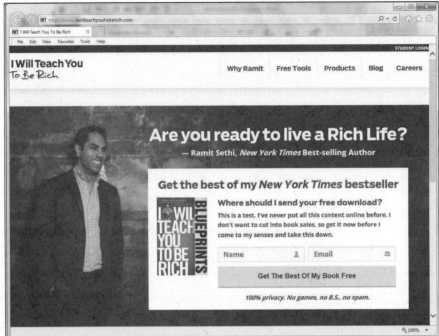

Figure 17-12:
The I Will
Teach You
To Be Rich
blog.

site. One key to reaping major value from a guest post is to make sure that when readers come back to your site from your author bio link, they have something valuable and impressive to see.

Possible fatal mistake: Your own site is not ready for prime time. One great guest post won't make up for your shoddy site design and poorly written content. If you don't have your online home in tip-top shape, don't invite anyone to visit it. You don't want to do more harm than good. Another possibly fatal mistake is to use exactly the same bio for every guest post you write. Doing so will make you guilty of duplicate content. Try to handcraft each bio by changing it in some way.

Conduct follow-up and promotion when the post is published

Think about how you will promote the post before it's published. Reach out to anyone you cited in the post. After the post is published, send links to all your social media platforms, your email list, and your newsletter list. This is where you get to demonstrate social proof by showing that a popular blogger published your content. Make sure to share the posts on social media platforms more than once. Not everyone sees them the first time.

Possible fatal mistake: Not immediately answering any comments or requests generated by the post. You want to grab opportunities when they are presented. Your profile will be at its highest right after the publication on a major blog. Take the time to respond to requests that come your way in a timely fashion.

Starting your own guest blogging program

If you've gained a bit of traction from your blog but need to enhance and diversify the content, you might want to try accepting guest posts on your own blog. Obviously, you won't get a massive response if your blog is relatively new. But everyone appreciates an up-and-coming blog that shows promise.

Your best bet could be to create a small outreach program rather than sitting back and waiting for requests to come to you. Here are a few things you can try:

- ✔ **Contact people you know:** No matter how new your blog is, you probably personally know other people in your niche. Reach out and ask them to write a post for you on a particular topic. Explain that you are trying to enhance your content and think that they would have something important to say. Work with them on their posts to ensure that the posts work for both them and you.

- ✔ **Request the written answer to one question:** Write to an expert you admire and ask him whether he would be willing to give you an answer to a question that you want to turn into a blog post. Don't write to the most famous blogger; he won't have time. Pick someone who is an expert in the field and who would appreciate the opportunity to promote it on his site.

- ✔ **Invite someone from a community of which you are a member:** If you are a member of a group, perhaps on LinkedIn (and you should be, by the way), ask a member if she would be willing to collaborate with you on a post or write one of her own for your blog. This will help you meet people and build contacts.

Everything related to content promotion takes time. Patience is the order of the day. Even the most prominent influencers talk about the vast amount of time it took to grow their blog. Well-known influencer and blogger Chris Brogan said that it took him eight years to get his first one hundred subscribers (`http://chrisbrogan.com/wont-stop-blogging/`). I hope you won't have to wait that long, but do be willing to put in the time to make things happen.

Check out the next page for a mind map of this chapter's content, and download a color version at `www.dummies.com/contentmarketing strategies`.

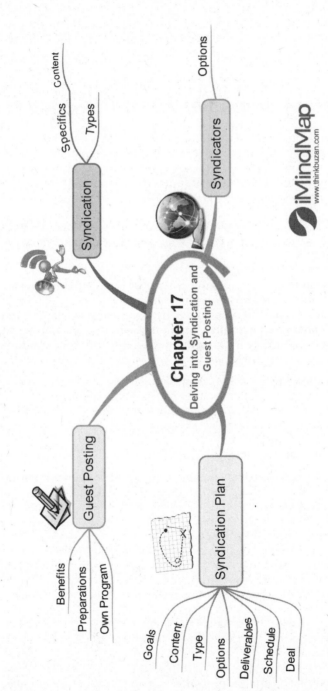

Chapter 17
Delving into Syndication and Guest Posting

Syndication
  Specifics
    Content
  Types

Syndicators
  Options

Guest Posting
  Benefits
  Preparations
  Own Program

Syndication Plan
  Goals
  Content
  Type
  Options
  Deliverables
  Schedule
  Deal

iMindMap
www.thinkbuzan.com

Courtesy of ThinkBuzan.

Chapter 18

Working with Influencers

*I*n today's marketplace, many types of people make up the constellation of customer influencers. Sometimes a family friend can supersede any referral made by your hand-picked celebrity. It's important to know your audience and understand what really matters to them. The key to using influence is putting the customer at the center of your content-marketing efforts.

In this chapter, you look at how content marketers can harness the role of influencers to satisfy a customer's greatest needs and make their brand indispensable. You examine both the accepted industry expert and the influencer whose word of mouth (WOM) recommendations drive conversions.

Discovering the Evolving Role of Influencers

First, what is social influence is? Pam Dyer, host of the Pamorama.net blog (see Figure 18-1) and one of the Forbes Top 20 Women Social Media Influencers, defines social influence as the following:

> *Social influence occurs when a person's thoughts, feelings, or actions are affected by others. Essentially, influence is the art of persuasion — the ability to cause a change in mindset or actions so someone thinks or behaves in a certain way. In the world of social media marketing, influence is currency.*

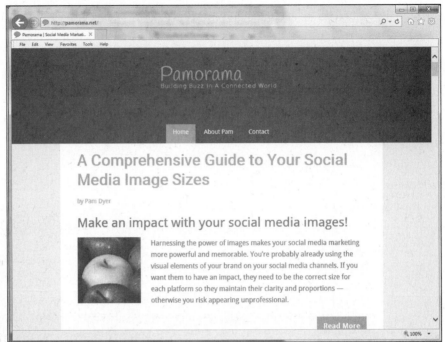

Figure 18-1:
The
Pamorama.
net blog.

I choose this quote as our working definition among others because it clearly spells out the three principles that must be present to influence others. To have influence, something or someone must do the following:

- **Impact the person's feelings.** Although most people believe otherwise, logic is not the way to influence someone. You must touch people to get their attention and allow them to focus on primitive emotions. Most information goes right by us unless it taps into our lizard brain (the part of the brain that controls such things as addiction, happiness, and the fear response.)

- **Cause a change in mindset.** Influence must cause movement that impacts your mindset. You may start out as neutral or even negative. Persuasion causes you to move in the direction of the influencer.

- **Rest on a trust relationship.** Influencers have "emotional capital" with their audience. They are trusted, which keeps the lizard brain from invoking the "fight or flight" response and instead focuses on positive emotions.

Persuasion is not trickery or deceit. The best types of persuasion help educate buyers to understand that your solution is the best. After you've done that, price is not an impediment to selling. You've allowed the buyer to persuade herself.

Understanding the six principles of persuasion

In his seminal book, *Influence: The Psychology of Persuasion,* Robert Cialdini identifies six principles at the heart of persuasion. (You might want to check out his blog, shown in Figure 18-2, at `http://www.influenceatwork.com/`. Also see the upcoming sidebar "Social proof and reciprocity: Better together?")

Figure 18-2: Influence at Work.

Cialdini's principles are closely followed by content marketers, and they can help you identify why your customers respond to some tactics more than others. Here's a quick overview of these six principles:

✔ **Reciprocity:** This principle is about keeping a relationship in balance. You want to reciprocate to someone who gives you something. There is no stated contract, but people instinctively want to make sure that they don't take more than they give.

✔ **Social proof:** This is another principle which remains unspoken but is understood by most. People like to eliminate the amount of risk they take in everyday life. One way to do this is to make sure that others have made the same decision you are about to make and have been pleased with the consequences. No one wants to be the first person to try something. Content marketers know that they need to show customers that others have used and raved about their products.

✔ **Liking:** It's well known that people want to do business with people they like. Dealing with likable people and brands is easy and certainly preferable to dealing with someone who is difficult. It is that simple. If your customers like you or your brand, they are predisposed to do business with you.

✔ **Authority:** People believe in experts. If you have a title after your name or are an acknowledged authority in some field, people believe what you say. If an authority recommends you, you are more likely to be chosen.

✔ **Scarcity:** This principle has been abused by marketers since the beginning of advertising. People hate the idea that they can't have something because its quantity is limited. When something is scarce, people want it all the more. Content marketers have recently extended this principle and called it *fear of missing out* (FOMO), which includes the value of physical goods as well as the fear of losing out on an experience that can't be repeated. I discuss this idea of FOMO further in Chapter 8, which is about the buyer's journey.

✔ **Commitment and consistency:** People's image of themselves dictates their behavior. For example, if they consider themselves to be generous, they would not like to find themselves acting in a miserly way. They want their behavior to be consistent with who they are. If they make a commitment, they want to believe that they will keep it.

Social proof and reciprocity: Better together?

Robert Cialdini's well-known "Towel Reuse Study" has garnered much attention. He looked at the impact of changes he made to small signs left for patrons in their hotel rooms. In randomly assigned rooms, he left a sign that asked patrons to reuse towels because it was good for the environment. In the other rooms, he asked them to reuse towels and noted that other guests had recycled their towels at least once during their stay. Here you see social proof in action. Twenty-six percent more of the guests who received the second sign recycled their towels. The simple fact that other guests had recycled made it more likely that these guests would do so, too.

Another study cited by the American Psychological Association (http://www.apa.org/monitor/2011/02/persuasion.aspx) returned to the topic of towel recycling. This time, the topic related to the reciprocity principle. The sign referencing the environment was used, and another, randomly distributed sign said, "We already donated to an environmental cause in the name of our guests. Would you join us in this effort to cover our costs?" This sign testing the reciprocity principle achieved a 21 percent greater response than the first.

Understanding why influencers matter more now

A trusted friend or family member has always been a social influencer. But online, influencers matter even more than they used to because of the glut of information coming at your customer from all sides. No one can read and understand everything on the web that he wants to know. People need help in the form of customer reviews, recommendations, and communities united around common topics.

According to Forbes, shoppers have completed 70–90 percent of their research before they ever speak to a salesperson.

It is both a blessing and a curse that users can investigate products or services they want to buy before ever talking to a salesperson. Rather than turning to a salesperson, they find trusted sources who can explain the benefits of a product without displaying a vested interest in making a sale. That's where influencers come in.

Influence marketing provides several benefits, including:

- **Lending credibility:** We all know that a sales page on a company's website is given very little credence. It's great to find out about specific product features, but most customers are too cynical to believe the hype. When an influencer recommends the product, it's given much more weight. You can capture brand awareness through recommendations in a way that you can't with your own ads.

  In a study by Dimensional Research, respondents found that 90 percent said that positive reviews impacted their buying decisions. Eighty-six percent said their buying decisions were influenced by negative online reviews.

- **Cost-effective targeting:** It is easier to tap into a community of people interested in your topic than it is to create one from scratch. Influencers have already done the hard work.

- **Positioning and copy:** Many content marketers overlook the opportunity to learn from their audience's influencers. How do they talk about the product? Are they tapping into specific emotions or using special language? They show you what content resonates with your audience. Paying attention to their appeal and what their audience wants to hear is an important takeaway for you.

- **Finding out what channels are their favorites:** Influencer audiences point the way to the channels your potential customers spend time on, thereby saving you a huge amount of time and pointing the way to the best advertising venues.

- ✔ **Developing brand awareness:** Having an influencer discuss your products can develop enhanced brand awareness. Not only is the influencer discussing your product, she is implicitly endorsing your brand.

- ✔ **Helping build your online community:** Building an audience from scratch is difficult and time consuming. Anything that you can do to encourage self-selected members of the influencer's group to join you as well is a great boost.

- ✔ **Fronting a specific campaign:** You know that some campaigns are more important than others. If you are a start-up and customers are seeing your product for the first time, collaborating with an industry insider can make all the difference.

Understanding how to measure expert influencers

How can influence be measured? A lot of controversy exists among content marketers about how to measure influencer clout. Marketers dislike the way some clout-ranking companies give a high rating to an influencer based solely on the number of Twitter followers he has or the amount of attention he garners on Facebook. The key to measuring influence is by looking at a range of factors.

Klout (http://Klout.com), a clout-ranking company, published an e-book called *Identifying and Measuring Influencers in Social Marketing with @Klout* (http://simplymeasured.com/blog/2014/06/03/guide-identifying-and-measuring-influencers-in-social-marketing-with-klout/#i.i2feei17drdc5z) in which Klout identified three attributes of influences:

- ✔ **Reach:** Does the influencer have your target audience as a subset of hers? Does she have the social followers and real-world influence to impact your potential customers? Is her audience large and responsive?

- ✔ **Relevance:** Do the influencer's content topics align with yours? Does his content have the quality your audience expects?

- ✔ **Resonance:** Do the influencer's authority and authenticity attract the audience you are trying to reach? This is important to determine. You want to be sure that you don't have more of a niche audience that does not resonate with your influencer.

Recognizing Influencer Types

You may be surprised by the wide range of influencer types. When you say *influencer,* what usually comes to mind is a celebrity or family member. But influencers come in five types:

- ✔ **Friends, family, and work colleagues:** This is the category of influencer with which you are most familiar. These influencers make up the person's social graph on social media platforms. They are known as positional influencers because they constitute the person's inner circle.

- ✔ **Subject experts:** This group has demonstrated expertise in a particular topic or area of interest. They are thought leaders and others who work to gain recognition by virtue of their knowledge. When they recommend something, their audience listens. These people generally have titles such as trendsetter, thought leader, authority, or even analyst.

  A subset of this group is the gadfly. The gadfly is known for saying controversial things and disrupting the status quo.

- ✔ **Professionals in high positions:** You recognize these influencers because they have jobs that confer expertise on them. They are the captains of industry, the politicians, and the local business leaders. Their credibility is measured by the size of the position they hold and the people over which they have power. Titles for these people include decision maker or industry leader.

- ✔ **Celebrities:** This group is easy to identify. Its members have high profiles and are written about in magazines and newspapers. Celebrity influence is very high and usually unpredictable. Fashion designers and others often give celebrities their merchandise free in the hopes that the celebrity will be photographed wearing it. That kind of publicity can't be bought. The downside to using celebrity influencers is that you may be subject to criticism if their behavior does not comport with your brand.

  A subset of this group is the professional brand. These are the people who are stars in their specific industry. For example, they could be a YouTube star or Internet marketing star.

What kind of influence do you think you could wield if you had nearly 63 million followers on Twitter, 44 million on Instagram, 72 million on Facebook, and more than a million YouTube subscribers? A great deal — if you're Taylor Swift. She told Apple in 2015 that she wasn't going to allow her album *1989* to stream on Apple's service because of its decision not to pay artists during Apple's three-month trial period. Apple quickly relented and agreed to accommodate the artists in some way. Swift accomplished this concession by placing an open letter to Apple on her Tumblog (`http://taylorswift.tumblr.com/post/122071902085/to-apple-love-taylor`), demonstrating that influencers can impact even the world's most valuable brand.

Are you targeting millennials? If so, be careful who you choose as your celebrity. MediaPost, an online publishing resource for advertising professionals, reports that "Authenticity is most important among the very desirable youth market (ages 12–29)" (`http://www.mediapost.com/publications/article/251664/rethinking-celebrity-endorsements-authenticity-an.html?edition=83523`). Even the most popular celebrity must have a true connection to your brand to satisfy this group.

✔ **Your raving fans:** This is the group that you love to nourish. This group's members are the people who chat up your brand and do the work of a citizen sales force. Their buzz is organic and never dies down. These are the people who influence by being your best brand ambassadors. I discuss them further in the "Enhancing Word of Mouth (WOM) with Advertising" section, later in this chapter.

Finding the Right Influencers

If you've read the previous sections of this chapter, by now you're probably convinced that influencers matter. But how do you find the influencers who are right for your audience? Assuming that you're starting from scratch, the following sections look at how to find the right influencers and approach them.

Discovering the influencers you need to target

Say that you've considered the influencer types described in the preceding section, "Recognizing Influencer Types," and have decided to focus on self-selected experts for now. These are the top thought leaders and bloggers whom your target audience reads and follows. (At some point, you will also want to consider the other types, of course, such as raving fans.)

Following are several immediate actions you can take to find influencers using three free online tools — BuzzSumo, Followerwonk, and Alltop:

BuzzSumo

To find influencers through the BuzzSumo tool, follow these steps:

1. **Go to** `https://app.buzzsumo.com/influencers` **to use the influencer search.**

   Look at the left side and select the filters you want to use. In Figure 18-3, I've selected bloggers and influencers.

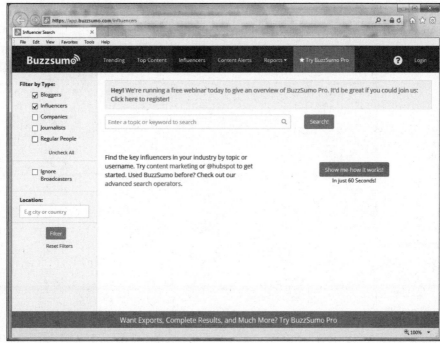

Figure 18-3:
Filters on
BuzzSumo
for
influencer
types.

2. Type in the topic of your niche.

I typed in **pet food**, as shown in Figure 18-4. After typing your topic, you receive a list of results. (For a longer list, you need to sign up for the Pro version and pay a fee.)

From this list, you can start to research influencers.

3. Select the ones you want to research further and put them on a list in an Excel spreadsheet or Google Doc.

Followerwonk

Follow these steps to work with the tool on Followerwonk:

1. Go to http://followerwonk.com.

On the page that opens, you see a tab called Search Bios.

2. Click the Search Bios tab and type in the topic of your choice; In this case, I typed pet food.

Followerwonk returns a list of all your Twitter followers who cite pet food in their profiles, as shown in Figure 18-5. Add the names you want to look at further to the list you created.

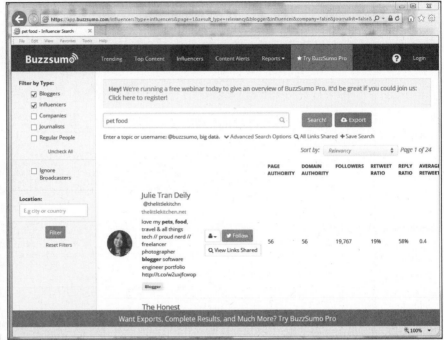

Figure 18-4:
Results of
pet food
search on
BuzzSumo.

Figure 18-5:
A list of
Twitter
followers
who cite pet
food in their
profiles.

Alltop

Alltop provides a collection of the best blogs on various topics. To find those blogs, follow these steps:

1. **Go to** `http://pets.alltop.com/`.

   You get a display of the top blogs in the topic, as shown in Figure 18-6.

Figure 18-6:
Results of search on Alltop.

2. **On the list of blogs, look for duplicates and see which ones show up most often.**

   Don't forget to consider bloggers that aren't at the top of the list. They may be more open to collaborating because they are not bombarded daily with offers.

You can always do a simple search on Google for your topic, such as pet food influencers, and see which blogs are returned. You can also search related terms, such as "pet resources," to see what you find.

Don't forget that you can also search Google using your terms as hashtags and keywords.

Developing a system

After you pick the influencer(s) you want to work with, you should establish a working system to define your roles. This is important because you want to make sure that everything goes smoothly. You may feel a bit intimidated working with your influencer for the first time, but you want to ensure success. The last thing you want to do is alienate someone who is important to your audience.

For this reason your system should have a documented plan.

I provide an influencer worksheet that can help you create just such a plan. You can download this worksheet at www.dummies.com/extras/contentmarketingstrategies.

Working with your influencer includes documenting the following:

- ✔ **The overall goal of the campaign or collaboration:** Each of you will have different goals for participating. You should make sure that it's clear what each of your goals are.

- ✔ **Deliverables:** Document what the campaign deliverables will be. Are you going to put on a webinar for the influencer's audience? Who will take care of the promotion and the technical aspects?

- ✔ **Roles:** Some influencers may want to front the campaign, whereas others may want you to take the lead. If the influencer has to spend time preparing a presentation, you want her to know that up front.

- ✔ **Decisions about editorial content:** Will you have to get approval for all the content in your campaign? Does the influencer want to run through everything beforehand or is he leaving the details to you?

- ✔ **Success measures:** How will you know whether the collaboration was a success? Decide beforehand what measures will be used.

Make this process as informal or formal as you think it warrants. The key is that you do it. It's not uncommon for people to be disappointed by those with whom they've collaborated because they did not have clear parameters before they began.

You also need to establish some predefined metrics that will let you know whether your association with an influencer is valuable. You may not have revenue returns immediately (unless you are specifically selling a product or service). However, you do want to make sure that you have tangible results. Although the ROI will be difficult to measure, here are some to consider:

✔ Increase in followers tied to that influencer

✔ Increase in requests for sales demos or leads or materials

✔ Increase in your mailing list tied to a specific landing page that you established for the campaign

✔ Increase in sales of the product or service if applicable

✔ Increased traffic of new visitors to your website right after the campaign

Uncovering New Influencers

Influencer marketing continues to change with the influx of new channels and technology. A relatively new phenomenon is the social media platform celebrity. That's an influencer who becomes popular on a specific platform based on the content that influencer creates just for that platform. Musicians, beauty bloggers, and others have posted tutorials that have catapulted them to fame. Social media creates its own media stars. Two innovative ways that influencers are being discovered are

✔ **On social platforms that have their own celebrities:** Because social media platforms have no barrier to entry, anyone with a good story to tell and a pleasing personality has a shot at becoming famous. This fame can then be parlayed into a line of physical goods, such as makeup, or a gig with a brand that wants to appropriate your celebrity for its media campaign.

Adweek reported on several brands that used these self-made celebrities to promote their own products with great success (`http://www.adweek.com/news/advertising-branding/brands-next-big-celebrity-deals-may-be-social-media-stars-162270`). For example, during the 2014 Christmas season, Old Navy ran a "White Elephant" game that gave away prizes for 12 days. To boost its profile, Old Navy asked 12 Vine (`https://vine.co/`) influencers to participate. Digiday reported that it got more than 7.6 million Vine loops (vines that are played to their conclusion are counted as one loop), more than 16,000 revines (a reshare of a vine), and 45,000 likes from this campaign. It also got a 50 percent increase in followers on Vine.

✔ **By creating algorithms on social platforms to find more catalysts:** Another way in which social platforms are using influencers is to uncover and target them for their own publicity purposes. Uncovering new influencers and using their clout is serious business.

A case in point is Facebook's filing of an ad patent that would reportedly identify new influencers. The way it works is that Facebook will be able to identify the people who share content and then get the most reshares. Every advertiser would be interested in knowing who they are and paying to advertise directly to them.

If you know the influencer's website but not his specific email address, you may want to check out Email Hunter at (`https://emailhunter.co/`). This tool isn't a license to spam someone, however. Be respectful.

Influencing with Customer Advocacy

As most content marketers agree, getting WOM from happy customers is the best advertising of all. If you can encourage your own fans to be your de facto sales force, you can expect great results. By organizing your most ardent fans, you can multiply your brand's profile. One type of advocacy is typically known as brand ambassadorship, which is a program that has a company's most loyal customers provide testimonials and other positive information to prospects. The program can be as large or small as makes sense for your audience. When people join your ambassador program, you can offer them free stuff, discounts, or special group meetings.

One key benefit of an ambassador program is that you will be privy to feedback that you probably wouldn't get from other sources. Remember, these are your fans, so their criticisms are heartfelt. They want to make the program better. Consider them to be your most intense focus group.

One example of brand ambassadorship is the Champions Program (`http://www.brainshark.com/campaigns/champions-program.aspx`; see Figure 18-7), created by Brainshark, a sales enablement company that helps customers create high-end video sales presentations. (See Chapter 9 on sales enablement.) Their case study was reported by Truman Tang on the Influitive blog (`http://influitive.com/blog/brainshark-social-media-case-study/`).

Tang reported that Brainshark knew it had an avid group of fans who loved its products. The key was to figure out how to get those fans to increase their advocacy on social media. To this end, the company created an online community staffed by Brainshark's star employees and called that community Brainshark Champions. The community invited customers who had given testimonials and case studies on the company's website. Customers were categorized into four groups: (1) active users; (2) social content sharers; (3) customers nominated for their loyalty by employees; and (4) community leaders and influencers. To demonstrate its commitment, the company provided the community with exclusive training and networking about Brainshark products. Obviously, this offering served as a real incentive to raving fans.

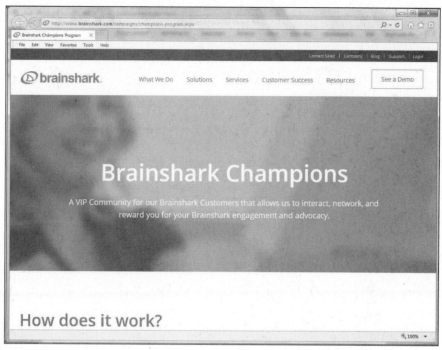

Figure 18-7:
The
Brainshark
Champions
Program.

The program was very successful and won Brainshark the Forrester Groundswell Award for 2014. One success measure showed a 106 percent boost in Twitter activity. Clearly, a program like this would be worth considering for your fan base (http://groundswelldiscussion.com/groundswell/awards/detail.php?id=1060).

Another example of a very active brand ambassador community is the one run by Evernote (https://evernote.com/community), the online content catcher. With more than one hundred million users, Evernote must be doing something right. It started its ambassador program in 2011 with an eye toward highlighting different use cases. Evernote picked users who were both passionate about Evernote and expert in their own field, and the company wanted to offer something valuable to these users. For example, a user who is curious to see how to solve a particular problem with Evernote might find an ambassador who can offer tips and hints. In Figure 18-8, you see a listing for Paperless Living Ambassador Jamie Todd Rubin.

You can also see a link to Rubin's website (http://Jamietoddrubin.com), shown in Figure 18-9, on which he mentions his ambassadorship in his blog heading along with his own considerable skills. Clearly, this is a win-win for both the ambassador and the company.

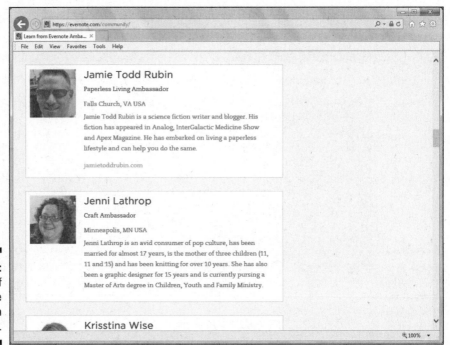

Figure 18-8:
Example of
Evernote
listing for an
ambassador.

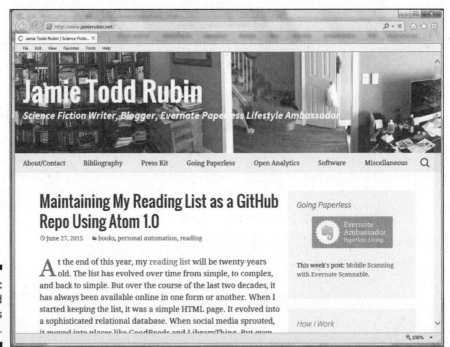

Figure 18-9:
Jamie Todd
Rubin's
website.

Enhancing Word of Mouth (WOM) with Advertising

As powerful as a collaboration with an industry influencer can be, we know that word-of-mouth (WOM) recommendations are equally important. When you adopt WOM as a content marketing strategy, you can get results that are even more effective. The best way to deploy WOM as a strategy is to understand its power as an advertising tactic that is called Word of Mouth Advertising (WOMA).

WOMA refers to actively using tactics to encourage WOM. Rather than use hope as a strategy to accelerate WOM, you proactively seed your campaigns with WOMA.

 A study at the University of Auckland Business School (`https://faculty.unlv.edu/gnaylor/Lang_Hyde.pdf`) found that three major benefits accrue to companies when WOM is used. They are (1) greater enthusiasm for a company and its products; (2) increased brand awareness; and (3) greater customer loyalty.

Connecting with your audience

An article in Forbes reports that 64 percent of marketing executives believe that word of mouth is the most effective form of marketing. Only six percent say that they have mastered it. That's an astounding number! So why is using WOMM so difficult? Suzanne Fanning, President of WOMMA (`http://womma.org/`), thinks she knows why. She believes that marketers have a hard time with WOMM because they use it to "collect rather than connect." By this she means that marketers are focused on counting followers, tweets, and likes rather than actually connecting with the very audience who loves their products (`http://www.forbes.com/sites/kimberlywhitler/2014/07/17/why-word-of-mouth-marketing-is-the-most-important-social-media/`).

You can easily see how this lack of connection results in a failed strategy. Most marketers show off their social media numbers as though they directly translate into revenue. What's missing is the knowledge of the level of advocacy behind those numbers. Many of your followers can have only a very casual interest in your brand and not be very effective ambassadors.

Identifying factors for WOMA

It's important to understand what factors must be present to trigger WOM. The conditions have to be right so that people feel comfortable sharing content with their trusted network. According to a study by consulting service McKinsey & Company (http://www.mckinsey.com/insights/marketing_sales/ a_new_way_to_measure_word-of-mouth_marketing), three factors are critical to triggering WOM, as explained in Table 18-1.

Table 18-1	Three Critical Factors that Trigger WOM
Factor	*Must Be Present to Trigger*
What's said	Important product or service features
Identity of the messenger	Trusted advisor
Environment	Trusted channel where the message seen

Paid Influencer Programs

If you want to go further and develop an ongoing influencer program for your company, you may want to consider paid influencer programs. A report called "2014 Influencer Marketing Benchmarks," by RhythmOne (http://www.rhythmone.com/advertisers/influencer-marketing), found that "on average, advertisers who implemented an Influencer Marketing program received $6.85 in earned media value for every $1.00 of paid media."

Here are a few influencer programs you may want to investigate:

- **GroupHigh** (http://www.grouphigh.com): Shown in Figure 18-10, GroupHigh is a PR and marketing software provider that helps companies find influential bloggers.

- **RhythmOne** (http://www.rhythmone.com): RhythmOne is a company that provides influencer marketing and unites advertising across all devices. (See Figure 18-11.)

- **Tapinfluence** (http://www.tapinfluence.com/): Shown in Figure 18-12, Tapinfluence has a Software as Service (SAS) platform that helps brands find influencers and create co-branded content.

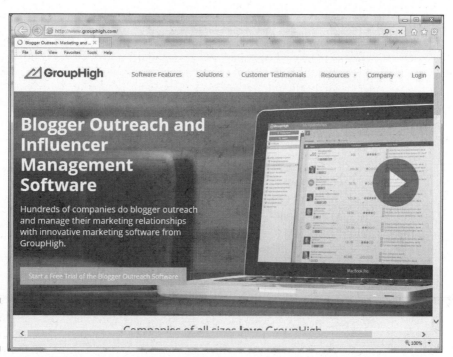

Figure 18-10:
GroupHigh.

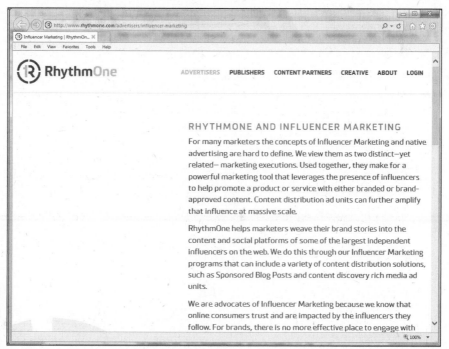

Figure 18-11:
RhythmOne.

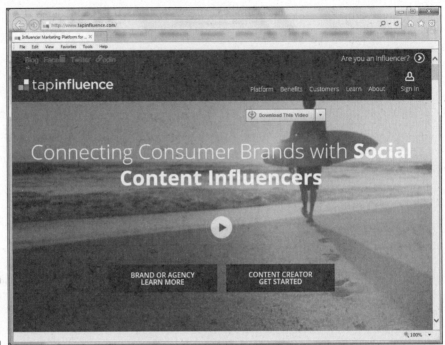

Figure 18-12:
Tapinflu-
ence.

Check out the next page for a mind map of this chapter's content, and
download a color version at `www.dummies.com/contentmarketing`
`strategies`.

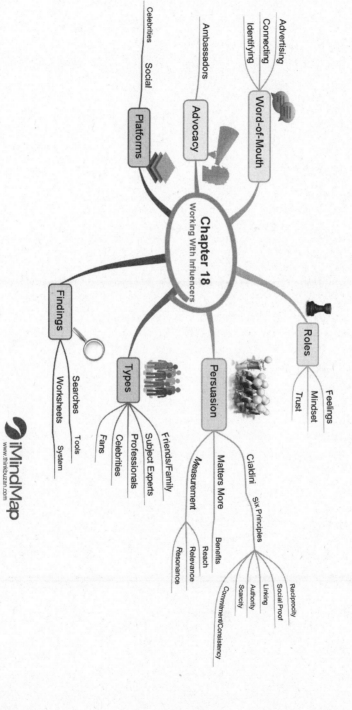

iMindMap
www.thinkbuzan.com

Chapter 18
Working With Influencers

Word-of-Mouth
- Advertising
- Connecting
- Identifying

Advocacy
- Ambassadors

Platforms
- Celebrities
- Social

Findings
- Searches
- Worksheets
  - Tools
  - System

Types
- Fans
- Celebrities
- Professionals
- Subject Experts
- Friends/Family

Persuasion
- Measurement
  - Resonance
  - Relevance
  - Reach
- Matters More
  - Benefits
- Cialdini
  - Six Principles
    - Reciprocity
    - Social Proof
    - Linking
    - Authority
    - Scarcity
    - Commitment/Consistency

Roles
- Feelings
- Mindset
- Trust

Part V
Using Check-Back Analysis

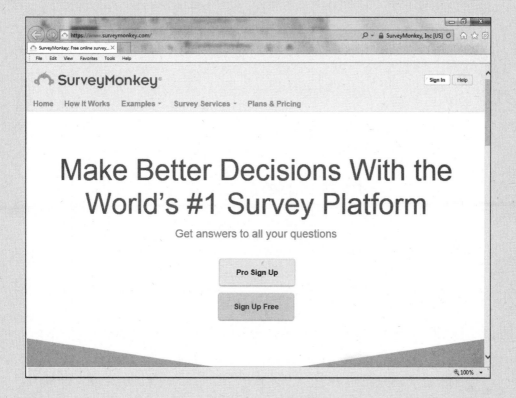

Want to focus on improving your bottom line? See how to reevaluate your business model to generate more revenue at www.dummies.com/extras/content marketingstrategies.

In this part . . .

- ✔ Your business model and brand are organic entities that need reassessment on a regular basis. I show you how to determine whether changes are needed.

- ✔ Failure is a part of your journey to content marketing success. See how to determine what needs to change and how to get renewed buy-in for those changes.

Chapter 19

Reassessing Your Business Model and Brand Value

In This Chapter

▶ Reevaluating your business models

▶ Looking at refreshing your brand

▶ Understanding brand failures

▶ Identifying new measures

As anyone who has been part of a business team knows, failure and change are part of the business lifecycle. You hear advice about "failing faster" and embracing change. But how do you go about it? This chapter begins Part V of the book by covering the last of the Five Cs, Check-Back Analysis. (I explain the Five Cs in Chapter 1.)

In this chapter, you reassess the efforts you document in Chapter 3 to determine whether you want to make changes. You want to see whether you can take additional steps that will lead to greater success.

To get the full value from this chapter, you're best off reading Chapter 3 first and downloading the worksheets.

You can download all the worksheets for this book at www.dummies.com/extras/contentmarketingstrategies.

If you wonder how often you should make reassessments, I recommend that you let no more than three months go by before you reevaluate what you're doing. This amount of time will give you enough data to evaluate your results. The sooner you identify problems, the easier changing course will be. I'm not recommending that you do a big overhaul each time you make an assessment. Rather, I recommend that you carefully assess your effectiveness on an ongoing basis. Some people prefer six-month intervals, but because things change so quickly on the web, you may fall behind before you realize it's happening.

If you're a solopreneur or small business, you know that speed is one of your greatest allies. If you're a large company, you know that the quicker you call attention to a problem, the more likely you are to make a dent in the bureaucracy that exists. In the end, only you can determine the intervals that make sense for your company.

Validating Business Models

I begin this section with a brief recap of why business models matter when working on content marketing strategy. (See Chapter 3 for an in-depth explanation.) We want to understand our business models because they tell us what value our products have for our customers.

In Chapter 3, you look at the dilemma of a fast-food company. The company needed to determine what "job" a customer hires its milkshake to do. The company found that customers buy milkshakes because they want something to do with their free hand during their long commute and that they want a drink that helps them stave off hunger until lunchtime. So this information told the company what it could do to make its milkshake do its job. But what does the information tell the company about its content marketing?

The customers' responses tell the company that producing content containing questions such as"How can you make your long commute less boring?" and "What can you drink on the way to work to keep yourself satisfied until lunch?" engages its audience. This type of content provides you with insight into the minds of your customers so that the content will be personal to them. These insights are critical to content marketing success. Rather than take a shot in the dark about what your audience wants to know, you can deliver just what it wants and keep it entertained.

Looking at change

When you begin your business model reassessment, you first need to ask yourself whether you are still in the same business you were several months ago. If you haven't read Chapter 3, this might seem like a strange question. But after you look at the issues concerning changes to business models and brand, you know that it's not strange at all. Obviously, if things change, your content marketing strategy must change as well.

So what can signal that a change is needed? You might want to revise your model if any of the following have occurred:

✔ **New competitors have jumped into the market.** You suddenly have more competitors than you did before. To avoid being a commodity, you need to figure out how to differentiate your products and services.

✔ **Your company has merged, been sold, or changed some other way.** Such changes inevitably bring internal changes. If a merger is involved, you may need to accommodate new brands or eliminate products.

✔ **The economy has shifted downward.** Obviously, you have no control over this trend, but you need to understand how it will impact your business model. For example, will people now view your product as a luxury?

✔ **Some of your products or services have changed or been discontinued.** Obviously, this circumstance requires a rethinking of your model from top to bottom.

✔ **Your profit margins are shrinking.** Lower profits are a sign that you need to change something. Try to pinpoint what's different in operations.

✔ **Government regulations have been added.** If your company has new regulations to comply with, your business model may be affected.

✔ **Barriers to entry have changed.** When you started out, there may have been high barriers to entry in your field. This means that someone starting a business like yours would be faced with high hurdles to get into business. With the advent of new technologies, the barriers to entry may have lowered, making more competition a certainty.

Revising your business model canvas

In Chapter 3, you looked at working with the business model canvas by Alex Osterwalder and Strategyzer. You should return to it now and see whether any revisions are necessary. Using this tool should make it very easy for you to determine what's changed since you filled it out. (Find it at `https://strategyzer.com/canvas?_ga=1.164112764.256400004.1437491350`.)

Make sure to ask yourself the following questions:

✔ Have you added or dropped any customer niches?

✔ Are some social media channels performing better than others?

✔ Have you lost or changed any critical vendors?

✔ Do you require more resources? If so, why?

✔ Have new expenditures become necessary?

There may be no major changes to the business model canvas that affect your model. But you will probably have revisions that you want to note so that when you come back the next time, you are up-to-date. Vendor changes and social media channel wins, among other developments, can become very significant down the road.

Reexamining your brand worksheet

In Chapter 3, I tell you about the brand worksheet that you can download at www.dummies.com/extras/contentmarketingstrategies. If you haven't done that yet, I recommend that you do it now. On the worksheet, you choose the following types of data to track and analyze: (1) general company measures; (2) brand awareness measures; and (3) brand loyalty measures. The good news is that because you pick specific measures to track, you will have items to evaluate after several months.

On the worksheet, you choose specific measures based on my suggestions. If you choose different ones, be sure that you understand what your reason is (or was, if you did this earlier) and why that measure matters.

When you look at the data you gather, ask yourself the following types of questions:

- ✔ **Have any of the company measures changed significantly from your baseline numbers?** For example, has your gross revenue taken a hit?

- ✔ **Has your reach (the number of customers that you reach with your content) diminished for some reason?** Has your publishing schedule changed?

- ✔ **Have the number of customer purchases changed?** Have you made changes to current products that would prompt a drop or an increase?

If you didn't fill out the worksheet when you read Chapter 3, don't give up. The best time to start something is now. Your next evaluation is only three months away.

Enhancing your business models

After you reevaluate your business models, you should look at whether you can add or subtract something to enhance what you are already doing. As you know, to grow a business, you can do three things: (1) increase the number of customers you serve; (2) increase the amount paid for a transaction; and (3) increase the frequency of the purchase. Using these three basic categories, here's a look at what you might do to increase growth.

✔ **Increase the number of customers you serve.** Gaining customers requires that you do some of the following:

- Actively look for new niches in the marketplace.

- Look at your current audience to see if you have attracted new customer niches based on something that has changed in the environment.

- See whether you can expand your reach to new domestic locations or countries.

✔ **Increase the amount paid for a transaction.** Can you increase the price of your product? This is a tricky one, but can be done depending on how your product is perceived. Can you introduce a premium version?

Can you bundle more with your product? Try adding such things as training, webinars, and specialized content.

✔ **Increase the frequency of the purchase.** Can you get people to use more of your product? For commodity products like shampoo and tooth-paste, this is a possibility. Increasing the frequency is tougher for online tools that don't have built-in usage amounts, but trying to figure out ways to do it is worthwhile.

Reviewing Your Brand Status

When you look at brand measurement, you should consider aspects such as brand recall and brand recognition. Large corporations have brand managers whose job is to focus exclusively on this area. Smaller companies often find that the marketing team is the de facto group in charge of brands.

As discussed in Chapter 3, your brand is fixed in the mind of your customer. You don't want to make changes if everything is working. You might, how-ever, have to make changes if something in the brand environment has changed. Check to see whether any of the following is true:

✔ **You're in a rut or stagnant.** If your customers and even your employees don't have much enthusiasm for the brand content you're producing, some kind of boost might be needed. You don't need to do something drastic. Perhaps redesigning your e-book covers and the look of your blog posts will help.

✔ **Your culture is not in line with your brand.** Many companies understand that if their culture doesn't support their brand, they will be perceived as inauthentic. Authenticity is a critical component of any brand today. For example, when customers buy something from Zappos (http://zappos.com), shown in Figure 19-1, they know that customer service is paramount. The company culture tells employees what's important and how they should treat their customers. In turn, this behavior gets identified with the brand. Zappos founder Tony Hsieh is famous for saying that "your culture is your brand." If your culture is not aligned with your brand, you need to make changes.

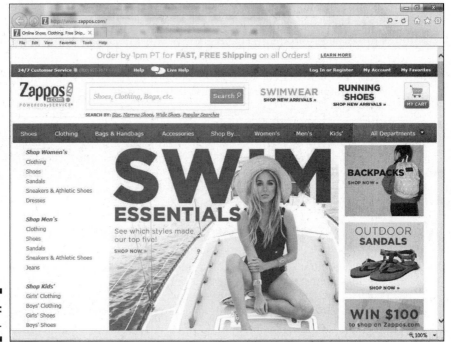

Figure 19-1:
Zappos.

According to an article from NewsCred, a content marketing software company (http://newscred.com), 72 percent of marketers find branded content more effective than magazine advertising.

Refreshing Visual Branding

When you make changes to your branding, don't be surprised if customers balk. When people are used to something they like, they get nervous when you change it. They are not looking at your brand in a strategic way as you are. They just decide whether they like the change or not. Be cautious and expect some dissent. You may even find that some critics come from within your company.

Understanding what your branding means

A classic branding mistake was made by Tropicana Orange Juice (owned by Pepsi). In 2009, the company decided to freshen up its Tropicana Pure Premium orange juice container by removing the iconic orange with the straw in it, shown in Figure 19-2. Customers immediately reacted negatively. Tropicana received a barrage of letters, email messages, and telephone calls. Some people said that the package looked like "a generic bargain brand" or a "store brand." They demanded that the iconic branding be put back on the package.

Figure 19-2: Tropicana's iconic orange juice label.

Management quickly complied with this request even though the company had just launched advertisements with the new packaging. The reason for complying? Even though the outcry was from a small percentage of the audience, it was composed of their most loyal customers. Smart. According

Renaming a brand service

At the time of this writing, a different kind of rebranding was undertaken by Nestle Waters North America (`http://www.nestle-watersna.com`). Its home and office water delivery service was called Poland Spring Direct. As the company began to expand its product offering to include such items as flavored teas and juices, it decided to change its name to reflect the breadth of its products. Its new name is called ReadyRefresh by Nestle. To support this change, the company displays a web page devoted to explaining the change (`https://eservice.readyrefresh.com/Pages/FAQ/FAQReadyRefresh.aspx`).

This name change is a good illustration of what I discuss in Chapter 3 regarding brand purpose. As mentioned there, Clayton Christensen recommended naming your product after your brand's purpose so that customers can clearly tell that a product will meet their needs. Calling the service ReadyRefresh communicates the benefit to the customer and doesn't limit the product offering to one brand of water.

to the *New York Times* article, "Tropicana Discovers Some Buyers Are Passionate About Packaging," by Stuart Elliott (`http://www.nytimes.com/2009/02/23/business/media/23adcol.html?_r=2&`), Neil Campbell, president at Tropicana North America in Chicago, says that listening to your most loyal customers is the key to maintaining your brand power.

So what did the Tropicana marketers take away from their branding mistake? I think one of the answers lies with an understanding of what their branding signified to their customer. Clearly, the customers were buying "pure premium" juice. They wanted to buy and be recognized for buying something that was designed to communicate value.

When the package changed to resemble a less expensive brand, these customers became angry. They were going to be paying the same price for something that looked inferior. This kind of branding mistake shows that understanding the emotional value that your customer places on your brand is critical.

Surveying about brand awareness

When working on your brand reassessment, you may want to consider taking a survey to determine how well your branded content is performing. With luck, you have tracking data that shows you how well your content is performing on social media channels. But have you surveyed your customers to get their sentiments?

The survey process is very straightforward and many online tools are available for you to use. But a survey can be hard to get going unless everyone on your team is on board with the idea. Learning what customers really think can be scary. (Think about what you see on social media every day.) But if you really want data that doesn't come through a filter, you need to survey your customers. Here's the quick version of how to implement a survey:

- ✔ Get buy-in from your managers for the purpose.

- ✔ Pull together a team to write questions or designate one person to round up what needs to be asked. Without a clear vision about what you want to know, the survey will not be useful.

- ✔ Pick a survey tool. (See the next section, "Locating a survey company.")

- ✔ Create survey questions and get approval.

- ✔ Run the survey using the tool of choice.

- ✔ Analyze answers.

- ✔ Share data with everyone in the company who could use it to take action.

Locating a survey company

You can find lots of good online survey tools. Here are two you might want to consider:

- ✔ **SurveyMonkey** (`https://www.surveymonkey.com`): See Figure 19-3. SurveyMonkey is a leader in the industry. It offers free and paid versions of its tools. Zoomerang is another well-known online survey company that has recently merged with SurveyMonkey. All new signups are being directed there.

- ✔ **Zoho** (`http://www.zoho.com/survey`): See Figure 19-4. Zoho offers unlimited free surveys as well as other software tools.

Check out the last page of this chapter for a mind map of this chapter's content, and download a color version at `www.dummies.com/content marketingstrategies`.

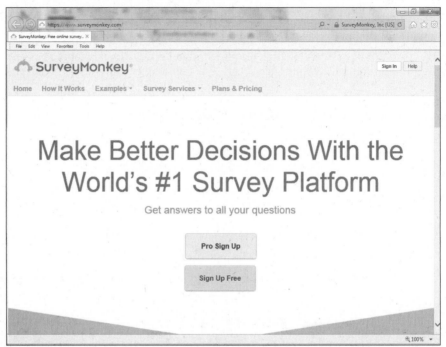

Figure 19-3:
Survey
Monkey.

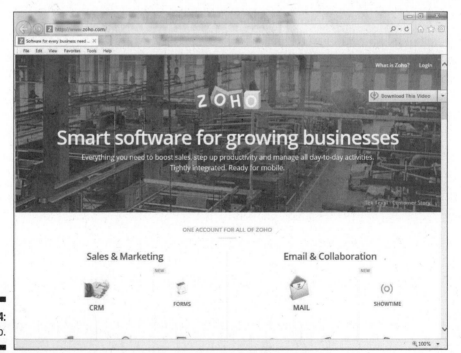

Figure 19-4:
Zoho.

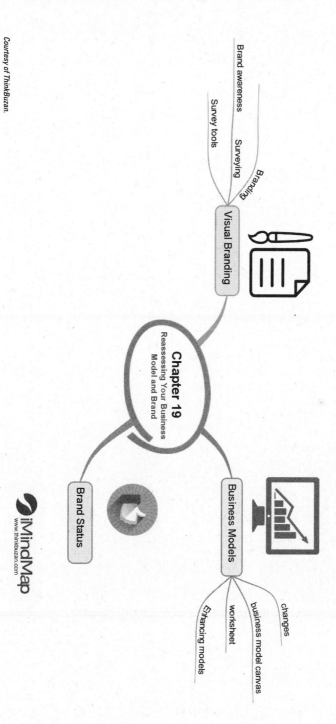

Courtesy of ThinkBuzan.

Chapter 20

Reviewing Your Content Marketing Strategy

*W*e all need (and, I hope, want) to learn from our mistakes. A good assessment of your strategy comes of learning from your failures and devising a better plan. You won't always hit a home run; your strategy will need revisions. Eighteenth century military commander Helmuth Karl Bernhard Graf von Moltke is famous for saying "No battle plan survives contact with the enemy." The same holds true of your content strategy.

In Chapter 19, you reevaluate your business model and brand plans. In this chapter, you discover how to evaluate and improve your content marketing strategy.

Allowing for Failed Experiments

You've probably heard the phrase "fail fast," used by Agile software developers. The phrase is meant to remind people to experiment — see what doesn't work and make quick adjustments. The definition of failure is framed as merely a course of action that needs alterations rather than a dead end. Perhaps Thomas Edison was the first agile developer. He is quoted as saying, "I have not failed. I've just found 10,000 ways that won't work."

Content marketers can take some lessons from Agile developers whose goal is to work with greater speed and efficiency. In his article "Go Agile: Adapt

12 Principles to Content Marketing," Jeff Freund, CEO of Akoonu (http://www.akoonu.com), adapts the principles of Agile development to Content Marketing ((http://contentmarketinginstitute.com/2014/10/go-agile-adapt-12-principles-to-content-marketing; see Figure 20-1). I include five principles here that I think are critical to content marketing success:

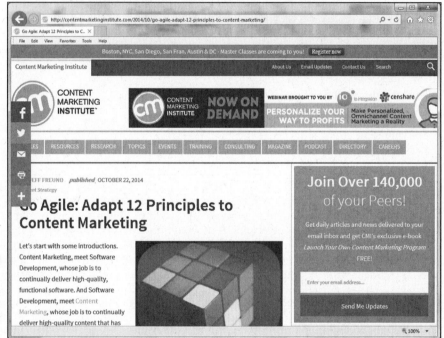

Figure 20-1:
Content
Marketing
Institute.

✔ **Your highest priority is the continuous delivery of quality content:** There should be no confusion here. You want to consistently deliver high value content.

✔ **You can always change content requirements right up to their creation:** You need to demonstrate flexibility and not feel that anything is set in stone. If you get better information, you should be willing to revise content when necessary. This is a hard one for some people to accept.

✔ **Deliver content frequently:** You need to be prepared to meet the needs of each channel. If, for example, a social media channel needs several posts a day to meet your goals, you need to be prepared to provide just that.

✔ **The business side must work collaboratively with the content creators:** This is another call to break down silos. (See Chapter 5 for details on dealing with silos in companies.) Strict divisions just won't work anymore.

✔ **Content should be measured based on its furtherance of business goals:** This is the major tenet of content marketing strategy discussed in this book. Your content should serve your business needs, and you must have a clear understanding of what those goals are at the outset.

Whenever you look at revising a strategy or making new plans, you want to consider the pace at which you will make changes. Are you going to upend the table and start over or take small steps? Make sure that everyone is on board with your decision.

Looking Back at Your Content Marketing Strategy

In looking back at the plans that you made concerning content and strategy, you need to focus on several major areas. They are:

✔ Business goals

✔ Key performance indicators (KPIs)

✔ Content maturity

✔ Ecosystem

Read on to look at each of these topics in turn to see how you can make your content strategy even better going forward.

Reviewing goals and KPIs

Reviewing business goals and KPIs are at the heart of your strategy. If you do a good job looking at and revising what you've done, you will stay on the path to content marketing success.

At this point, you might find flipping to Chapter 1 helpful to remind yourself of the components that go into developing your strategy.

To review your goals, focus on two key strategy areas:

- **Mission statement:** Most mission statements don't change in the short run. But looking back to make sure that your actions are congruent with your statement is always good. If, however, you do see a shift at some point, you obviously need to revise your statement, which in turn signals the need for major changes in goals and KPIs as well.

- **Goals and KPIs:** Your entire content marketing strategy is based on meeting your business goals. Table 1-1 in Chapter 1 helps you to select KPIs based on possible goals. If you documented these KPIs, you can look back now at the results and ask yourself:

  - *Has my strategy been successful so far?* Are the company goals still the same? Do I need to add or delete anything?

  - *Are the measures I've chosen the right ones?*

  - *Do I still enjoy the same level of buy-in that I had at the beginning?* If not, why not? What actions should I take to get it back?

  - *Has a person been assigned to play the Chief Content Officer role?* Have certain people been assigned to manage the strategy, and do those people understand their responsibilities?

Assessing content maturity

In Chapter 10, you consider Kapost's Content Maturity Model to determine where your company is along the continuum. You're asked to characterize your group as one of the following:

- Novice
- Practitioner
- Intermediate
- Advanced
- Expert

If you've done that evaluation, or when you do, ask yourself whether you've made any progress. Have you broken down silos, created systems, or developed solid channel plans? When you've made progress, look at the designations and definitions in Chapter 10 again and evaluate how you can make even more progress.

If you have stagnated, determine what you need to do to get your group moving again. It may seem like a small thing to make this reassessment, but in reality, you need to take small, continuous steps to achieve your goals. Here are three important behaviors you need to encourage in your team to make progress on this continuum:

- ✔ **Collaboration:** You must stress the value of collaboration throughout the organization. You will get better quality content and engender pride from your staff.

- ✔ **Commitment:** Your executive staff must be on board and financially supportive of any content marketing efforts. You need to have the right tools and staff to get the job done.

- ✔ **Innovation:** You need to encourage the staff to try new things and to think creatively.

 If you're interested in learning about a business process that helps you make continuous progress, see the book, *One Small Step Can Change Your Life: The Kaizen Way* (Workman Publishing Company, Inc.), by Robert Maurer. It discusses the use of kaizen, a method to help you take small steps to reach big goals.

Reevaluating Your Ecosystem

In Chapter 10, you look at how to create a map for your company's ecosystem. (See also Chapter 16 for a look at the PESO model.) If you created the map, you now have a good evaluation tool to work with. You can look at each of the map areas and evaluate your results as follows:

- ✔ **Paid media:** The first obvious question to ask yourself regarding your paid media is, "Are each of the strategies in this category generating revenue or having some tangible effect on my business?" Paid media refers to your ads, native advertising, and any other sponsorship on which you spend money. Do you know whether they are providing something of value?

  It is not unusual for companies to spend money but not take the time to evaluate whether they are getting enough bang for their buck. In a time of tight money and dwindling budgets, this may seem surprising, but it frequently happens. Are you one of these companies?

  To prevent this lack of awareness from existing, go through each category in Table 20-1 and look at the measurements you're currently using to determine whether you are successful.

Table 20-1	Paid Media Evaluation	
Type	*Measures Used*	*Result (Success or Not)*
Social media ads:		
Facebook		
Twitter		
Other		
Native advertising		
Sponsorships		
Pay per click		

You should also determine whether the measures you are using are still effective and consider changing them. Determine whether the audience you want to reach is still found on these specific platforms. They may have shifted their use and you are no longer reaching them in the numbers you expect.

As discussed in Chapter 16, the use of paid ads on social media is increasing. This increase is occurring because these platforms are expanding their use of advertising and giving the ads a higher priority. Emarketer reveals that in 2015, Facebook owned 65.5 percent of the social ad market.

✔ **Earned media:** You knew that you needed to take an active role in encouraging earned media. You created campaigns, events, and other activities to get media attention. One thing you want to remember is that earned media has increased value because people believe experts and influencers. You should look at the influencers you chose and determine their value to your audience. When doing your evaluation, here are some questions to ask yourself:

- *Should I be deepening my relationships with specific influencers or perhaps finding new ones?*

- *Am I satisfied with the metrics I've chosen to use to measure my results?*

- *Do I need to engage PR professionals or change the ones I'm employing?*

✔ **Shared media:** Obviously, you don't have control over content sharing. The only actions you can take are these: (1) Make sharing easy from a technical standpoint by providing sharing icons; and (2) Provide the content that you're certain has the best chance of being shared. (See Chapter 15 for more about sharing.) Here are some questions to ask yourself:

- *Have I uncovered some new trends that will interest my audience?*

- *Are some formats more popular than others?*

- *Am I listening to my social media audience and reflecting their interests?*

✔ **Owned media:** Your owned media is under your control and can be revised in any way you see fit. Your analytics should be guiding you to make improvements to content, design, and formats. Questions to ask yourself include:

- *Am I totally clear about the topics my audience wants to know about?*

- *Does my website design impede my customers from finding the right content?* (See Chapter 10 to review your website map.)

✔ **Syndication:** You need to evaluate whether you're getting the value you expected from your various syndication deals. Some questions to ask yourself are the following:

- *Is syndication still the right strategy for my company?*

- *Am I effectively measuring the results I'm getting from my syndication deals?*

- *Do I need to drop some deals and find others?*

Check out the next page for a mind map of this chapter's content, and download a color version at www.dummies.com/contentmarketing strategies.

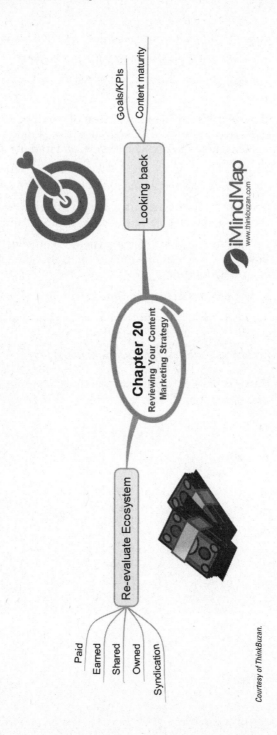

Courtesy of ThinkBuzan.

Part VI

The Part of Tens

the part of tens

Find out how to avoid the 6 things content marketers forget to do when they are creating content at www.dummies.com/extras/contentmarketing strategies.

In this part . . .

- ✔ Want to avoid the top ten content marketing problems that most marketers face? I tell you how.

- ✔ You need to keep up-to-date on content marketing strategies and tactics. I recommend the top 10 content marketing blogs that you should be reading.

- ✔ Check out ten free content marketing tools that you should use to enhance your efforts.

Chapter 21

Ten Problems Content Marketers Face

In This Chapter

▶ Working with a limited budget

▶ Forgetting to create content that fits the buyer's journey

▶ Dealing with decreasing content quality

As every content marketer knows, even if you try to do everything right (as I'm sure you do), you always face problems. In this chapter, I reconsider the "Five *C*s" framework introduced in Chapter 1 to examine some of the problems you may encounter.

To recap, the Five *C*s are

✔ Company focus

✔ Customer experience

✔ Content creation

✔ Content promotion

✔ Check-back analysis

Following are ten problems that content marketers may face, spread across those categories.

Company Focus

The question to answer in this category is, What do you want to achieve and how will you make it happen? The problems in this category revolve around setting a company strategy and creating goals and objectives related to your content marketing. The next sections describe two of these problems.

Inadequate budget

This problem is usually high on everyone's list of content marketing problems. No matter your company size, you can always use more money and or resources. But if you are significantly short on budget or resources, you need to demonstrate to management how your competition is beating you.

Lack of buy-in

See Chapter 4 for an in-depth discussion of buy-in. If you don't get buy-in from other staff, you have to deal with the situation directly. Content marketing projects are complex enough without adding opposition to the mix. First try speaking to the staff member or members themselves. If you get no mitigating response, you may need to involve others.

Customer Experience

The question to answer in this category is, Who are your prospects and how will you serve them? In this category, the problems are related to what kind of experience your customers have when they engage with your company. Read on for some of those problems.

Your content isn't categorized for the buyer's journey

You know that effective content marketing puts your customer at the center of your strategy. If you don't provide content that supports each part of the buyer's journey, you are not allowing your customer to learn everything she needs to know to choose you. Regardless of whether you do that, be assured that your competitors will.

Your content isn't personalized

If your customer feels that he is just another faceless prospect to you, you are not doing a good job of personalizing your content. Technology tools allow for varying degrees of customer personalization. The key to making this tactic work is to determine what kind of personal experience your customers want to have at each touchpoint. Do they want to have something simple, such as having newsletters address them by name, or something more advanced, such as receiving discount coupons based on their last purchase?

Content Promotion

The question to answer in this category is, How will your prospects find your content? Problems in this category relate to being able to get your customer's attention. I describe some of those problems next.

It seems as though no one is listening

If your content marketing is just getting started, you can fully expect to feel as though no one is listening — it takes time to build a readership. But rather than sit around hoping to be found, your company should engage guest posters and evaluate syndication deals. If you have been around for a while and the data still suggests that no one is listening, you need to do a better job of developing your customer personas. You may not be talking to the right audience.

You're not working with the right partners

Have your recent campaigns fallen flat? One reason could be that you are not working with the right partners to develop some synergy and excitement. Sometimes you need to bring in more marketing muscle to engage a bigger audience. Major companies like Pepsi often partner with TV shows or celebrities when they launch a campaign. You can do the same on a smaller scale. Many "Internet famous" people would be happy to partner with you. For example, you could get a person who is well-known in a specific part of the business world to do work with you in exchange for some publicity.

Content Creation

The question to answer in this category is, Who, what, and how will you create quality content? In this category, the problems are related to the value of your content and the ability to choose topics that your audience cares about. Following are some of the problems that may arise.

Running out of good ideas

All the content marketing advice you see says to keep a running list of ideas so that you never run dry. But what about really good ideas? Not all ideas are created equal. You may find that you don't see anything very stimulating on your list. One good way to generate new ideas is to ask a guest poster who disagrees with your company's method of doing something to write a post. Ask that guest poster to take a post that's already been published and rewrite it to include her opposing opinion. Then ask for feedback from your audience. That might help generate some new topics. If you can add some humor, you might get a greater response.

Decreasing content quality

Decreasing quality is the content marketer's worst nightmare. If you find that you are losing blog readers and newsletter subscribers, you may be providing poorly written content. Look back at your approval process and see whether everything is being properly vetted.

Check-back Analysis

The question to answer in this category is, How will you know that you met your goals? Problems in this category relate to measuring and meeting your goals. Read on for what some of these problems may be.

Not effectively monitoring customer sentiment

Millions of conversations are happening online. Are you listening? If your company doesn't adequately analyze social media data, you are missing out on key information about your customers. Don't make a half-hearted attempt. Find free online tools to help you gather information.

Inadequate measures to determine action

Your company has set specific goals of all kinds. It has business goals, operational goals, sales goals, and more. One problem you may encounter is that no one is accurately measuring what your department needs to know. This can be a very real problem for content marketers, who may command less attention. If you know of specific data that you want collected, make sure to lobby for it. Your profile in the company will rise when you can show that your efforts are making a significant contribution.

Chapter 22

Top Ten Blogs on Content Marketing

In This Chapter

▶ Discovering top-notch content marketing blogs

▶ Finding out which blogs have cutting-edge information

▶ Getting advice from content marketing experts

Have you ever stopped to think what the Internet would be without blogs? As much as we all hate the word *blog*, we love to scour the web to find just the right blogger to impart her pearls of wisdom to us. Blogs exist for almost every topic on earth, and they have a set of readers to go with it.

In this chapter, I serve up some of my go-to blogs for information about my favorite topic — content marketing. This list is by no means an exhaustive one. I could name many others, but then it wouldn't be a Part of Tens chapter. Following — in alphabetical order (because I would hate to imply that one is better than another) — are the blogs you should consider reading.

Buffer

https://blog.bufferapp.com/

It's software; it's a blog. Buffer is a relative newcomer to the list. Joel Gascoigne, cofounder, launched the Buffer software tool in 2010. It quickly gained a large following because it solved a real problem by letting you schedule your social media posts on a timetable that made sense for you and your readers. Because the people at Buffer understand the social media space, they have great posts about all things marketing, including content marketing. Kevan Lee is at the editorial helm.

Content Marketing Institute

http://contentmarketinginstitute.com

If you're interested in the content marketing space, you likely already know about Joe Pulizzi and the Content Marketing Institute. It's the gold standard for information about content marketing. It publishes magazines, consults with businesses, and probably has a guest post from all your favorite content marketers. Joe hosts the popular Content Marketing World event each year.

Convince & Convert

http://convinceandconvert.com

Jay Baer, who started Convince & Convert in 2008, bills himself as a "hype-free digital marketing strategist," and I have to agree. He offers no-nonsense advice about all things marketing in the form of fun videos and posts.

Copyblogger

http://copyblogger.com

Blogger Brian Clark is a veteran in the content marketing space. He started this blog in 2006! His site offers training, software, podcasts, and just about any form of information ready to help you. Writers Sonia Simone and Demian Farnworth are always great reads.

Oracle (Eloqua) Content Marketing Blog

https://blogs.oracle.com/marketingcloud/content-marketing-2

Eloqua, a marketing automation company now owned by Oracle, offers a wealth of information specifically devoted to content marketing. The site divides the information into three categories: measurement, planning, and production, and it includes webinars, e-books, and in-depth guides.

HubSpot Marketing Blog

http://blog.hubspot.com/marketing

HubSpot is an inbound marketing software company that has a variety of blogs devoted to online business building. Joe Chernov, VP of Content, is doing a wonderful job of keeping HubSpot on the cutting edge. Its marketing blog has guides and substantial posts about how to improve your content marketing.

Marketo Content Marketing Guides

http://www.marketo.com/content-marketing/

Marketo, a marketing automation software company, offers an incredible amount of high-quality guides, infographics, reports, e-books, and webinars on the topic of content marketing. This site is a one-stop shop for all things content marketing.

QuickSprout

http://www.quicksprout.com/blog/

Neil Patel is a remarkable writer with a great deal of business success. Although many of his posts exceed 4,000 words, they are very informative and flow really well. He writes about content marketing and online tactics that will help your business grow. Check him out.

Social Media Examiner

http://socialmediaexaminer.com

I'm a big fan of the Social Media Examiner blog. Founder Michael Stelzner and guest posters do an excellent job of sharing the most up-to-date information using an easy-to-read style. Michael also hosts Social Media Marketing World, an exciting yearly event.

Social Triggers

http://socialtriggers.com/

Derek Halpern is at the helm of this blog, and his personality shines through. He's direct, straightforward, and always delivers great information. Definitely worth a look.

Seth Godin

Okay, I guess I meant "Eleven Top Blogs," because no marketing blog list of any kind is complete without Seth Godin (http://sethgodin.com), even if I'm putting him in here out of alphabetical order. I include him here as I would on any blogging list I compile. He's a visionary and a must read.

Chapter 23

Ten Free Tools for Content Marketing

- -

In This Chapter

▶ Analyzing the performance of existing content

▶ Optimizing your content for search engine optimization

▶ Writing memorable content

▶ Creating engaging visuals

▶ Scheduling your team

▶ Collecting and storing content

- -

As you know, this book covers content marketing strategy along with some tactics and tools. I mention all the tools I recommend in this chapter in other chapters throughout the book. I single them out here because they have free versions that do a good job. I chose tools that help you with six key functions: (1) analysis; (2) optimization; (3) writing; (4) creating visuals; (5) scheduling; and (6) collecting and storing content. I note which category they are in, in their description.

If you want a cohesive content marketing platform, you need to buy one that is constructed to have all its parts working together to accomplish everything you need. If you're just getting started, and you're not sure what you want, consider one (or more) of these tools.

BuzzSumo

http://buzzsumo.com

This great tool helps you analyze published content in a variety of ways. You can look at different post topics to see which ones are most popular on the social platforms. You can also find influencers in those topics. By analyzing the content that's most popular, you get a clear indication of what you should be writing about. Check it out.

Dropbox

http://dropbox.com

This is a storage tool that helps you sync and share your content. When you store content on Dropbox, you have a local version on your computer and a synched version in the cloud. You can collaborate with others and always have an up-to-date version of your content.

Emotional Marketing Value Headline Analyzer

http://www.aminstitute.com/headline/

This valuable writing tool was created by the Advanced Marketing Institute. As I mention elsewhere, people make decisions based on their emotions although they believe they are using logic. For this reason, the Institute created a tool that helps you zero in on the "emotional marketing value" (EMV) of your headlines. If your headline is not intriguing, your customer won't stop to read it. After you type in your headline into this tool, it tells you whether it appeals to the intellectual, empathetic, or spiritual side of your customer.

Evernote

http://evernote.com

This is a cloud-based online collection tool that provides a central repository for all the content you want to save and review. Evernote calls itself the workspace for your life's work. It's great for collecting web research, visuals, and PDFs. You can have content available to review whenever and wherever you want.

Google Webmaster Tools

https://www.google.com/webmasters/tools/

Google Webmaster Tools are in the optimization category of this chapter, although they are more basic than that. They help Google do a good job of analyzing your site so that you can optimize it. You have to sign up for them, so if you haven't already, you should.

Grammarly

http://Grammarly.com

This is a great writing tool that finds errors and makes you a better writer. If you use Microsoft Office, you can invoke the software from a plug-in and analyze your writing inside the program. It analyzes such things as style, vocabulary enhancement, sentence structure, and punctuation.

Piktochart

http://piktochart.com

This is a visual tool that helps you create infographics. Infographics are visual depictions of statistics, and they are hot right now. This tool makes it easy for nondesigners to create professional- looking infographics that can be shared on blogs or other social sites.

Screenpresso

http://screenpresso.com

This is a visual capture tool that packs a big punch. You can capture images and annotate them. You can capture video in the free version, but it has branding in the content. One great feature is that it lets you capture an image and then extract the text in the image. This works well and saves a lot of time. Imagine that you had to copy the statistics and text from a graphic for a report. With Screenpresso, you get a text file ready to use. That's easy!

SEO SiteCheckup

http://seositecheckup.com/

This tool helps you optimize your content to ensure that your customers can find you. The free tools include a `Meta`-tag analyzer, a Google search results preview, a check of the most common keywords on your site, and a keywords cloud that visually shows you the frequency of your site's words.

WordPress Calendar

https://wordpress.org/plugins/editorial-calendar/

This is a scheduling tool that works within WordPress. You can drag and drop scheduled posts, and the interface makes this tool easy to use.

Index

About the Author

Stephanie Diamond is a thought leader and management marketing professional with 20+ years of experience building profits in more than 75 different industries. She has worked with solopreneurs, small-business owners, and multibillion-dollar corporations.

She worked for eight years as a Marketing Director at AOL. When she joined, there were fewer than 1 million subscribers. When she left in 2002 there were 36 million. While at AOL, she developed a highly successful line of multimedia products that brought in an annual $40 million in incremental revenue.

In 2002, she founded Digital Media Works, Inc. (DigMediaWorks.com), an online marketing company that helped business owners discover the hidden profits in their business. She is passionate about guiding online companies to successfully generate more revenue and find their company's real value.

As a strategic thinker, Stephanie uses all the current visual thinking techniques and brain research to help companies get to the essence of their brand. In 2014, she founded the Content Marketing Toolbox (ContentMarketingToolbox.com) where she helps companies accelerate their growth by communicating their value using content to customers using all the latest techniques.

Stephanie received a BA in Psychology from Hofstra University and an MSW and MPH from the University of Hawaii. She lives in New York with her husband and Maltese named Colby.

Dedication

To Barry, who makes all things possible.

To my family, for their encouragement and love.

Author's Acknowledgments

It has been my distinct privilege to write this book. I want to offer thanks to Wiley Publishing, Inc. for letting me write this book for its audience of smart readers.

The following people were especially important in creating this book, and I offer very sincere thanks:

To the great creative group at Wiley, Acquisitions Editor Amy Fandrei, Project Editor Susan Christophersen, and Technical Editor Michelle Krasniak. They made this project great fun to work on!

To the very innovative iMindMap/OpenGenius Group, starting with the amazing Tony Buzan, Chris Griffiths, Krystian Morgan, Natacha Pope, Oliver Spear, and their team. Thanks for working with us on the great mind maps throughout this book.

To Matt Wagner, my agent at Fresh Books, for his continued hard work and support on my behalf.

Finally, thanks to you for choosing this book to learn about content marketing strategies. I wish you enormous joy on your exciting journey into content marketing.

Publisher's Acknowledgments

Acquisitions Editor: Katie Mohr

Project Editor: Susan Christophersen

Technical Editor: Michelle Krasniak

Editorial Assistant: Matt Lowe

Sr. Editorial Assistant: Cherie Case

Project Coordinator: Antony Sami

Cover Photo: ©iStock.com/VLADGRIN

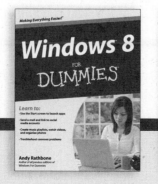

Math & Science

Algebra I For Dummies,
2nd Edition
978-0-470-55964-2

Anatomy and Physiology
For Dummies, 2nd Edition
978-0-470-92326-9

Astronomy For Dummies,
3rd Edition
978-1-118-37697-3

Biology For Dummies,
2nd Edition
978-0-470-59875-7

Chemistry For Dummies,
2nd Edition
978-1-118-00730-3

1001 Algebra II Practice
Problems For Dummies
978-1-118-44662-1

Microsoft Office

Excel 2013 For Dummies
978-1-118-51012-4

Office 2013 All-in-One
For Dummies
978-1-118-51636-2

PowerPoint 2013
For Dummies
978-1-118-50253-2

Word 2013 For Dummies
978-1-118-49123-2

Music

Blues Harmonica
For Dummies
978-1-118-25269-7

Guitar For Dummies,
3rd Edition
978-1-118-11554-1

iPod & iTunes
For Dummies, 10th Edition
978-1-118-50864-0

Programming

Beginning Programming
with C For Dummies
978-1-118-73763-7

Excel VBA Programming
For Dummies, 3rd Edition
978-1-118-49037-2

Java For Dummies,
6th Edition
978-1-118-40780-6

Religion & Inspiration

The Bible For Dummies
978-0-7645-5296-0

Buddhism For Dummies,
2nd Edition
978-1-118-02379-2

Catholicism For Dummies,
2nd Edition
978-1-118-07778-8

Self-Help & Relationships

Beating Sugar Addiction
For Dummies
978-1-118-54645-1

Meditation For Dummies,
3rd Edition
978-1-118-29144-3

Seniors

Laptops For Seniors
For Dummies, 3rd Edition
978-1-118-71105-7

Computers For Seniors
For Dummies, 3rd Edition
978-1-118-11553-4

iPad For Seniors
For Dummies, 6th Edition
978-1-118-72826-0

Social Security
For Dummies
978-1-118-20573-0

Smartphones & Tablets

Android Phones
For Dummies, 2nd Edition
978-1-118-72030-1

Nexus Tablets
For Dummies
978-1-118-77243-0

Samsung Galaxy S 4
For Dummies
978-1-118-64222-1

Samsung Galaxy Tabs
For Dummies
978-1-118-77294-2

Test Prep

ACT For Dummies,
5th Edition
978-1-118-01259-8

ASVAB For Dummies,
3rd Edition
978-0-470-63760-9

GRE For Dummies,
7th Edition
978-0-470-88921-3

Officer Candidate Tests
For Dummies
978-0-470-59876-4

Physician's Assistant Exar
For Dummies
978-1-118-11556-5

Series 7 Exam For Dumm
978-0-470-09932-2

Windows 8

Windows 8.1 All-in-One
For Dummies
978-1-118-82087-2

Windows 8.1 For Dummi
978-1-118-82121-3

Windows 8.1 For Dummi
Book + DVD Bundle
978-1-118-82107-7

Available in print and e-book formats.

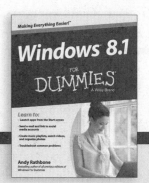

Take Dummies with you everywhere you go!

Whether you are excited about e-books, want more from the web, must have your mobile apps, or are swept up in social media, Dummies makes everything easier.

For Dummies is the global leader in the reference category and one of the most trusted and highly regarded brands in the world. No longer just focused on books, customers now have access to the For Dummies content they need in the format they want. Let us help you develop a solution that will fit your brand and help you connect with your customers.

Advertising & Sponsorships

Connect with an engaged audience on a powerful multimedia site, and position your message alongside expert how-to content.

Targeted ads • Video • Email marketing • Microsites • Sweepstakes sponsorship

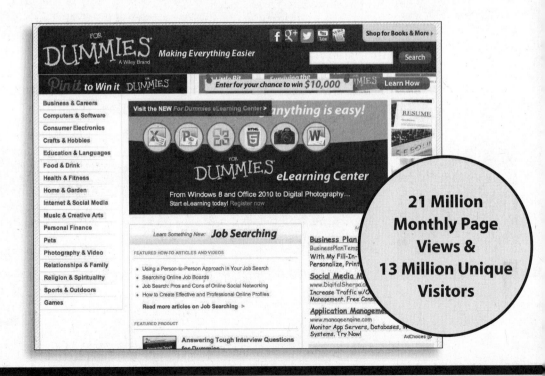